Stops Along the Way

By
Charles
Ticho

Stops Along The Way by Charles Ticho
Copyright 2021 by Charles Ticho
ISBN 9781957863009

All rights reserved. No part of this publication may be reproduced, distributed, or transmitted in any form or by any means, including photocopying, recording, or other electronic or mechanical methods, without the prior written permission of the publisher, except in the case of brief quotations embodied in critical reviews and certain other noncommercial uses permitted by copyright law.

Other books by Charles Ticho:
M'Dor L'Dor — From Generation to Generation: A Family's Story of Survival

Selected stories have been previously published by
The Jerusalem Post and *The Jewish Standard*

Charles Ticho
7305 Kirkland Village Circle
Bethlehem, PA 18017
Phone: (610) 691-7813
Cell: (201) 707 2498

Cover Photo Illustration and Design:
   Lisa Massey Buffer, Pam Lott and Robin Ticho
Creative/Editorial Director: Pam Lott
Book Design: Gayle F. Hendricks
Manuscript Review: Angel R. Ackerman

Published by Parisian Phoenix Publishing Company,
Easton, Pennsylvania USA
www.ParisianPhoenix.com

C O N N E C T with the publisher:
ParisianPhoenix
parisbirdbooks

Contents

Preface	1
The Sacred Scroll of Boskovice	3
M'Dor L'Dor From Generation To Generation	8
Politics In Days Gone By	13
Life In the Ghetto	17
The Shop On Main Square	21
The House at U Templu 10	26
The Railroad and the Carriage Team	31
Fond Memories Of Brno	34
The Winds of Change	39
Brotherly Love	45
On The Move	49
Our Maternal Sage	61
The Gathering Storm	65
It Took a Miracle	68
A Rosh Hashanah to Remember	73
The Bar Mitzvah That Almost Wasn't	77
Wounded Hero	85
A Matter Of Life And Death	89
On Becoming Ninety	93
My Cousin Henry	98

In The Footsteps Of History	100
Benito Mussolini Saved My Life	104
A Reach Into The Dark	112
Jewish Tears	119
Unwelcome Featured Speaker	125
Hands Across The Void	127
A Brother's 90th Birthday Wish	130
A Letter to an Older Brother	135
An American's Yom Kippur in Israel	137
Lost Generations	141
A Bus To Jerusalem	146
Lifescape: The Work Of Anna Ticho	153
Out Of My Will	158
Mitzpe Ramon in 1954	162
The 75-Year-Long Secret	168
Director's Recollections	173
Being Jewish	182
Will The Holocaust Ever End?	185
The Man On the Piano and the Cooked Goose	188
The Wonders Of America	191
WQXR and the Bohemian Payment Plan	195
Going Up In Smoke	197
A Student's Life in IIT in the 1940'S	199
The Show Must Go On	204
What a Bargain	207
Watch What You Say	209
You Played It Too Loud	212
A Lesson In Economy	215
Gil's Funeral	217
You Would Never Guess What I Did	219
The Frozen Heart Attack	224
Take One — Cut!	228
Kind And Gentle Lloyd	232
Organizing The Chicago Directors Was Risky Business	237
Tit For Tat	242
Crime Does Pay	245
Gravestones In The Desert	250
Acknowledgements	254

Foreword

The Ticho family: A legacy

I first "met" Charles Ticho by email in 2017 when he began submitting ruminations on his iconic aunt, Jerusalem's own Anna Ticho. His colorful, heartfelt accounts easily found a home in the pages of the publications I edit at *The Jerusalem Post*.

From her arrival in Palestine in 1912, Anna's influence on the Israeli artistic scene was significant and reverberates to this day. The Jerusalem home she resided in with her husband, Dr. Albert Ticho — appropriately known as Ticho House — is today a popular art gallery and center of culture.

Distinctive figures of yesteryear can often seem mysterious and inaccessible, yet happily, Anna's nephew Charles is here to shed intimate light on the woman she was and the family from which she came.

Who were the Tichos? Charles takes the *Post's* readers back to their roots and into the

cobblestone streets, homes and shops of the small Czech town of Boskovice, telling us of the synagogue's sacred scroll, a 75-year-old family secret and of family characters like his cousin Frantisek, a wounded hero, and his Aunt Gisella, a talented knitter. Tales of their cunning escape from the Holocaust transition to the establishment of a new foothold in America, memorable travels to Israel, one very meaningful Yom Kippur and a reunion with a long-lost friend of 55 years.

Finally meeting Charles and his wife Yochi in person in February 2020 (what pre-pandemic timing!) in Ticho House's namesake cafe Anna felt like a reunion of old friends, as I sensed the life, times and work of generations colliding and enduring.

The Ticho patriarchs and matriarchs would be proud of the saga Charles Ticho so vividly and movingly portrays in *Stops Along the Way*. Their flame, unextinguished by the Holocaust, continues to burn ever brightly via Charles' pen.

Erica Schachne
Editor
In Jerusalem and
The Jerusalem Post Magazine
October 2021

Preface

On the night of March 14, 1939, our father awakened us and asked us to get dressed quickly. He handed us two small suitcases that, apparently, had been prepared earlier for emergency purposes and we left our house and entered the waiting taxi for the Brno train station. We boarded a night train for Prague along with many other anxious, worried and confused people. In Prague, Father bought tickets for a train from Prague to Switzerland and we, Father, my little brother Steven and I jumped into a taxi for the ride to the westbound train's station. We never made it.

In central Europe, Czechoslovakia was one of the few countries where cars drove on the left side of the road — like they still do in England. However, most of the European countries, including Germany, drove on the right. Our taxi was suddenly confronted by a big truck about a half-a-mile away heading straight at us on "our" side of the street. Our driver just managed to get out of the way by driving the car onto the sidewalk. The truck rumbled past us without even slowing down. He was followed by what seemed like an hour of such

Charles working on the manuscript. Contact sheets of photos line the wall behind him.

trucks rolling past us, each one with a load of soldiers seated in the truck and towing various instruments of war behind. The soldiers were not dressed in the familiar green of the Czech army but in the unusual gray of the German Wehrmacht. The short history of our beloved independent Czechoslovakia, born in 1919, had come to an end after just 20 years of peaceful democratic rule.

This is how the Holocaust began for me and now, as I write this some 82 years later at age of 94, it has never really left me. The Holocaust was such an unbelievable event in the annals of human life on earth that, so far, no one has been able to describe it in a meaningful manner. There are simply no words in our language to describe it. It lives with me every day and it rises up at the most unexpected moments. Like the day I was driving to Jerusalem.

The day before there was news on the radio about a forest fire in the vicinity of Jerusalem. The following day, as I was on my way to Jerusalem, I was suddenly confronted by acres and acres of burned trees. I thought of the thousands of dedicated Jews who had dropped coins into collection boxes to pay for these trees and, suddenly, each of the blackened trees became a monument to a Jew who was burnt during the Holocaust and I had to stop the car because my tears were blocking my view. Yes, the evil of the Nazis keeps pursuing me through the decades causing pain and grief.

Like my cousin Ilan, who learned a half century after the war that the man he called "father" throughout his life, was not, in fact, his father.

Or like my dear wife, Jean, who met her biological mother only at the age of 52 — in a photograph.

Or like the house in Boskovice, where my grandfather was born, that belonged to our family for over a century but was seized by the Nazis and sold to strangers.

Or like a sacred Torah scroll that was featured in our grandson's Bar Mitzvah but may have also served my father, my grandfather or even my great-grandfather during their Bar Mitzvah ceremonies in a small town in Europe centuries ago.

Yes, the Holocaust reaches back centuries and will, undoubtedly, also reach forward centuries into the future. It is this belief that has driven me to write this book in order to recall and retell some of the experiences, the stops along the way, where the Holocaust has touched me, shaped me and affected me, and created my memories.

I was blessed and was miraculously saved and came, along with my parents and brothers, to the United States to start a new life. There, additional unusual and memorable events, more stops along the way, marked my progress to my 94th birthday, the day when I concluded writing these stories —

— my STOPS ALONG THE WAY.

The Sacred Scroll of Boskovice

Boskovice's Town Hall with its impressive bell tower.

Few tourists, visiting the Czech Republic these days, visit the small town of Boskovice. It isn't usually part of a tourist's itinerary. As a matter of fact, while the capitol of the Czech Republic, Prague, is today one of Europe's major tourist attractions, all of Moravia is considered to be off the beaten path and is usually ignored by visitors. Boskovice, an ancient and modest-sized town, is located in the center of Moravia and was probably founded in the 11th-century and, at one time, had one of the largest Jewish communities in the country. The first mention of a Jew in the town's records was around 1343. By 1589, there were 148 Jews living in 25 family houses. At the turn of the 18th-century Boskovice had an active yeshiva and by the mid-19th-century the Jewish population comprised one-third of all Boskovice inhabitants.

Today the town features the ruins of a 13th-century Gothic fortress, St. Jacob's church, an Empire Chateau, a large and very old Synagogue, and a Jewish cemetery. This final resting place of Boskovice Jews was founded in the 17th-century and is one the largest in the Czech Republic. The unique large Synagogue was built in 1698 and in 1705, Jeshaya Maler and Loeb from Krakow, painted beautiful decorations and Hebrew liturgical texts on many of the interior walls.

During the Holocaust, all the Jews of Boskovice, including all the members of the Ticho family, were deported to the Terezin Concentration Camp and from there to Auschwitz where they were murdered. The fourteen of these deported Jews, who somehow managed to survive the Holocaust, did not return to Boskovice. There are no Jews in Boskovice today. The large synagogue survived, but from 1942 up to the 1990's, was used as a storehouse. All the walls were painted white. In 1999 a restoration began and it was then when the beautiful and unique old murals were discovered and restored.

For centuries, Boskovice was known as a center of prominent Talmudist scholars. The most famous of these is Samuel ha-Levi Kolin (also known as "Machazit HaShekel") who is buried in the local Jewish cemetery. His gravestone is the goal of many pilgrimages to this day. In 1851 the town was honored when the Boskovice rabbi, Rabbi Placek, was appointed Chief Rabbi of Moravia and served until 1884.

In 1942, at the height of the German Nazi power, a group of members of the Prague's Jewish community devised a way to bring the religious treasures from the deserted communities and destroyed synagogues to the comparative safety of Prague. The plan was that, after the anticipated Nazi victory, a "Museum of an Extinct Race" would be established. The Nazis were persuaded to accept this plan and they ordered all Jewish communities to send their ritual objects to Prague. More than 100,000 artifacts were brought to the Prague Jewish Museum. Among them were about 1,800 sacred Torah scrolls that were stored in the closed synagogue at Michle, a small town outside of Prague. There they remained forgotten and abandoned until they were discovered and were brought to the Kensington Congregation in London.

Today, Sub-Carpathian Russia has been absorbed by its neighbors and the Slovaks have decided to go their own way. Typical of the unconfrontational nature of the Czechs, the parties split amicably and Bohemia and Moravia now form what is today the Czech Republic. One could easily assume that the

Hebrew sign on building in the Boskovice ghetto area. Hebrew caption states: "Black on White, Remember the Disaster" which may be a reference to a great fire in 1832.

ethnic Czechs living in Moravia, surrounded as they were for past centuries by militant countries such as Germany, Austria, Poland and Russia, might have been the victims of constant turmoil. Actually the opposite was true. Moravia, located off the path of the Crusaders, away from the conflict between the Catholic Church and Protestant firebrands and of relatively little economic and political importance, was usually bypassed and ignored as power struggles made the rest of Central Europe a focus of many conflicts.

So it shouldn't be a great surprise that even today, most of the visitors to Boskovice are not foreign citizens but rather Czech nationals. They climb the lovely, wooded mountain to visit the fortress that once dominated the valley below or tour the castle at the bottom of the hill which was, and still is, the seat of the Mansdorf-Pouilly family, the aristocrats placed there by the Austro-Hungarian Empire centuries ago to keep the Czechs under control and to "protect" the Jews.

It was the unique position of Moravia, away from the turmoil and turbulence that affected the rest of Europe, that created an unusual and fertile atmosphere for the Jews living in this region. While the kings in Prague and the emperors in Vienna formulated rules and edicts governing the lives of

Boskovice cemetery gate entrance.

Jews, in Moravia these laws and regulations were often ignored or not enforced. As a result, Jewish life, with few exceptions, tended to be civilized and humane.

Visitors to Boskovice can wander a few yards from the castle and visit the well-preserved section of the town that once constituted the Jewish ghetto. They can walk the few narrow streets and look for signs of the Jewish life that once thrived there or examine the tombstones of the well-preserved Jewish cemetery or visit the old synagogue. This synagogue was already one hundred years old, when a local scribe sat down to carefully and painstakingly start the creation of a perfect copy of our sacred scripture, the Torah. By the time my grandfather was born in 1846, the Torah had already served three generations of Jews as they gathered each day and on the Sabbath to practice the faith taught to them by their previous generations. In 1899, when the Torah had already reached the venerable age of eighty-five, it may have served during the Bar Mitzvah of my father, Nathan Ticho. And when World War I started, the now century-old Torah scroll continued to mark the passing of each year as it provided the sacred readings each time the congregation met to pray.

Collective view of the Jewish cemetery from the west with the city center and the parish church in the background in the early 1950's. Today housing developments have reached the gates of the cemetery.

Then, on March 15, 1939, the Nazis marched into the country and soon many things changed. The synagogue of Boskovice was ordered closed and all of the congregation's possessions, including all Torah scrolls, were shipped to Prague. Today, after a millennium of Jewish life in Boskovice, there are no more Jews in this city. The only things that remain are the synagogue, the cemetery, the streets and houses of the former ghetto, and the sacred articles collected by the Nazis now stored and cared for in Prague by the Jewish Museum. This included the now two-hundred-year-old Torah scroll. It and 1,564 other Torah scrolls were discovered by a British art collector. He returned to London and found a generous philanthropist who financed the purchase and the transfer of these holy scrolls to the Kensington Synagogue in London. There, for over forty years, they were stored, cared for, repaired, restored and made available to synagogues and worthy institutions all over the world.

After decades of searching for a home, the Boskovice Torah scroll was placed into my hands and crossed the Atlantic. Today, this sacred parchment, this honored and beloved scroll, this Holocaust survivor, resides in the warm and friendly surroundings of Congregation Brith Sholom in Bethlehem, Pennsylvania, passing on its power and inspiration from one generation to the next.

Today, the 200-year-old Boskovice Torah Scroll has a secure and loving place of honor in the Brith Sholom synagogue in Bethlehem, Pennsylvania, USA.

M'Dor L'Dor
FROM GENERATION TO GENERATION

For hundreds of years my family, the Ticho family, lived, thrived, and persevered in the small Moravian town of Boskovice in the Czech Republic.

And then, in one dreadful blow, they were all gone. Today there isn't a single Jew in the town.

As I approached my birthdays in the low 60's, I decided that perhaps someone ought to preserve the history of our family and that someone should record the experiences of Jews, in general, and of our family members, before, during and after the horror now known as the Holocaust. About fifteen years later, I had the honor and joy to distribute copies of my book "From Generation to Generation" to family members, friends and several institutions. All along, the purpose of this book was not, and is not, to tell my life story, but rather to endeavor to pass on to the younger generations and to the generations yet unborn a sense of the Holocaust, the birthright and history of our family and a feel for our Jewish heritage.

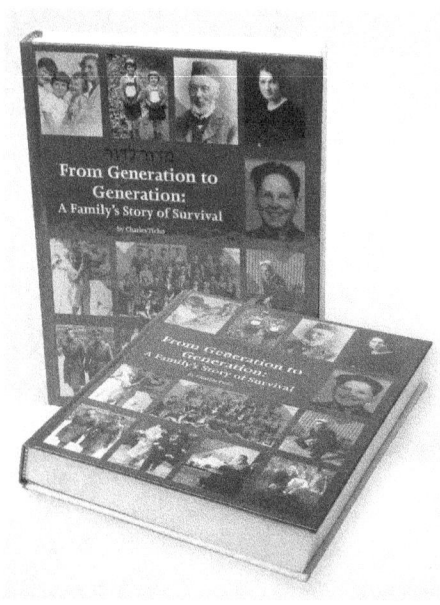

Above: Charles (l-r) with his grandchildren Hannah, Connie, and Nathan Ticho, and Ambassador of Israel, Raphael Givr, at the dedication of the Spielberg plaque in 2004.

Left: In 1939 Bill Klein (right) meets Harold Ticho as he arrives in America.

It is in this spirit that I've undertaken other projects like the restoration of the house in Boskovice where my grandfather, Yitzchak Zvi Ticho, was born, cause a plaque to be placed on the birthplace of Anna Ticho, restore the graves of our grandparents in Boskovice and Berlin, place a plaque to remember the Jews who were locked up in the Spielberg fortress, participate in the restoration of the synagogue in Boskovice and undertake the tracing of our family tree as far as we could manage.

It was also in this spirit that, in 1998, I led a delegation of family members to the Czech Republic where we visited the many sites connected with the history of the Ticho family. Four years later, I brought our daughter Robin, her son Michael and our son Richard for a similar visit in order to make them aware of the roots of the family. And then, in 2004, I returned to the family sites with my son Ron, his wife Pam and their three children, Nathan, Hannah and Connie.

> **III. Ester Ticho (1906)**
>
> Here is buried
> a modest being, respected
> and chaste,
> a jewel of her mate and a diadem
> of her children.
> Constantly and faithfully she sought
> to fulfil all the mitzvot,
> thereby transmitting the Jewish spirit
> to grandchildren and greatgrandchildren.
> The summers of her life were overturned
> before they could be filled.
> Her days were not many
> and their end was filled with illness.
> Her children mourn her deeply
> and to the spouse of her youth
> (there remains) no joy,
> nor the loftiness of her nobility of spirit.
>
> Here died Ester Ticho
> daughter of our teacher and rebbe Aharon Beer,
> the first day after the sabbath 18 sivan
> 668 of the small count.
> (May her soul be inscribed in the Book of Life)

Ticho tombstones in Boskovice Cemetery — Itzchak Ticho, his sister Nettie Broch, and Esther Ticho.

A key element of this last tour in 2004 was a gathering of our family, along with the ambassador of Israel and some twenty members of the press, on Brno's Spielberg fortress to dedicate a memorial plaque, which we sponsored, to the Jews who were imprisoned there by the Nazis during World War II. And it was also in this spirit that we undertook to make a special presentation during Nathan's wonderful Bar Mitzvah celebration in December 2004.

Nathan was the star of this event, reading the portions from the Torah, reciting his Haftorah and handling two English presentations like a professional. His knowledge, his wit and his self-assurance made all of us proud and grateful to have lived long enough to enjoy that day. This event also gave us an opportunity to dramatize the *M'Dor L'Dor* (generation to generation) concept.

The Bar Mitzvah of Nathan Ticho, the great grandson of the Nathan Ticho born in Boskovice in 1886, was dramatized during the ceremony as the Holocaust Torah Scroll from Boscovice was passed from generation to generation to the hands of the rabbi.

In honor of our grandson Nathan's Bar Mitzvah, after decades of searching for a home, the Boskovice Torah scroll, this inspiration of dozens of Jewish generations, this survivor of the Holocaust, crossed the Atlantic and became part of the celebrations. My wife Jean and I had the honor, in the tradition of *M'Dor L'Dor*, from generation to generation, to present this sacred parchment to our son Ron who, in turn, passed it to his son Nathan who placed it into the hands of Rabbi Juda who placed is alongside the other scrolls in the synagogues' Aron Kodesh, Holy Ark.

It is in this *M'Dor L'Dor* spirit that I have endeavored to pass this story of our family and to the future.

Gate to the ghetto from the Hradni Street as it looked in 1928. A truck knocked-off the upper portion of the gate. It was rebuilt but not restored to it's original form.

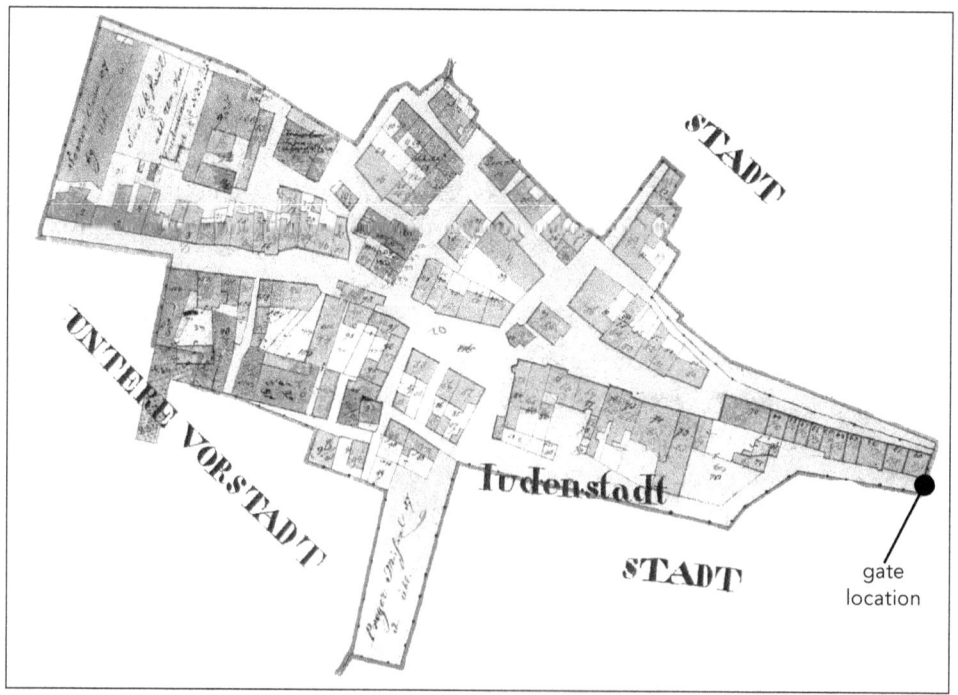

Sketch of the permanent layout of the Jewish quarter of Boskovice, 1826, MZA Brno.

Politics In Days Gone By

In the 1850's the Austro-Hungarian empire was like a goose trying to maintain some order among a horde of unruly goslings. The country encompassed nearly a dozen various ethnic groups that had their own ambitions, loyalties and allegiances. Each group had its distinct level of loyalty to the government in Vienna. The area that, these days, comprises the Czech Republic was not much different. At one time the Czechs controlled an impressive piece of Europe with Prague as its capital. But, in the struggle between the Roman Catholic Church, as represented by Austria, and the Protestant firebrands under the Czech flag, the Czechs lost and for three centuries thereafter were obliged to live under Austrian rule.

To maintain some order, the Vienna authorities introduced some pseudo-democratic laws including voting. Now, to maintain a German majority in the Vienna legislature, the Austrian administration concentrated on maintaining good relations with German-speaking groups throughout its vast empire. In the areas that are today's Czech Republic, the principal recipients of this preferred attention were the Jews.

To encourage the Jews in our family's hometown, Boskovice, to vote as a German ethnic group, Vienna went to some lengths to maintain friendly relations with the Jews of the city. The Austrian government designated the local count to be the *Schutzherr* (protector) of the Jewish ghetto. For this service the Jewish community contributed to the count's treasury and the count, in turn, took interest in the affairs of the Jewish families under his benign protection. In the 1800's, for example, the reigning Count Mansdorff donated a new administration building to the Jewish community and paid for the construction of the ghetto's new main well. Later, an equally generous count donated an area of land adjacent to the ghetto where a small grammar school could be built and where festivals and athletic activities could be conducted.

A familiar anecdote that was popular in the ghetto told of the occasion when the count was discussing Jewish affairs with the Dayan. The question came up: "What is a Dayan?" The Dayan, the Jewish elder explained to the count, is like an assistant rabbi who deals with matters that should not take up the rabbi's valuable time. For example, a Dayan may be called upon to decide whether a certain goose, duck, or chicken is kosher and can be cooked and eaten by Jews. If, as a result of a careful inspection the bird is declared not kosher, it cannot be eaten by Jews and must be discarded. "Well, in the future" the count very generously offered, "just bring such an un-kosher fowl to my game-keeper, and I would be happy to replace it with a matching bird from my farm." The Dayan gratefully accepted this generous offer and went on to explain that a Dayan might also be concerned with the *Mikweh* (the ritual bath) where the Dayan must decide when a woman may engage in intercourse after having menstruated. "Well," the count is reputed to have said,

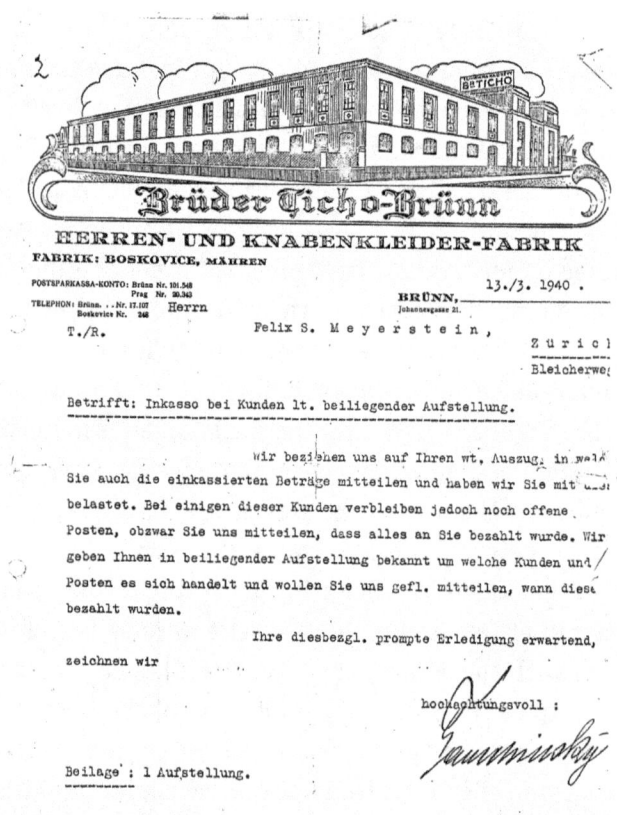

The 1940 letterhead of the Brothers Ticho Factory in Boskovice. In this letter the new Nazi "owners" demand that any money collected from customers must be sent to the factory. As a result, my father was deprived of the funds he had hoped to use during our escape.

The 1928 map of the first Czechoslovakia.

"I am perfectly happy to help and replace a duck, a goose, or a chicken but, when it comes to the countess, I am sorry, but there I must draw a line."

The occasional favorable treatment of the Jews, of course, generated resentment among the Czech population. They considered the Jews to be traitors to their ambitions to have their own independent country. So, the Jews had to walk a thin line between support of the Vienna court and the Czechs' political aims. This also raised a conflict within the Jewish community itself as the older generations leaned towards the support of the Vienna government while the younger generation, particularly those who went to Vienna to study, came home with ideals favoring the Czech position.

> ... *the Jews had to walk a thin line between support of the Vienna court and the Czechs' political aims.*

Of course, all of this underwent a major reorientation in 1918 with the end of World War I and the defeat of Austria. The former empire was now partitioned into several pieces. One of these newly created countries was Czechoslovakia, an assembly of four provinces, Bohemia, Moravia, Slovakia and Sub-Carpathian Russia. The Jewish ethnic minority in these areas now became a fervent supporter of the Czech cause. For me that meant to be a loyal and ardent supporter of all things Czech. I was a great fan of all the sports teams that represented Czechoslovakia in international sports — soccer, ice hockey, tennis, skiing and athletics. I also joined in the cheering when King Carol of Romania visited Brno because Romania, Yugoslavia and Czechoslovakia created the Little Entente, a security pact to come to each other's defense if attacked. We also supported France and England because they expressed interest in our country. Of course, when the German tiger growled they all turned tail and abandoned us.

After World War II ended in 1945, our father made an effort to seek restitution of some of the family's possessions that were seized by the Nazis. After six years of turmoil and war there was little to recover of the valuables like paintings, furnishings and jewelry. The Germans had raided all our bank accounts and traded away all our investments. The only thing they could not take with them was the real estate — the houses, the factory and lands that my father owned before the war. When the Communists seized power in Czechoslovakia in 1948, all efforts to recover the properties to the rightful owners stopped. The Communist Czech authorities had no inclination to negotiate with anyone. For 41 years the miserable Communist regime held the country in a tight grip. It wasn't until 1989 when, in the so called "Velvet Revolution," the communists were ousted and were replaced by a democratic administration. By that time, my father and my brother Steven had died. Steven became a very good and successful lawyer and had led the efforts to recover our property. With his passing, the recovery of the properties fell into my inexperienced lap.

After the revolution, the Czech government was at least willing to listen to claims. They allowed the building on Janska Street in Brno, that was jointly owned by us and cousin Karl's family, to be returned to us and I also received the possession of our house on Dolni Street 5. However, they flatly refused to discuss the Brothers Ticho factory in Boskovice. It was seized by the communists and was now operated by government-assigned owners. The house at U Templu #10, that the Fuchs family owned, where my grandfather was born, that became the property of Uncle Jacob and that I had rebuilt and restored to keep it from collapsing, was sold by the city to new owners and recovery was rejected. There was another large apartment house on Minoritska Street that was owned by several Ticho uncles, that was not returned to me despite of the fact that I was declared the rightful owner.

So, despite of the fact that our side won the war, we sustained substantial losses. Who was it that said: "War is Hell"? Whoever it was, was certainly right.

Life In the Ghetto

"Your grandfather limped." I was completely surprised by this bit of startling information that I heard one day from my Aunt Gisella while sitting in her apartment at 3600 North Lake Shore Drive in Chicago.

It was around 1998 and Aunt Gisella (my mother's oldest sister) was in her late 90s. As usual, she was seated in front of the picture window of her apartment on the 17th floor overlooking Chicago's Lincoln Park and Lake Michigan. And, as usual, her hands were busy. She could no longer create wonders with her knitting needles, crochet hook, or scissors and thread as she had done all her life. Her hands and fingers were now twisted from arthritis, and her eyesight was poor. But this did not stop her. She just switched to larger needles, thicker thread, and to designs that enabled her to create beautiful Afghan bed covers and blankets which she gave away to family members and which, today, are still prized possessions in the various households.

In all the years that I had spoken to my parents and to other family members about my grandfather, the fact that he had a pronounced limp was never mentioned. "Yes, father did limp," Uncle Alfred, his youngest son, confirmed to me years later when I asked him. To my surprise Alfred could not tell me why. Alfred continued: "We had too much respect for our father to ever question him on this subject. He limped, and that was that. It might have been a childhood deformity, an injury (don't forget, a broken bone in those days without X-rays was a major problem) or, for that matter, it could have been a self-inflicted wound to avoid service in the Austrian army during the war of 1866. We just never spoke about it or even mentioned it."

Ignatz Zvi Ticho, my paternal grandfather, born in 1846, was 20 years old when the war between Prussia and Austria broke out and was, certainly, a candidate for the army. A limp would excuse him from serving. Besides, many Jews opposed the German military forces in this war. At one point, Ignaz's friend, a certain Mr. Vogel, the secretary of the Jewish Community in Boskovice, was asked by a German Army officer: "Which road is the way to Kunstat?" Mr. Vogel proudly responded: "I will not aid our enemy. Find your own way," "Very well," commanded the officer, "you will now ride with us 'til we get there, and then you can walk back home." Mr. Vogel stubbornly stuck to his position and spent three days walking back home. Thereafter the Czechs, as well as the Jews of Boskovice, considered Mr. Vogel a patriot and a hero.

The 13 living children of Ignatz Ticho treated their father and mother with the greatest respect. At home they spoke German and, when addressing their parents, they would never use the familiar "du" form, but always addressed them in the honorific third person "Sie" manner. Even Dr. Isidor Reiniger, who had married Sarah, the oldest of the children and who was familiar with the cause of his father-in-law's limp, never discussed it. He would not even discuss it when I asked him, decades after Ignaz had passed away.

The children also respected their father's wish not to be photographed. Nevertheless, during a visit to a spa with his sister, Nettie, he sat on a park bench and rested his eyes while reading and wearing, as usual, a skull cap. Aunt Nettie got a street photographer to take his picture while he was in this pose. Years later, the family engaged an artist by the name of Gustav Boehm to make a drawing of Ignatz based on this photograph. Mr. Boehm selected Victor, from among the 11 sons of Ignatz Ticho, as best suited model to sit for him so he could replace the closed eyes with open ones. This portrait and a matching one of his wife Laura (Esther) and the many copies are in the hands of family members and are the only pictures ever made of my paternal grandparents.

Yitzchak Zvi Ticho photograph.

The Ticho house in Boskovice was an enlightened Orthodox Jewish home. The kitchen was kosher, the Sabbath was strictly observed, Ignatz always had his head covered, and the holidays were major events in the life of the family. (My father, Nathan, could readily recite by heart all the daily Hebrew prayers.) Ignatz's father, Abraham,

Gustav Boehm's painting based on the photograph of Yitzchak Zvi Ticho and the matching portait of his wife Laura Esther Ticho.

(my great-grandfather) was the *Dayan* (assistant rabbi) of the congregation and Laura (Esther) Baer's father was the rabbi of Holesov. The children were brought up in this atmosphere of Jewish traditions and learning while, at the same time, being exposed to the outside world in their relations with non-Jews in trade and everyday contacts.

The life of the Ticho family was centered in house number #56 and in house #18 on the U Templu (near-the-temple) Street 10, which the Ticho family shared with the Fuchs family. The Fuchs family lived in that house when Abraham Ticho (my great-grandfather) first married Esther (Rezi) Fuchs. Mr. Fuchs was the Shames (caretaker) of the synagogue. One of his tasks was to visit the Jewish families and offer for "sale" the aliot (Torah recitations) for each service. The income from these donations paid for the upkeep of the synagogue as well as Mr. Fuchs' salary and the salaries of the rabbi and cantor. The contributions were voluntary, but certain minimums were usually suggested. These often changed depending on the economic level of the individual approached as well as on the current needs of the congregation. The price of these honors would rise from time to time and when Fuchs was questioned as to who decided on the price increases, his brief answer often was: "I conducted a meeting with myself."

Boskovice, a town of respectable size and standing in the Czech Republic, took great pride in the manner religious services were conducted. Nevertheless, after an addition to the synagogue was completed, the community invited the cantor from the Brno synagogue, the second largest city in the country, to come to Boskovice and officiate during the festive and joyful opening of the completed and enlarged temple.

After the services, a large crowd remained around the building with many commenting on the beautiful presentation and voice of the imported cantor from Brno. These comments, that were overheard by the local cantor, became a major irritation that finally caused the injured local cantor to burst out with: "Do you have any idea how much we paid the Brno cantor to sing here this evening? If I would get such a salary, I too could sing as well as he does!"

1890's photograph of Boskovice Main Square, The A. J. Ticho store is at the left edge of the photographs.

Close up of the A. J. Ticho store.

The Boskovice Main Square now.

The Shop On Main Square

"Your grandfather was the first Jew in Boskovice to buy a house outside the ghetto," said my uncle Alfred with obvious pride, as I was interviewing him for my book *From Generation To Generation*, "Yes, he bought a house right on the main square and opened his shop at the front door of this house."

Like most towns and villages in the Czech Republic, Boskovice has a main square where the town's main streets meet. In Boskovice, the main square is dominated on one end by the town's church and at the other end by the impressive tower of the city hall. The main square was, of course, the focus of all major events. This is where the new army recruits would march off to serve in the Austrian Army, where all parades took place, where all demonstration were centered and where all the market days took place.

When, in the 1870's, the Jews of Boskovice were granted the right to purchase property outside of their ghetto, my grandfather, Yitzchak Zvi Ticho, was the first Jew to take advantage of this new law. He purchased a two story house right on the main square. This became the home of the Ticho family and the location of the A.J. Ticho textiles store. I learned that information from my uncle who was very proud that his father was so courageous as to expose himself and his family to the turmoil that often occurred on the main square.

One day, while chatting with my cousin Dr. Arthur Reiniger, the son of Uncle Isidor, I happen to mention my grandfather's courage. Arthur, always a jolly and humorous friend, smiled and said: "Wait a minute, young man, I guess you don't know that, while the house was actually outside the ghetto and on the main square, the back yard opened into the ghetto. So, the family was never too far from reinforcements in case they were needed."

Many of the Jews of Boskovice were traders who gathered their merchandise on handcarts or horse carts and traveled around the countryside selling their goods. After the end of the Sabbath, these men got ready and departed early Sunday morning. Those with hand carts favored nearby villages while those with greater loads and a horse to do the heavy work covered much of the county. Most were away 'til Friday noon when they returned to Boskovice in time to wash up and get ready for the Friday evening services and Shabbat dinner with the family. Saturday was a well-earned day of rest, time with the family and, perhaps, a beer or two in the local pub.

My grandfather's move to the main square was a clever business decision. Yitzchak Ticho decided that instead of him wandering around the county seeking customers, he would let the customers come to him. With its location on the main square, A.J. Ticho was a busy place. In addition to textiles, the store featured sewing supplies, ribbons, trim and, of course, needles and thread. It was particularly busy on market days when farmers or their wives would bring their produce to the market. Booths and stalls covered the whole town square and people from all over the county would arrive to buy their supplies. Transactions of all kinds took place. Many farm families made various handicrafts in the wintertime and brought the ceramics, carvings, knitted clothing, and metal objects to the market. If you looked long enough and visited the market often enough, you could find most anything. And, of course, market day was also a good time to renew acquaintances, exchange the latest gossip, argue about politics and share several local beers.

My Grandfather's move to the main square was a clever business decision.

In those years nearly all clothing was hand made by the women of the farm families. A good housewife was expected to have sewing skills and provide the required apparel for the family. The head of the family and his wife may invest in a tailor-made outfit to wear to church and on special events, but all the rest was home-made, patched, repaired and handed down from family member to family member. The major gift at a wedding was a foot-operated sewing machine. This was a valuable tool because many farm housewives did the sewing for the

Brothers Ticho clothing factory. The factory would prepare the designs, cut the cloth and then bring it to selected farmhouses where the items were sewn.

The main town square also became the center of A. J. Ticho's principal competition in Boskovice, a store run by the Schwartz brothers. And, for a brief time, A. J. Ticho had a second competitor. In the Ticho store a secret code was used when our grandfather suspected that a customer might be a possible shoplifter. *"Zwei auf Zehn"* (two on ten) was the way grandfather Ignatz advised his employees to keep two eyes on the ten fingers of a customer. A long-time employee by the name of Kurtilek decided to leave A. J. Ticho and open his own store that he proudly and pointedly identified as "The First Christian Textile Store in Boskovice." To profit from some of the anti-Semitic feelings among the Czech customers, he revealed the secret of the *Zwei auf Zehn* code words to the public suggesting that the Jews running the Ticho store looked down on Christians and did not trust their Czech customers. "Besides," he claimed publicly, "my merchandise is less expensive than Ticho's." To this final insult Ignatz responded with a counterclaim: "That is hard to believe," stated grandfather publicly, "how can Mr. Kurtilek's merchandise be less expensive than ours since Kurtilek buys merchandise from us." This was too much for Kurtilek, and he filed a libel lawsuit against my grandfather in court. Ignatz's claim was not a rash statement. The books of A.J. Ticho did actually contain an entry of a sale to Kurtilek in the past. It was a minor transaction, but enough to cause Kurtilek to lose the lawsuit and greatly damage his own reputation.

My grandfather would often boast: "I keep the smart sons here in my business. The others can go to Vienna and study at the university." In fact, three of his sons, Max, Joseph and Solomon did go to Vienna and became lawyers and Albert became

Father Nathan and his brothers (L-R) Jacob and David on the way home from Saturday morning services.

a physician. Three sons, "the smart ones" Jacob, David and Chaim joined their father's business and substantially expanded the operation. Ultimately, after grandfather died, they moved it from Boskovice's main square to the heart of Brno, the second largest city in the land. Unfortunately, Chaim died of leukemia in 1928. Nevertheless, Jacob and David caused the business to thrive — 'til the Nazis destroyed everything in 1939. Jacob and David were arrested and were sent to the Terezin concentration camp. There, Jacob, despite of the efforts of his niece and nephew, starved to death. David was sent to the Warsaw ghetto.

Jacob and David Ticho.

One day, we received a desperate postcard in our home in the United States. In this card, Uncle David begged us to send insulin to Warsaw that he urgently needed to care for his diabetes. We fought the authorities for several months to get permission to buy the insulin without a doctor's prescription. Then, after the United States entered the war, we could no longer ship anything from the United States directly to Poland. We had to ship the insulin to a friend in Switzerland and beg him to send it to Warsaw. He did, but many months passed and we never heard from David again.

That marked the end of A. J. Ticho.

Chaim Ticho

Joseph Ticho and Family

Grete and Max Ticho

Dr. Albert Ticho

Solomon Ticho and Family

The House at U Templu 10

"I consider it a great honor and a sincere pleasure to unveil this memorial plaque to a great man and a great family." With these words His Excellency, Raphael Gvir, the Ambassador of Israel to the Czech Republic, concluded his brief remarks in the small-town square in front of the house at U Templu Street 10 in Boskovice in June 1998.

Earlier the cantor of the Brno synagogue and a small chorus had chanted a brief prayer and the vice-mayor of the city had welcomed everyone to the event. A crowd of about 90 invited local people and dignitaries and perhaps another 50 local folks who happened to stumble onto this ceremony waited eagerly. Also present were 27 members of the Ticho family from England, Israel, South America and the United States who came, on this Sunday morning, specifically to attend this dedication and to tour the Czech Republic. Windows of surrounding houses were open with curious residents peering out. Children squeezed through the crowd to get a better look. Now they all stood silently, with eyes on the ambassador, waiting to see what happens next. Two newsreel cameramen and some reporters were covering the event.

The ambassador paused briefly, waiting for his last sentence to be translated into Czech, then stepped towards the wall to pull down a white sheet that was covering the plaque. He gripped the cloth and pulled down. Nothing happened. He tried again. The cloth remained in place. There was a moment of embarrassed silence. "This is no way for this ceremony, after all the work that has gone into it, to end," I said to myself and joined the ambassador for one more pull. The cloth came down revealing the plaque and filling me with

BEFORE: The house at U Templu #10 in Boskovice before restoration. The house belonged to Uncle Jacob but had been sold to "new" owners.
AFTER: The same house after restoration.

great emotion. Some of the family members joined me with a tear or two. The crowd applauded, and I felt a great sense of accomplishment. It had been a long road, and I had just saved a piece of our family's history.

During the past few years, with the help of a dedicated and skilled genealogist, we were able to trace the Ticho family back eight generations to the late 1600's. They all lived, married, raised families and died in Boskovice, a small town in today's Czech Republic. This town was a major spearhead among the Jewish communities of the land, an effort in which the Ticho family played a substantial role. I also learned the important role that the house at U Templu Street 10 (By the Temple Street 10) in Boskovice played in our family history. In 1846, the house belonged to the Fuchs family. The head of this family was the deacon of the large town synagogue and was a well-respected member of the Jewish community. His daughter, Esther, was married to Avraham Ticho, the *Dayan* (assistant rabbi) of the community, my great-grandfather and the highly esteemed head of a major branch of the Ticho family.

On March 27, 1846, Esther Ticho left her home at house number 56 and came to the Fuchs house at U Templu 10 (city registered house number 18) in order to be with her mother as she delivered her sixth child and second son, Yitzchak Zvi Ticho, the man who one day would become the father of 13 children, grandfather of 35, my grandfather and the family root of countless other family trees and branches thereafter.

> *...when I first learned of the significance of this house, it was in great disrepair.*

In 1995, when I first learned of the significance of this house, it was in great disrepair. So much so, that no one lived in it. The roof leaked, the chimney needed rebuilding, the exterior was in shambles and the house was near collapse. Old real estate records indicated that Abraham Ticho, my great-grandfather, purchased the house in 1843. When Abraham died, the house was passed on to his son, Yitzchak and then to Yitzchak's eldest son, Jacob. The house was in the family for over 100 years until it was seized by the Nazis in 1940. After World War II the house was nationalized by the

Communist Czechoslovak government, and then the town authorities sold it to two Czech families.

I decided that it was important that this house should be preserved. It is hard for me to explain why I felt so strongly that this piece of our family history should not fall victim to time and neglect. During an earlier 1996 visit in Boskovice, I learned that another house that played a major role in our family's history no longer existed. The house on the main square of the town that my grandfather, Ignatz Hirsch Ticho, (Yitzchak Zvi Ticho) bought and where my father and all his siblings were born, had been torn down and replaced by a new building. Now, I felt that the house at U Templu 10, this last vestige of the life of our family that had stretched over several centuries in this town, must be preserved.

I approached the two owners of the house at U Templu 10 (one owned the downstairs and the other the upstairs) with a simple proposal: Allow me to replace the roof, rebuild the chimney and repair the exterior of the house and I will ask you for just two things — first, allow me to place a plaque on the outside of the house and second, agree not to sell the house for 15 years. After a few weeks, an agreement was signed, and the reconditioning of the house began. I was anxious that the work be completed by the time of the "June 1998 Ticho Family Festival" in Israel that was followed by the family gathering in Boskovice for the dedication of the plaque. While this is my personal campaign, I was eager to have other family members share in the restoration of our ancestral home. To my great pleasure several did with small and large donations and by attending the dedication.

It is through a very fortunate set of circumstances that the family of Ignatz Ticho not only flourished, but also managed to survive the Holocaust with most of its family members alive. It might have been the strict and formal Jewish upbringing in the Ignatz Ticho household that resulted in such a great bond among the 13 adult children that translated into an intense, dedicated, and unified effort to save the family. Or, it might have been just sheer luck. In any event, when, after World War II the survivors of one of the greatest human tragedies gathered, many offspring of Ignatz Zvi (Hirsch) Ticho were among the fortunate few who were alive. Today, some 75 years later, these survivors have built many large thriving families of their own in Israel, the United States of America, Argentina, Uruguay, Australia, and England and, true to the spirit of their forefathers, continue to live and act as one large extended Jewish family.

It is my sincere wish that, like I did, other members of our family will take their children and grandchildren by the hand and bring them to Boskovice and Brno and say: "This is where our forefathers were born, here is where they prayed, here is where their children played, where they lived, and this is where they were laid to rest. This town was once the beating heart of a Jewish community that lived here for over a 1000 years and, throughout the few good times and some bad times, held firm to the teachings of our religion and made the survival of our Jewish faith possible."

The plaque (above) reads in Hebrew, Czech, and English: "In this house, on March 27, 1846, was born Ignatz Hirsch Ticho, a scholar and the founder of the Ticho family."

The Railroad and the Carriage Team

As the 19th-century approached its end, some fundamental modifications in the life of the Jewish citizens of Boskovice, a town in central Moravia, began to take effect. Pipes were installed to bring water to homes. There was no longer the need to trek two or three times a day in order the haul heavy containers of water that were needed in the very large Ticho household. With running water came the luxury of indoor plumbing. Then the wonder of electricity arrived and miraculous lamps replaced the dangerous candles and gas lamps. It was also time to make progress in transportation.

But in this field, Boskovice lagged far behind. Although the town was an important industrial center in the late 1800's, the Austro-Hungarian railroad magnates in Vienna decided not run the Vienna-Brno-Prague railroad line through the town. Instead, the line skirted the town some four or five miles to the West through the Skalice railroad stop. Thus, Boskovice travelers who wished to use the railroad were obliged to climb on board a carriage and depend on a coachman and a horse to provide the required transportation to reach the Skalice station.

There were many tales told about this Boskovice to Skalice transportation "system." My father once relayed the following, perhaps apocryphal, story to me: It is about a young man who hired the coach for the trip to Skalice. When the coach approached an incline, the coachman turned to his passenger and said: "Sir, it is such a lovely day and you are a young man — why don't we give the horse a break and climb up this rise alongside the coach?" The young man agreed and the three, coachman, passenger and horse walked up the hill. At the top of the hill the coachman turned to his passenger once more and said: "The horse worked so hard getting us up the hill, lets walk downhill — it's so easy." And so they did. This happened several times on the way and when they arrived at the station the passenger addressed the coachman with: "I came here

... it was customary to send fur coats and fur-lined sacks to the station to keep passengers warm ...

because I have business in Brno. You came here to pick up some baggage. But tell me please, why did the horse have to come along?"

Two carriages shuttled back and forth to provide the service between our town and the Skalice station. Two Jewish coachmen, who were in intense competition, operated these horse-drawn carriages. Traffic was lively and space on the coaches was limited. Traveling along the road was slow because the horses had several slopes to overcome. Therefore, in the winter when members of the family were expected to arrive by train, it was customary to send fur coats and fur-lined sacks to the station in order to keep the passengers warm during the trip. On occasion this caused problems and confusion as to which furs belonged to whom.

It stands to reason that the construction of a railroad spur to connect our town, Boskovice, with the main railroad line at Skalice was always in the air. This project was frequently debated but did not seem to materialize. In our town, the family of the industrialist Loew Beer made many charitable donations that, in addition to a house of prayer, he also supported an old folks home and an orphanage. In the old folks home lived a Jewish man who was known to everybody in town simply as Cousin Mosheh. He was an elderly, stooped man who leaned on a cane and always seemed to have a droplet under the tip of his nose. Cousin Mosheh, who had no living relatives, had a fascination about the proposed phantom spur railroad. Every news item regarding the project fired him up with eagerness, and every dashed hope depressed him. But he never lost hope that someday the branch railroad track between Boskovice and Skalice would come into being. Small wonder that he was the butt of many cruel jokes. Mischievous and nasty people would mention in his presence that a team of engineers had arrived in order to survey the area. Of course, that would ignite Cousin Mosheh who would immediately set out for a futile search for these fictitious engineers.

But then, suddenly one day, the project truly became a reality. Cousin Mosheh was elated. He would follow the team of engineers doing the surveying without let-up. When the engineers' work neared the Skalice station, he even rode each day on the coachman's bench, which was free, in order to be close to all the activities. When construction began, one could find him every morning at the construction site, and he was able to answer with accuracy, pride and detailed factual information all the jocular questions that were directed at him. He relished the attention that he was now enjoying.

Then came the day of the train's dedication. Cousin Mosheh received a special invitation to the festivities from the Boskovice stationmaster. He was also personally greeted by the stationmaster of Brno, the county chief, and all the other dignitaries. Then he was invited to ride in the deluxe salon coach on the inaugural trip of the train. Finally, after the festive train arrived in Skalice, the 88-year-old man was presented with a lifetime pass for free rides on the Skalice-Boskovice railroad.

The local newspapers, of course, featured this story in several editions. These included several photographs of Cousin Mosheh as he was honored. He became famous and known not only to the Jews in town but to the whole population in the county.

It is doubtful that this could ever happen again.

Boskovice relics.

Fond Memories Of Brno

A Childhood with Three Brothers

It must have been one of my mother's happiest days — April 20, 1931. On that day the fourth male child was added to our own special branch of the Ticho family tree. To Harold, Leo, and me the name Stepan Felix Ticho was now added. Stepan in Czech, Ishtvan in Hungarian, Steven in English or Stephan in German was selected to give the child an internationally accepted name. *Felix*, which means "happy" in Latin, was added as a wish for his future. His Hebrew name, after the recently departed Uncle Heinrich, became *Chayim* which means "life" in Hebrew. Unfortunately, neither Felix nor Chayim protected my little brother from a tragic end which he encountered much too soon.

In 1937, in spite of the political turmoil in Central Europe, life was still essentially carefree for me at the age of ten.

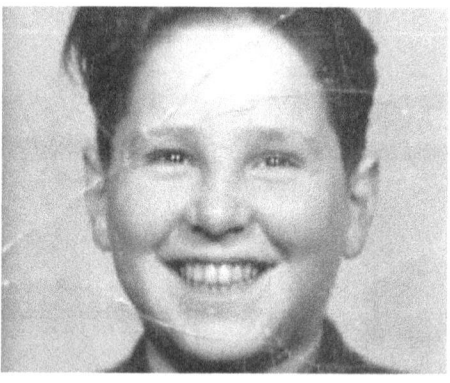

By the time this passport photo was taken two years later conditions had changed drastically.

A day after the happy event, our governess escorted me to a place with which I would soon become very familiar, the private hospital on the Sadova Ulice (now Drobneho Ulice) in Brno, Czechoslovakia, in order to meet my new brother. I am certain that the little baby duly impressed me. But what I remember most about the event was that this new member of the family was introduced to me as my birthday present. Steven was born April 20th and my birth date was April 21 — just one day later. I just did not think that the baby was an appropriate gift for my fourth birthday.

Fortunately, my disappointment was quickly dissipated when my mother gave me a very fascinating toy. It consisted of little multi-colored wooden cubes that one could put into a honeycomb frame to make all kinds of creative designs. That, I felt, was a more appropriate gift. For years thereafter during our childhood, Steven's and my birthdays were celebrated on the same day always creating a very embarrassing comparison of the gifts that each one of us received. I always felt very uncomfortable, because my gifts appeared to be more costly and larger than Steven's. Steven never complained but I was embarrassed and felt awful.

I visited this hospital on two more occasions. When I was about 9-years-old I had my tonsils removed there. That was fun because I got to eat a lot of ice cream because, I was told, ice cream reduced the discomfort caused by the operation. Some time later I was at this hospital once again to be subjected to one of the most painful experience of my life — to that date. Some two years earlier I woke up in the middle of the night with a strange feeling. The left side of my face felt all twisted up. I had a strange sensation in my head, and I could not talk or see clearly. I moaned loudly and our governess, who slept in the same room with us, turned on the light and called for my parents. This seizure lasted for about two minutes and, when it ended, my bed was all wet. No, I had not wet the bed. In a panic and not knowing what to do, the adults had doused me with cold water hoping to end the emergency with this shock treatment. It did not really help. The seizure ended on its own. Needless to say, this became a matter of great concern of my parents.

My parents frantically searched for a medical answer. We now started regular trips to Vienna to see several "specialists." The seizures did not affect me in any other way, so these trips were like little vacations when I could visit with relatives in Austria and have a few days off from school. There did not seem to be a simple explanation for the seizures so, along with the visits to the doctors, came a variety of prescriptions as the doctors tried this and then that.

These medicines, of course, had to be taken at regular intervals according to the doctor's strict orders. Robert Stern, my grammar school teacher, was advised of these procedures and my mother stressed the urgency of having the medication taken precisely on time. Mr. Stern, who underneath was really a great person, a well-loved teacher, and an excellent educator, apparently was annoyed by this additional obligation and made it a practice to announce to the class: "Now we must interrupt our studies while I make sure that Ticho takes his pills." One day I had a seizure in his class and, thereafter, he never made a joke of the matter again.

After a while, I developed a method of stopping a seizure before it really got started. If I was awake and I felt a seizure coming, I would quickly grab my left cheek both inside and outside and pull on it hard until the feeling would pass. It worked most of the time. At night, was a different story. I continued taking different medications that did not seem to be doing much for me. At this point the doctors decided to subject me to a spinal puncture. To this day I have no idea what the purpose of this procedure was. All I remember was that I was taken to the hospital, the nurses undressed me and set me down on a table. I was bent over until my head touched my knees and was held down while a needle was inserted into my spinal column. I don't know whether something was removed or something was added. All I recall is that my head hurt indescribably. I made my displeasure known with the loudest screams that I could muster.

Now, to all my other problems, was added a skin condition. At various places on my body I would develop a boil. One formed on my face, another on the back of my neck, and under my knees. Dr. Huth, the dermatologist I was visiting, was mystified. All he could do was drain the boils and keep them clean. For nearly six months I suffered and the situation was getting worse. By then it was 1939, the Nazis had seized Czechoslovakia, my seizures had stopped, and Steven and I were living without our parents. A cousin, Claire Rooz, was now taking me to Herr Doktor Huth whenever my boils got too large. On one of these visits the good doctor asked what medications I was taking. When Claire told him, the doctor literally flew out of his chair, which was not easy since he was a very big and stout man. He rushed over to his library, seized a large book, stormed through the pages until he reached what he was looking for. Then, triumphantly, showed my cousin that I was suffering from an acne caused by a reaction to the bromide medication I was taking. He ordered me to immediately cease taking this drug.

Over the next few months everything healed nicely leaving me with a few marks that I still have today. And thus, at last, the whole seizure episode came to an end. I never learned whether it was the medications that solved my problem, whether the spinal puncture cured me, or whether I simply grew out of the problem. In early 1939, just before my 12th birthday, I had my last seizure and have had none since. When we visited Dr. Huth the very last time, the German anti-Jewish regulations no longer allowed him to practice medicine. Rather bitterly, this outstanding and highly regarded physician showed us his new equipment, a box of plumber's tools, with which he was now hoping to earn a living.

I am afraid that the medical problems of the four boys gave my parents a great deal of heartache. Within a year of Steven's birth, we were back to three boys again with the death of my brother Leo from a middle-ear infection. This tragedy was followed shortly by a serious bout with scarlet fever that nearly killed my older brother Harold. When it was not disease, then accidents pursued the family. Harold was struck by a truck while riding a bicycle and broke his hip. For months he was confined in a toes-to-waist cast while the doctors tried to restore the use of the hip joint. They were only partially successful and the problem was not really overcome until Harold underwent a hip joint replacement operation some 60 years later. Little Steven also started out with his share of medical problems. The family soon discovered that he needed help with his eyes, and special glasses were prescribed that kept one eye blocked. This was supposed to strengthen the other eye. For several years Steven had to walk around with these strange glasses or with a patch over one of his eyes. Then he developed a form of allergy that caused his little body to develop water blisters on his skin. The science of allergies was not as advanced as it is today, and the doctors kept searching for the cause of this reaction. Nothing helped. Bandages on his arms and legs were usual sights as we tried to keep the affected areas clean.

> *... our father was in a concentration camp ...*

It was not until Steven reached the age of 9 when the problem, like my seizures, seemed to disappear on its own. By that time, the Nazis had invaded Czechoslovakia, the persecution of Jews had begone, our father was in a concentration camp, our mother was in Switzerland and, somehow, medical problems suddenly became irrelevant.

Stops Along The Way

Adolf Hitler at Prague Castle, 1939.

The Winds of Change

April 21, 1937 was my 10th birthday. That was, perhaps, the last time that our whole family and I celebrated a happy celebration together. Soon things changed dramatically. The initial shock for me was when, a few month after this birthday, my older brother Harold was sent to Switzerland to study.

Then, in 1938, the German army marched into Austria and that country became part of the Greater German Reich. The Austrians lined the streets, cheered and lustily *Heil Hitler*ed as the German Army arrived in their country. Now disquieting reports became a major concern of our family in Czechoslovakia. Half of my father's family was located in Vienna, and we started to hear about their problems. My cousin Ernst, who was studying law, was arrested, and sent to the Buchenwald, a severe concentration camp in Germany. The German government established many such concentration camps.

These camps were prisons, which the Germans used to jail the enemies of the Third Reich, communists, Jews and whomever did not agree with their policies. In these camps the prisoners were subjected to very harsh treatment, and many died from overwork, disease, beatings, suicide, or starvation. Later, the Germans built other camps where the conditions were much, much worse.

Pressure mounted on my uncles and their families. Uncle Joseph, Max, and Sami who were attorneys in Vienna, were told that they could no longer have non-Jews for clients. Uncle Joseph was also arrested, and Uncle Max was publicly humiliated. Uncle Victor, who had a jewelry store, had a Star of David painted on his store window and non-Jews were told not to buy from him. And Uncle Isidor, this wonderful, dedicated doctor and humanitarian, was told that

Uncle Joseph and family made their way to British-controlled Palestine.

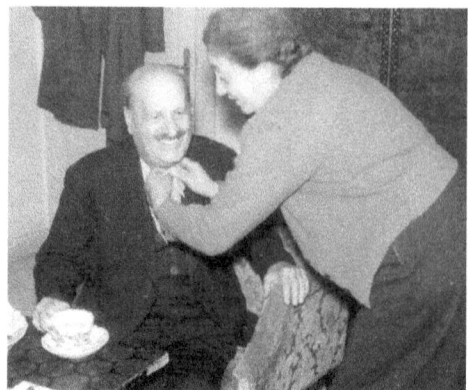

Dear Uncle Max, a highly respected attorney, suffered great humiliations at the hands of the Nazis. He and his remarkable wife, Margareta, settled in Jerusalem.

from now on he could only treat Jews. The families were talking about leaving Vienna.

In 1937, my cousin Harry, the son of Uncle David, was sent to England to study. Harry's older brother, Robert, who had returned from California after completing his degree in agriculture, left for Palestine. My uncle Alfred arrived from Palestine, married his niece Ella Reiniger, and urged the family to make plans to leave Europe. Uncle Alfred would send documents, money, and instructions that enabled many Ticho family members to leave Vienna and make their way to Palestine. Things seemed to be coming apart.

Our school population started to change. Friends, with whom I had grown up and gone to school with since kindergarten, were suddenly gone. Some were going to Palestine, but many were departing for places I had heard about only in my geography lessons. I took my atlas and looked up Cuba, Shanghai, Uruguay, South Africa, Australia, Costa Rica, Hong Kong, India, Australia, and many other strange-sounding places. Some friends just disappeared. One day, they were in school and the next day they were gone. It was sad seeing so many friends leaving. At the same time, new students were arriving at the school. These were from Jewish families who fled to Czechoslovakia running away from Germany, Austria, and other countries such as Poland, Lithuania, Latvia, Estonia, and Russia.

A new crowd of people was now seen on the streets of Brno, my hometown. These were groups of men dressed up in white shirts, short leather pants, and white stockings. They would march through the streets singing German songs and carrying a flag different from our Czechoslovak flag. Gangs of these people would wait for our Jewish school day to end and follow some of us from school.

They would call us dirty names and occasionally chase us and beat us up when they caught us. We learned to keep our eyes open and walk to and from school through small back streets. Sometimes some of the older boys in our schools would send a few of us little kids ahead and wait until we were attacked. Then they would show up and beat up on the guys picking on us.

These rebels were part of the German ethnic party led by a Sudeten German named Konrad Henlein (1898–1945). The Sudetenland was the part of Czechoslovakia that bordered on Germany and many ethnic Germans lived in that part of the country. For 20 years, under the democratic rule of President Masaryk's Czechoslovakia, these Sudenten Germans, along with the other ethnic minorities in the country, enjoyed full freedom to go to German schools, enjoy German theater, read German newspapers and books, have their own sports organizations and political representation. Henlein insisted that they were, nevertheless, a persecuted minority and was now agitating to get that part of Czechoslovakia to join Germany.

In 1938, our family in Vienna was slowly disappearing. Uncle Max, Joseph, Sammy, and their families left for Palestine. Uncle Victor and family came through Brno on his way to France. Uncle Isidor and Aunt Sara came to Brno from Vienna and moved in with one of our uncles. My cousin Trude, Uncle Joseph's daughter, went to Bombay, India. Jacob's son Otto and family departed for Palestine. Cousin Anna Kolari (Reiniger) and family left for Montevideo, Uruguay, and Uncle David's daughter, Lisa Weiss, left for Australia. Other older first cousins scattered to other parts of the world. By now, I was very disturbed and concerned.

Our summer vacation that year was quite different from previous years. In 1938, we went to Cortina deAmpezzo, a famous ski resort in Italy. In the

Uncle Isidor and Sara were sent to the Terezin concentration camp. Most of the older prisoners in this camp starved to death.

Uncle Victor and family wandered through Europe and settled in New York where he earned a modest income as a jeweler.

Uncle Samuel and family made their home in Jerusalem where his wife, Rosa, resumed her dental practice.

summer it is a breathtaking location in the mountains. Harold joined us from Switzerland and we spent a great two months hiking and sightseeing. Our governess, Gusti Miksch, was with us and she taught us several German and Italian marching songs which we sang as we went exploring the many trails marked in the valley. For a little while we forgot what had been troubling us back home in Brno. But then a strange thing happened. When school vacation ended, we did not return home. Instead we left for Zurich, Switzerland. We stayed there for about six weeks awaiting political developments in Europe and in Czechoslovakia.

What to do? Was it safe to return to Czechoslovakia, or should we remain in Switzerland or leave for another country? We learned that the Swiss authorities would not let us stay. If we left for Palestine or some other country our family would lose all our possessions in Czechoslovakia. The pressure on my parents must have been terrific. In mid-October 1938, our parents decided that it might be safe for us to return to Brno. Their decision almost cost all of our lives.

I got back into school (my second-year gymnasium) a little late and had to do some catching up. My parents hired a tutor to help me. Even with his help, it was difficult to concentrate. There were so many things going on. I was 11-years-old, and I was no longer kept in the dark as to what was happening. We heard many reports of Jews who were abused right in our own country by the German gangs. This was happening particularly in the northwestern part of Czechoslovakia that bordered on Germany and where many ethnic German people lived. Hitler demanded that these areas be surrendered to Germany. There was great excitement; people expected that a war between Germany and Czechoslovakia might start at any time. We learned about poison gases in school and started to prepare air raid shelters at the house. Gas masks were handed out to the citizens, and we learned to use them. It was all very frightening.

Despite the seriousness of the situation, the Czechs managed to maintain their usual wry sense of humor. The initials CPO started appearing in many places. The letters stood for *Civilni Protiletecka Obrana* (Civilian Air Raid Defense), signs that were now seen on shelter doors, helmets of wardens, emergency cars, first aid kits, and poison gas clinics. Among the Czechs rumors claimed the CPO really stood for *Co Plasite Obcany* (Why are you panicking the citizens?).

In November 1938, several Jewish organizations staged a special event in one of the theaters in Brno. Each group was scheduled to perform for an audience made up mostly of the children's parents. Some groups put on skits, some sang Zionist songs, some danced Jewish folk dances, and some demonstrated gymnastics. It was supposed to be a fun evening. Everything was going very well. Our group, the Barak Kvuzah of the Zionist youth organization *Techelet*

Lavan, (blue and white) had performed a skit about how life would be when we get to Palestine. Then there was an intermission. First there was an unusual murmur in the crowd, which grew and grew and became some very excited conversations. The show did not resume after the intermission.

My mother and father surprised me backstage and told me to get dressed. "We are going home, and hurry." A few days earlier, a Jewish refugee in Paris had fired shots at an official at the German Embassy. This evening, which became known as the *Kristallnacht* (the night of the broken glass), Nazi gangs throughout Germany staged anti-Jewish demonstrations destroying Jewish property, arresting tens of thousands of Jews, burning synagogues, and attacking Jews on the street. Word about these attacks reached our gathering in Brno along with rumors that gangs of anti-Semites were also roaming through our town staging similar attacks. The second half of the performance was canceled, and all of us rushed for the safety of our homes.

Things never became the same again. It would be a decade before we started to live a normal — but a much, much-changed — existence.

Interior view of the destroyed Fasanenstrasse Synagogue, Berlin, burned on *Kristallnacht*.

My brother Steven, at 2 years.

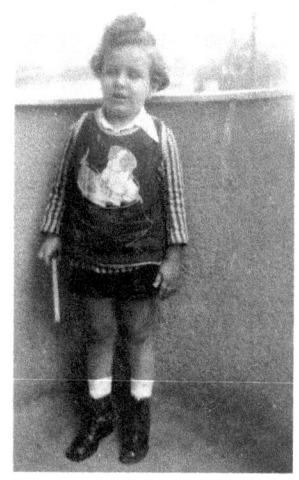
As a toddler.

At 8 or 9.

With Alfred, Irma and Fannie.

New arrival in the USA.

During his army assignment in Germany.

With Father Nathan in Chicago.

As a young professional and family man.

Brotherly Love

My brother Steven's birth on April 20, 1931, was the beginning of a close loving association between us that lasted until 1978 when I flew to Chicago to attend his funeral. Steven and I were destined to be close for a lifetime. To start with, he and I shared a room and a governess together. We ate together, played together, traveled together, shared vacations together, invented games, even a language, shared secrets, and plotted against adults — particularly our governess. While I was overweight most of my first 13 years, Steven was small and thin. He had blondish hair that my mother liked to comb into three large rolls that reached from front to back. When his permanent teeth came in his two front teeth protruded somewhat and gave him the slight appearance of a squirrel. He was even-tempered, and the two of us got along very well. We hardly ever fought and when both of our parents were pulled away from our home starting in April 1939, Steven and I became even closer.

We would take the streetcar together to school — he to the grammar school and I to the gymnasium (high school which started in the 5th year). Then we would meet to go home together. We did our homework together and went to the nearby park together by sneaking in through the bushes thus avoiding the "No Jews Allowed" signs the Germans had posted at all recreational facilities. As a result of this close relationship, we managed to overcome many of the problems that we had to face as the Nazis were taking our life apart. And when we had to travel together around war-torn Europe, we trusted each other and never had any doubts that we would succeed.

In Chicago and in New York, we continued sharing a room and continued our close association. It was not until I went to Israel in 1953 that our first separation occurred. By then, Steven had graduated from the same high school as I did, where he also followed me as a star on the Hyde Park High School soccer team. Despite our closeness, our personalities were quite different. Steven approached life with a great deal less seriousness than I did. He did not let school studies interfere with his relaxation, and his high school grades left a great deal to be desired. However, when he realized that he had to have good grades to get into a good college, he settled down in his senior year and suddenly became an honor roll student.

When he and several of his friends were facing the military draft, they decided they were all going to volunteer together to serve in the United States Air Force rather than be drafted into the Army and serve in the infantry. So they all went to the recruitment office together to sign up. Unfortunately, Steven foolishly confessed that, as a high school student, he had joined an organization called American Youth for Democracy. Now, at the height of Senator McCarthy's anti-Communist crusade, the AYD organization was listed as a possible Communist front organization. As a result, the Air Force turned Steven down while the rest of his friends all qualified. Steven was bitterly disappointed and, when he was finally drafted into the Army, he was determined, in his own words: "To do as little as possible." He then went about to carry out his plan.

During basic training he managed to become "ill" just as the eight-week course was coming to an end. He was then assigned to the quartermaster department where he distributed uniforms to new recruits for a few weeks until he was discovered and was put back to start the basic training course all over again. He did this three or four times. As a result, it was more than ten months before he finally finished the 8-week basic training course.

During this time he devised a plan to make a lot of money. "If I could buy a large car," he told me, "I could drive soldiers back and forth from the camp to Chicago, charge a fee, and make some money." He explained the plan to me and convinced me to loan him the money for the down payment on a large Buick and to pay for the insurance. The plan worked well for about three or four trips. Unfortunately, on one of the trips the car ended up on the side of the road on its roof totally destroyed. Fortunately, no one was seriously hurt, and Steven proudly boasted that he had enough foresight to turn off the ignition as the car was rolling over so that a fire would not start. The insurance payments partially paid back my loans. This was typical of Steven's approach to life that was, at times, both endearing and exasperating,

The Army now sent him to a camp in New Jersey where, while nobody was watching, he managed to hide his file so that he was not called to be shipped overseas. For the next five months or so, Steven stayed at this army base during the week doing odd jobs and spending his weekends enjoying life in New York City. During all this time he was not paid. It wasn't until he ran out of money and, at last, asked for his pay, that the Army "discovered" him and decided to ship him overseas to Germany. There he notified his commanding officer that he spoke German fluently and was promptly assigned to the luxurious position of personal driver for the colonel. After seven months of doing little more than driving the colonel around Germany, eating officer's food, and enjoying the privilege of shopping in the officers' supply stores, Steven was shipped back to the U.S.A. to be discharged. Thus, as promised, he fulfilled his threat to do as little as possible during his military service.

... he hid his file ...

At the University of Illinois campus on Navy Pier in Chicago, Steven proved again that, when he wanted, he could do outstanding work. His success there enabled him to study law at Northwestern University near Chicago. He successfully launched a new life as an attorney and as a newly married man. His family soon included three daughters, Terry, Karen, and Cydni, and, as his career blossomed, the family moved into ever-larger homes. His bright personality and his brilliant mind attracted many loyal friends and the respect of his colleagues in the legal profession. Our close relationship continued even after I moved to New York in 1962.

However, medical problems pursued him. At one point Steven was suffering from kidney stones in one kidney. While caring for this problem, the doctors decided to x-ray both kidneys. To everyone's shock a highly malignant cancer was found in the other kidney. This kidney was immediately removed. This completely accidental discovery certainly saved Steven's life, but the experience influenced him greatly. He had always approached life with a certain free spirit attitude. Now, he felt, he was living on borrowed time and became a gambler with his life. His marriage broke up, and he lived a lonely personal life while keeping active in his office. A night intruder came into his apartment on the 63rd floor of the Hancock Building and ended his life. At his funeral, I was asked to say a few words. But I knew that I could never do it. So, I wrote the following, and the rabbi was kind enough to read it for me:

STEVEN F. TICHO 1931-1978

How do you say goodbye to a brother?
A man that you loved above every other.
To the baby, when born, so tiny and frail,
Would worry his parents, for often he'd ail.
To the smiling young boy full of charm and
    such grace
Though his glasses and teeth seemed
    too large for his face,
Whose head was adorned with a curl on each side
That his mother would comb with such pleasure and pride.

Yes, how do you say goodbye to a brother
When you know that there never again be another?
To the youngster we teased in a cruel children's game
By threatening to reveal his unique middle name.
Yet Felix (which means happy) was a prophetic selection
For it suited his lifestyle to near perfection,
For he'd always accepted life's strange
    aberrations
And discovered the humor in most situations.

Oh – ... how do you say goodbye to a brother
As memories pile up one after another?
Of the boy, who with you, Europe crossed
To escape the dread fate of the Holocaust.
And whose Bar Mitzvah became a sign to all men
That the family had survived and will live once again.
Then he managed, while breaking
    most every rule,
To charm his way through school after school.

How do you say goodbye to a man
Who enjoyed life like few others can?
Who laughed at the pomp and punctured pretense
And of this mad world, could somehow some sense.
So even in the army, by strategic complaining,
He arranged for himself ten months' basic training.
And whose studies were often much of a jest
But as an attorney, he was one of the best.

How do you say a final amen
To a husband, a father, a family man?
Whose wisdom and help gave our life sense and order
And whose love and devotion had no limit or border.
Just mention a need, a task or a worry
And his help was there – ... and in a great hurry.
He dealt with our problems with strength and acumen
And the few times he stumbled just proved he was
    human.

How do you say goodbye to a friend
On whose word and bond you could always depend?
Who could turn darkness to the brightness of noon
By the simple action of entering a room.
Whose nature gained him, as everyone knows,
The love of his friends, the respect of his foes,
His partners' faith, and his staff's total trust
For he dealt with them honestly, fairly, and just.

How do you say goodbye to a soul
Whose journey was ended before reaching its goal?
Forgive us, dear Steven but life is so cruel
It gives us no guidance, or practice, or rule.
It leaves us alone in dumb disbelief
To suffer such torment, sorrow, and grief – ....
To stand here before you, with this terrible ache,
Our hearts filled with pain and near to a break.
We long for the power to make it all seem.
The frightening end of a terrible dream.
That soon we will wake to the sun's early call
And discover all this had not happened at all – ...
And we'll hear once again your favorite lesson:
"Smile – and try to be – a better person."
Yet miracles like these, alas, are but few
And a voice tells us softly: "It's true – ... it's all true."

Yes the time is at hand, the hour is now
We must say goodbye – though we just don't know how
Our hearts will recover and our tears will dry
And the pain will be lifted as time passes by.
And into our souls your example we'll burn
How to love every man and be loved in return.
So – sleep well dear father, husband, and friend,
Dear brother – your journey, alas, is at an end.
We'll miss you as long as we all shall live
We'll long for the love and kindness you'd give
We'll look for a partner, like you, to share
A joke, a drink, a bet, or a dare – ...
And we'll search, dear Steve, till the day that we die
For a better farewell then:
    "God Bless – ...and Goodbye."

On The Move

The major events in my brother Steven's and my early life were the summer vacations. We always spent them together and shared the adventures. The earliest vacations that I can recall were spent in a small town north of Brno called Krtiny in Czech or Kiritein in German. There we were housed in a villa belonging to a local physician. The villa had extensive grounds and a large garden, and we spent our days playing outside. We were watched over by a maid and a governess, and our parents visited us on Sunday. I don't recall whether Harold was with us, but in 1933 my older brother Leo, my younger brother Steven and I were spending our summer there when Leo became ill. After he died, we no longer went to Krtiny, and I never visited the village again.

The year 1934 marked a major move in our lives. Late that year the apartment house, that was being built for us by Architekt Drucker on Dolni Ulice 5 (now Erbenova Ulice 5) was completed, and our family moved from the old apartment on the Starobrnenska Ulice 9/11 to this

The house on Starobrnenska Street 9/11 (first house on the left) in which, from time to time, "ghosts" visited our bedroom and where, on the ground floor, the offices and warehouse of the Bratri Ticho men's clothing factory were located.

This is our house on Erbenova Street 5 that Nathan Ticho built in 1933. The Ticho family occupied the whole second floor. The window at the far right was the room Steven, the governess and I shared. Today, the space has been divided into three apartments. The house was returned to me after the Communists were kicked out of office. It was sold in 2006.

brand new, large and luxurious apartment that covered the whole second floor of the new building. One of the very few memories that I retain from the old apartment is the only really clear one of my older, deceased brother Leo. On this occasion I was pretending to be a painter and had climbed on a small table to paint the top of the tile stove that was located in the corner of our room. My oldest brother Harold and Leo got into an argument as to who had whose pencil and at one point one or the other pushed the table sending me flying. I fell and hit my head hard on the stove and, of course, started crying as injured 5-year-olds are prone to do. Father was summoned from the store that was located on the street level below the apartment and, after attending to my hurt feelings, decreed proper punishment for my siblings.

The other vivid and most unpleasant memory I have is the rather cruel method some of our servants used to try to make me behave or go to sleep. If I was particularly difficult, the door would open and a ghostly figure would come into the dark room making weird scary noises. Of course, the procedures had exactly the opposite effect, and I would scream my head off in fright. It was not until years later that I realized that the "ghost" that visited our room was our maid with a white sheet thrown over her head, holding a lighted candle underneath.

In 1935, my parents, for the first time, decided to take a summer vacation as a family. The five of us plus the governess, a driver, and a load of baggage piled into our large nine-passenger Skoda car and headed southwest to Yugoslavia and the beautiful spa at Bled. On the way, the overloaded car had to negotiate some steep mountain roads. At one point the car simply could no longer manage and started rolling back downhill. We were in real danger of simply going off the side of the road and down the mountainside. In desperation, our driver turned the wheel so that the car ran backwards into the opposite side of the road, up against the mountain, and into a ditch. The rear wheels sank in and the large trunk, which was attached to the rear of the car, broke open. We all got out and surveyed the damage. We were told that there was a town nearby and started walking. Two days later, after the car had been rescued and repaired, we arrived at the beautiful resort.

Bled is surrounded by beautiful mountains and is located on a large lake with a small island in the middle of it. A small, red-roofed church is on this island and can be reached by climbing up a hundred or more steps. The Yugoslav royal house also had a summer castle on the lake and, every once in a while, the royal Rolls Royce, with the royal emblem painted on the side of the door, would glide into town bearing the recently widowed queen into shops or cafes. King Alexander became a victim of an assassination in Marseilles just a year earlier. His two sons were also in Bled, and we would see them, all dressed in white, playing in the garden as we rowed our boat past the front of the castle grounds.

In 1936 and 1937, our summer vacations were spent away from the rest of the family as Steven, I, and our ever-present governess settled in the village of Nedvedice. I was always anxious to have more time with my parents. However, they often seemed to be too busy to spend the days with us. Occasionally, we would stay a day or two in the beautiful woods just north of Brno or go swimming in the nearby village of Bilovice. But, when I would beg my father to take me on an *ausflug* (an outing), he would take my hand and walk with me through all the rooms of our large apartment instead. Needless to say, I was very unhappy with this substitution.

Nedvedice is a village just north of Brno near a river and a beautiful, fortified castle, Pernstyn. We visited this castle regularly and got to know the staff

Surrounded by the foothills of the Alps is the breathtaking spa of Bled, Slovenia, with its beautiful lake and inviting island.

Pernstyn Castle

who would show us all the many rooms, staircases, corridors, balconies, secret doors, and ramparts. We were allowed to go places where the public was not admitted; we even entered the tunnels and cellars of the fortress. During our vacations in Nedvedice, we rented a room on the second floor of a busy country inn. It was the only two-story building in the village. The downstairs was a bar, restaurant, and kitchen. A barn, barnyard, bowling lane and a large garden were in the rear. The barn housed milk cows and horses, and the yard was full of ducks, geese, and chickens. Steven and I learned a great deal about these animals, but our particular favorite was a huge (at least he seemed that way in those days) St. Bernard dog called Sultan. On any day when it was not raining the four of us — Steven, the governess, Sultan and I — would take long walks through the forest and explore the hills surrounding the town. Sultan became the dog we were never allowed to have at home. Mother was frightened of all the diseases we could catch from a dog and always refused our request for a pet.

... We spent two wonderful carefree summers in Nedvedice ...

At one point, we actually acquired a wire-haired terrier. But a week later the dog was returned to the pet shop owner. Mother caught the dog licking Steven's face, and the poor friendly animal was banished. A few days later the dog showed up in front of our apartment house all alone. We were all surprised and pleased to see him except, of course, mother. The pet store owner was called to pick up the dog. He claimed that the dog had run away from the store and was so in love with our family that he managed to find his way back to our house all alone. We insisted that the dog's love should be rewarded, but my parents, rather cynically, suggested that the pet shop owner probably planted the dog in front of our house so that he would not have to refund the purchase price.

We spent two wonderful carefree summers in Nedvedice in 1936 and 1937. Things, however, changed drastically the following year. Summer 1938 saw the whole family together in Cortina D'Ampezzo and in Riccione de Marino in Italy. Cortina, a very popular ski resort, is also a gorgeous place in the summer. High up in the Dolomite Alps and surrounded by mountains, Cortina was an ideal place for long walks and hikes in the forest. In Riccione, on the Adriatic Sea,

The summer vacation in Cortina d'Ampezzo in 1938 turned out to be the last time our whole family would be all together for nearly three years. Harold and Steven enjoy the beautiful surroundings shortly before Harold left for the United States.

we spent our time on the beach. But, in truth, it was not really a true summer vacation.

The family was keeping an eye on events in Czechoslovakia waiting to see what was going to happen as the political pressure from Germany against our country became greater and greater.

THE LIGHT OF ENLIGHTENMENT

Between summer vacations there was always school. All of us went to the schools run by the Brno Jewish community. The Grammar School was in the rear of a large municipal building on what is now Shillinger Plaza. Robert Stern was my teacher when I entered kindergarten, and he remained with our class for the next five years as we progressed through the fourth grade. Mr. Stern was a patient teacher who got a very good response from most of the students. Once in a while he had to handle a disciplinary problem and, unlike some of the other teachers, would not use corporal punishment. The worst he would do was to ask you to take his note home and bring it back with your parent's signature.

I don't recall the exact nature of my offense that, one day, resulted in just such a punishment. For weeks I carried this dreaded note around trying to find an opportune moment to ask my father to sign it. I was plotting to find a way to avoid the punishment that I knew was coming. At various times, I asked my father to demonstrate how he signed his name. When he refused to do so, I started to practice what, I hoped, would be a convincing substitute. I finally thought I had the signature close to perfect and handed in the forged note. However, Mr. Stern was not fooled

The former Jewish High School building in Brno. The top floor was added after the war. It is now a municipal health clinic.

Stops Along The Way

My fifth grade class (first year in the gymnasium) with Professor Otto Ungar, our class counselor. I am in the center of the first row.

The boys of our class (second year gymnasium) insisted on having a photograph taken with Professor Hrdlicka (left). Professor Hrdlicka was both admired and feared. The photograph may have been simply a devious maneuver to get into the professor's good graces. He was respected and strict and it was rumored that he limped because he lost a leg in World War I. The other professor (right) is Otto Ungar, our home room teacher. I could not hold still and am the fuzzy image of the first row right side.

and, to my horror a few days later, I saw Mr. Stern speaking to my father in his office. My punishment was quite severe, and father went to great pains to explain to me the sanctity of a person's signature, the demands of honor and honesty, the pitfalls of not being truthful, and the need to accept responsibility for your actions. This was a lesson I never forgot.

Perhaps the most memorable person at the grammar school was Dr. Kurzweil, our religion teacher. For five years, this remarkable man made the Bible come alive for us. His lectures were adventures that brought reality to the stories, breathed life into the characters and, in the process, taught us the ethics, heritage, and the teachings of our religion. The pointer, that other teachers used to point on the blackboard or to punish evil doers, became a tool in his class. He would slash the air with it to illustrate battles, put it across his shoulders and pretend to be an angel, hit the desk with it to dramatize the power of God, stick an empty milk bottle on its end and pretend to be carrying a lantern or do the same with a piece of paper and call it a flag. We were actually sorry when the bell rang to end his class. Judaism became an integral part of my life thanks to this man's efforts. On the other hand, Mr. Donnenberg who taught Hebrew, which was also a required subject in this school, was remembered for a different skill. The only memory I have of him was that he would settle disciplinary problems by pulling the hairs of your sideburns — a most painful procedure.

Perhaps the most memorable person in the grammar school was Dr. Kurzweil, our religion teacher. For five years this remarkable man made the Bible come alive for us and, in the process, taught us the ethics, heritage, and the teachings of our religion.

At the end of the fourth grade, those students who had done well were promoted directly to the eight-year course in the gymnasium. This was a major move and a great change. Gone were the kindly Mr. Stern, Dr. Kurzweil, and the others, and we were now faced with a multitude of serious and very strict professors. Unlike American high schools where students go from class to class, at our gymnasium the class stayed together in one room and the professors came to you. Different professors, depending on the subjects they taught and the methods that they used, and the way they conducted their lectures had different levels of disciplinary problems. Professor Hrdlicka in the physics laboratory was a strict disciplinarian and demanded your full attention all the time. No humor or levity was allowed. Once, when he was demonstrating that water under pressure could be heated to more than 100 degrees Centigrade, the thermometer

Tall, gaunt, and sickly-looking Professor Blau could not keep order in his class. Few students paid any attention as he spoke, and he became the butt of an occasional prank. As a result of a severe disciplinary crisis, we discovered what a wonderful and sensitive educator he really was.

popped out of the cork, hit the ceiling, and came crashing down on the table. The class dared to laugh and was promptly awarded with a lengthy homework assignment to explain exactly why the thermometer had escaped the cork.

On the other hand, Professor Blau, who taught Czech, was the exact opposite. Tall, gaunt, and sickly-looking, this mild-mannered professor could not keep order in his class. We talked to each other, passed notes, read books, teased the girls, and ignored the professor. Poor Professor Blau. Few students paid any attention as he spoke, and he became the butt of an occasional prank. I can't recall what exactly we had done to him one day early in the school year but, apparently, it was so serious that Professor Blau decided he had had enough. He now threatened all of the boys with the ultimate punishment, i.e. writing their names into the class register. This would have meant a compulsory visit to the dreaded office of the director of the school, Professor Doktor Eduard Drachmann, a visit of your parents to the school plus additional punishments.

The class was stunned by the unanticipated ferocity of Professor Blau's threatened action. One of the students proposed a deal: "The class promises to be absolutely still during your classes for the rest of the year if you refrain from entering the boys' names into the class register." Professor Blau agreed to this proposal and for the next seven months we were perfect gentlemen and ladies in his class. To our amazement, we discovered a brilliant and interesting lecturer who captured our full attention even without the threat of punishment. Everyone's grade in his class rose and, what is even more important, our attitude towards all the other professors also changed. We became an outstanding class.

When the other classes heard of our "strange" behavior in Professor Blau's class, they were puzzled and considered us traitors.

THE LAP OF LUXURY

Our new apartment, that covered the whole second floor of the building, consisted of a large dining room with an adjoining "father's" room, a music room, a salon, three bedrooms, two bathrooms, kitchen, pantry, cold storage area, three balconies and hallways — 13 spaces I counted at one time. One of the most interesting rooms in our new apartment was the Winter Garden. This was a beautiful room with three floor-to-ceiling windows, with marble flooring, an aquarium, potted plants all around, luxurious furniture, a staircase down to the garden below and a tropical garden with a small waterfall. The wall above this tropical garden was designated for a mural.

One day, I was introduced to a jolly heavy-set man who was going to paint this mural. In my first year in the gymnasium, I was surprised to meet this same man again. He was Professor Otto Ungar, our art and homeroom teacher. His charm, wit, and patience made his class a joy to attend, and he was one of the most beloved among our professors. The Nazis sent Otto Ungar, like virtually all the Jews of Czechoslovakia, to the Theresienstadt Concentration Camp. During his confinement there he and several other artists decided to document the life and misery of the camp with drawings. These they would hide away carefully. Ultimately the Nazis discovered some of these drawings and, as punishment, broke the fingers of Professor Ungar's hands. Somehow Professor Ungar survived the Holocaust but died of typhus shortly after being liberated. Fortunately, several his drawings from Theresienstadt were saved, are published in many books, and are displayed at various Jewish museums, particularly in the Czech Republic. Each time I see one of his drawings on display, I am very proud that once, many years ago, he was my teacher and my friend.

My gymnasium school homeroom professor, Otto Ungar, along with several other artists, recorded the life in the Terezin Concentration Camp in drawings and paintings. Some of these were discovered after the war, such as this quick sketch by Ungar.

In my writings I have been picturing our governess, Miss Augusta (Gusti) Miksch, mostly in a negative manner. This stems from our discovery in 1939 that she was a Nazi party member. Prior to that revelation, however, Steven's and my relationship with her was very close and friendly. Miss Miksch, who was probably in her early 50s when she came to work for us, was a very intelligent and even-tempered person who knew how to handle us. Her greatest contribution to our education was the almost painless way she taught us hundreds and hundreds of facts. We played many games that were, at the same time, teaching tools. "I have a city which starts with a Z and ends with an H," she would announce. We could then ask 10 questions to guess the name of the city. Then it was our turn to pose a riddle. When we were not playing "Famous Cities," we played the same game naming countries, composers, poets, writers, scientists, rivers, inventors, statesmen, flags etc. — the variety never ended, and our knowledge expanded.

In the evening, while we were eating our dinner, which for the first few years of our life always consisted of porridge, Miss Miksch would read to us. We discovered Hugh Lofting's series of Doctor Doolittle books and eagerly awaited each new volume to be translated from English to German. Soon we had all 11 of those great books. We then started with another series of books. Each meal was an adventure, and the worst punishment that could be meted out to us was to cancel the story reading. But once the Nazis marched into Czechoslovakia, and our parents were gone, Miss Miksch became the enemy. Steven and I, along with Ladislav Kellner, our janitor's son, banded together to either ignore her or oppose her. Forty-two years later, the next time I met Ladislav he told me that Miss Miksch returned to her hometown in northwest Bohemia and, when the war ended, she was most likely forced by the Czech authorities to emigrate into Germany.

Most of our days were spent with our governess. Occasionally, however, we would get all dressed up and go visiting with our mother. One of her best friends was the wife of Doctor Politzer who had a very nice apartment on the Janska Ulice just a few houses away from father's office in Janska Ulice 21. Mrs. Politzer would always prepare bowls full of candy which she would set out in front of us. Our favorite was a bowl of M & M's that we would eye hungrily. Good manners prevented us from asking whether we could have some. So, we just sat there suffering for what seemed like an eternity until Mrs. Politzer finally remembered to ask us whether we would like some candy. "Very well," my mother would then say, "Very well, you can each take one." How can anyone take just one M & M! This was really cruel, and we

either cheated or we would sneak over to the bowl when we thought that nobody was watching and grab a handful.

Another place that I often visited was the office of Doktor Kapp, my dentist. It seemed like I was forever in need of dental care. There seemed to be no end to drilling, filling, more drilling, and more filling. All this was done without the benefit of an anesthetic, and I truly suffered. The only pleasant thing about these visits was the time I could spend in Doktor Kapp's dental laboratory. We would arrive for my appointments early to allow some time for me to spend in the lab. The technicians were very patient with me and showed me how to prepare an impression, how to make a reverse impression, mold a filling in wax, and then cast it in gold and polish it. I then graduated to crowns and small dental bridges. None of these were actually used on the patients (at least that is what I was told) but I got a lot of practical experience. By the time the Nazis arrived I had gotten to the point where I was going to learn to make dentures. By then, however, Doktor Kapp, who was Jewish, had to close his office and my teeth suddenly did not require so much care anymore. Everyone said I was a natural-born dentist, but I could not see myself inflicting on anyone the kind of pain that I had suffered. My experience, however, came in very handy in the future and my dentists were always quite amazed how well I understood what they were doing or trying to do inside my mouth.

The high points of the year were the Jewish Holidays and family events. During the holidays, particularly at Passover, the family would gather for a large Seder. And, with such a large family, there seemed to be a birth, circumcision, wedding, or Bar Mitzvah nearly every year. (Bat Mitzvot for girls were not as yet an accepted practice in those days.) For these events we either drove down to Vienna in our car, or family members arrived in Brno to attend the event. Sometimes even Uncle Albert or Uncle Alfred arrived from Palestine which seemed to us as if they were coming from the end of the world. When everybody got together it was most confusing for us young children. There was such a wide age spread in the family that keeping track of who was who and how they were related was nearly impossible. I actually had a first cousin who was 31-years-older than I! And that cousin had a son who was older than I! And then, every once in a while, a family member from my mother's side would arrive from Germany or from the United States to add to the happy confusion.

My father's business seemed to be doing well, and I assumed that we were financially secure. However, father never let us forget the need to save for the future while mother made a point to teach us to be charitable. She would cross the street if she saw a beggar so that she could give him or her a coin. Once she overheard one of our maids turn away a beggar who had come to our apartment door begging for some bread to eat. Mother made the maid run after the man to hand him a piece of bread and a slice of salami. Nothing ever got thrown out in our house. Mother made sure that any discarded clothing was given to charity. Throwing food into the garbage was a sin that she would not tolerate.

Nathan and Fannie Ticho in front of our apartment house at 6841 South Clyde Avenue in Chicago in the late 1940s. We lived there from 1943 till 1953 during our formative years.

Strangers who were in need would often sit in the kitchen having a meal and there were needy Jewish students at our Sabbath table or Seder meal. She was also generous in other ways. She would lecture us: "I don't care if the girl you marry does not have a shirt on her back as long as she comes from a good home, has character, and an education."

The years between these earliest childhood memories and the sudden maturity brought on by the Nazi era passed much too fast. These were wonderful, pleasant, and mostly carefree years spent within a close and warm family circle, among schoolmates that shared most of your life, exposed to art, music, and travels and based on a Jewish heritage and on Jewish ethical values.

But the sun shone much too briefly on this springtime, and dark and ominous clouds rose on the horizon that soon tore the fabric of our lives into shreds.

Our Maternal Sage

When our family first arrived in the United States in 1940 we were often invited to family events centered on our Mother's family, the Kleins. Sooner or later, at each of these events, either Uncle Julius Klein or Uncle Ernest Klein would rise, raise a glass of wine and speak about our Klein family forefathers. It was always a solemn occasion highlighted by recounting the work and fame of the great Rabbi Schick. This was all news to us. We had learned a great deal about the Tichos, our father's side of the family, but hardly anything at all about the Kleins, our mother's family.

Then in 1978, uncle Julius Klein mailed the following newspaper article to the family members to acquaint us with the accomplishments and reputation of Rabbi Moshe Schick of Hust, Hungary. Since then, I have had the opportunity to learn more about him in the Encyclopaedia Judaica where a page is dedicated to this great man.

Reading this article and Uncle Julius' comments, made me realize that the great Rabbi Maharam Moshe Schick was my mother's grandfather.

Here is the text of Julius Klein's letter that is addressed to uncle William L. (Bill) Klein, the younger brother of Julius.

FROM THE DESK OF JULIUS KLEIN
JUNE 28, 1978

Dear Bill,
Only a few days ago my attention was called to an article written about our great-grandfather, Maharam Schick — God Bless His Soul — that appeared in "Der Yid", the Jewish Newspaper in New York, , on January 21, 1977.

I would like you to have the translation and I am sure you will treasure this tribute to our sainted ancestor as I do.

Love

Julius

Translated from the Yiddish paper "Der Yid", Jan. 21, 1977 edition by Rabbi Irving Weingart

THE GAON AND TZADIK RABBI MOSHE SCHICK OF BLESSED MEMORY

The Maharam Schick

By Emanuel Baer

Our great sages have said (*taanit 7a*) "great scholarship of Torah can be achieved only by those who are humble of spirit" because humility is the very source of all other virtues. Rabbi Moshe Schick, who became the rabbi of Hust, Hungary, who was recognized by all as the greatest of Talmudic scholars, possessed the highest degree of humility — like the humility of Biblical Moses about whom the Torah says, "Moses was very humble." Rabbi Moshe Schick eschewed material things and was highly critical of those who pursued the quest of money as unbecoming to rabbis and desecrating the "Name of Heaven" — equally he was critical of those who were unworthy of wearing the "Crown of Torah."

Rabbi Moshe Schick was born around 1807 in Brezoveh, Slovakia, and he chose the name Schick when family names were required by governmental decree — it is an acronym of *"Shem Israel Kodesh"* implying the given Jewish name is most holy. His father Reb Yosef died when Moshe was six years of age and his mother, a daughter of great scholars, undertook to further his education. At the age of 11, he went to study at the yeshiva of his uncle Rabbi Isaac Frankel and after three years returned home a Talmudic master. Subsequently, he went to study at the academy of Rabbi Moses Sofer (Chasam Sofer) in Pressburg (today Bratislava, the capitol of Slovakia) where the head of the yeshiva immediately recognized his great erudition and who invited the young Moshe to be his house guest and eat at his table and discuss Torah on all Sabbaths and Holy Days.

Moshe's attachment and longing for this great teacher was so great that in later years whenever he mentioned Rabbi Moses Sofer's name tears would well up in his eyes. At the age of 20, Moses Schick married the daughter of Rabbi Peretz Frankel of Holitsh who supported him for ten years so that he could continue his studies without worldly cares and to enable him to surround himself with students as his scholarly fame spread.

At the highest recommendation of Rabbi Sofer, the head of the Pressburg Yeshiva, Moses Schick was chosen to his first post as rabbi of the small community of Yergen near Pressburg. In considering this offer, Rabbi Moshe Schick reckoned that, although Yergen was a small and poor community, it equally must also be small in sinfulness and the waywardness of its youth must be much less than in a large community. He became the dedicated teacher — the wise counselor and the great benefactor by word and deed.

It is related that one day a poor congregant came to the rabbi in tears that his feudal lord, to whom he owed a large sum of money and was unable to repay, was threatening his life. That very day, Rabbi Schick received his quarterly salary and he beseeched the poor congregant to take an envelope containing his salary to his lord as payment of the debt and that all would be well — and so it was. Such was his benefaction for others even though he and his family suffered deprivation. He once refused an increase in salary voted to him by the heads of the community arguing that since they had refused an increase of the teachers' salaries and of the ritual slaughterers how could he justify an acceptance. Only when the others received an increase did he accept his.

The grave of Rabbi Schick in Hust, Hungary, a goal of many pilgrimages.

As his grandson relates, his grandfather had a regular schedule of courses stating the hours and days when various subjects would be studied. His love of his students was indescribable, relates Rabbi Zalman Spitzer. One of his students would escort him to and from the yeshiva, all the while discussing Torah as not to waste even a precious moment. Alas, the small community of Yergen, where he served for 24 years, was not able to support a large yeshiva. Rabbi Schick left Yergen and became the Rabbi in Hust, Hungary. There he established a yeshiva with hundreds of students that over the years produced thousands of outstanding scholars that spread Torah learning throughout Hungary. Even though to be a rabbi in Hust, a Jewish community considered to be one of the finest in Hungary, was a great honor, he refused to accept his new position until the community agreed that all poor students would be financially supported.

He was steeped in study day and night retiring at the midnight hour and sufficing with only three hours of sleep. Doctors had informed him that his sight was failing and that he should curtail the unlimited usage of his eyes to which he answered "if not to study Torah of what need have I of sight." Eventually, he did go blind, necessitating a student reader.

Like the Biblical Aaron about whom it is said "that he loved peace and pursued peace," so too Rabbi Moshe Schick was instrumental in establishing peace and harmony in many a community by his intervention especially where the authority and dignity of the rabbi was involved, or when a religious disputation split the community. He was the firefighter who extinguished many a blazing community fire. On the other hand, he was zealous and fought like a lion against any religious innovations or modifications of Jewish law. He even fought against the change of a Jewish name given at birth by parents and against rabbis who gave certification to ritual slaughterers who were unqualified because of ignorance. Even though he was an Ashkenazi rabbi and Hust was a stronghold of Hasidim, his relationship with all the Hasidic rabbis was one of love and harmony and so was his relationship with all the great rabbis of Hust and other communities. Although Reform Judaism had made inroads in many communities but not so in Hust — where Rabbi Schick was on constant guard against reform infiltration.

Alas during his last years he went blind and suffered immeasurably from not being able to zealously study Torah, but yet he continued writing his "Responses" to questions asked of him by many and distant communities aided by the assistance of one of his students. He was eulogized by the noted Rabbi of Seagat and by the Gaon Rabbi Chayim Sofer.

On his monument is inscribed: "To our sainted Godly rabbi — known to all ends of the universe as the greatest of scholars. Rabbi Moshe, the son of Rabbi Joseph Schick who served in our community faithfully and devotedly for 18 years and who died at the age of seventy two at the dawning of the Shabbat, Rosh Chodesh Shevat 5639."

"May his Soul Be Bound In The Bond Of Life Eternal."

The revered Maharam Schick was the grandfather of Regina Schick Klein, mother of the Klein Brothers and sisters.

Regina Schick was your mother, Bill and Maharam Schick was our grandfather.

The Gathering Storm

I'm not sure when I started to suspect that something was wrong. It might have been when my parents would suddenly stop talking when I walked into the room. I was used to them doing that once in a while, but now they seemed to be doing it more often. I was also asked to leave the room more often than usual so that I would not hear what was being discussed. Suddenly there seemed to be an important subject that we, the children, were not supposed to know about. Needless to say, it was all very puzzling to us.

My mother's youngest sister, Josepha Klein, had been staying with us for many years. Unmarried and in her early 30s, she was one of our favorite relatives. She took us on walks, told us stories, read books to us, bought us presents, and told us about life in the United States where she had visited. One day, we suddenly learned that she was returning to the United States and was not coming back for a long time. Then, my mother's oldest sister, aunt Gizella, and her husband, Moritz Rooz, and three of their adult children arrived in Brno. They had been living in Berlin, Germany, and left there rather suddenly.

Uncle Moritz went to work for the Ticho Brothers Factory, and his son Walter, who was called Wolf at that time, opened a furrier salon. Their two daughters, Claire and Francis, also found work in Brno. *Tante* (aunt) Gizella became one of our favorite people. She was as dependable as a rock. She was always doing something, if she wasn't cooking or baking, she was knitting, crocheting, or doing some intricate needlework. Her cooking was a revelation after the simple meals the children ate at our house, and her baked goods and cakes were out of this world. A visit to Aunt Gizella's house was a holiday. Uncle Moritz was a quiet man who obviously was a firm believer in Jewish traditions. He had a great singing voice and Chanukah celebrations were a joy at his house as we sang all six stanzas of *Mah Oz Zur* (Rock of Ages). Yet, even though we learned to love our new uncle and aunt, their flight from Berlin seemed strange. In my 8-year-old world, these were major changes in what had been, until now, a fairly steady existence.

The new leader of Germany, Adolph Hitler. Official Portrait, 1938.

The quiet and security to which I had become accustomed was occasionally deeply disturbed by an ugly voice that I heard on the radio. Our house had a large, tall Telefunken radio. I learned to search for stations on different wavelengths and in different languages. At times, during this search, I would encounter a man who was screaming in a raspy voice and people were shouting and applauding. I knew he was speaking in German, but I could not understand him even though I spoke German fluently. I tried to understand what he was yelling about, but had real trouble making sense of his raving. Just occasionally, I would recognize the word *Jude* which means Jew in German. When my parents caught me listening to him, they would ask me to turn the radio off. Soon I learned that the voice belonged to the new leader in Germany, Adolph Hitler.

Now we started to hear some very distressing reports as to what was happening to some Jews in Germany. I was not told about these events. I just overheard little snatches of conversations: "Did you hear that Dr. Oppenheimer was fired from his job as the head of the State Hospital?", "They made Professor Rosen scrub the sidewalk with a toothbrush on his hands and knees in front of the university," "Jews can no longer go to operas, concerts, or any public events," "They burned the synagogue and the Torah scrolls were unrolled in the gutter," "Then they cut off his beard and made him spit on the *mezuzah*." These bits of highly disturbing conversations came ever more often. I was used to a little anti-Semitism, but this was more disturbing.

Things were now changing rapidly. In l937, the founder and first president of Czechoslovakia, Thomas Garigue Masaryk, died at the age of 87. He had been a most beloved leader and everyone was very sad. People cried in the streets and brought flowers and wreaths to memorials that sprang up in every town and village of the nation. The country truly felt as if it had lost a father. We had a very sad memorial service at the school and were surprised to see some of our tough professors with tears in their eyes and wiping their noses from time to time. Many people felt as if they had lost a member of their family. Jews, in particular, took the death very hard. President Masaryk had been a firm believer in democratic principles and always insisted that all religious and ethnic groups in Czechoslovakia be treated equally.

He requested that he be buried in a simple grave in the village cemetery near his favorite summer residence in Lany. My allegiance to this great man is such that I visit his grave when I am in the Czech Republic. It warms my heart to see the flowers on his grave each time I visit, and I am happy to see the occasional other visitors who come to pay their respects more than 83 years after his passing.

Pres. Thomas Garigue Masaryk

His death was a severe blow to the stability of Europe. I overheard my Uncle David say: "Now the Germans won't be afraid to start trouble." As a 10-year-old I wondered what he meant by that.

It took less than two years to make my uncle's prediction to come true.

Uncle David whose dire prediction, alas, became horribly true.

It Took a Miracle

Czechoslovakia became the first victim of Nazi Germany's aggression when its army rolled across the border in March of 1939. This was the first seizure of an enemy country. Prior to this event, Germany absorbed Austria, a German-speaking land that enthusiastically voted 90%-plus to welcome their invaders and form the "Greater Germany." But Czechoslovakia was different. There Czechs sullenly, many with tears streaming down their cheeks, watched the Wehrmacht parade before them and seize the country. Bohemia and Moravia now became a German puppet state called Protectorate Bohemia and Moravia. Slovakia became a Fascist state under the leadership, of all things, a Catholic priest, Father Joseph Tiso!

Since the Nazis came to power in Germany in 1933, many new laws were promulgated all designed to make the life of Jews as painful as possible. About 50% of the Jews in Germany emigrated while it was still possible. Now, in 1939, these same laws were applied to the Jews in the new Protectorate. Like the Jews of Germany, the Jews of the Protectorate made urgent plans to get away. These departures became ever more difficult. It wasn't just all the red tape the German authorities placed on these efforts; the immigrants faced a hostile world that had little or no desire to permit Jews to enter their country. The United States also went to great pains to follow suit by setting up quotas that strictly limited the number of emigrants that were allowed to enter the United States each year from every country.

In 1940, when we were already safe in the United States, we received a desperate postcard from my Uncle Isidor pleading for help. He had registered

Auschwitz concentration camp gate. *Arbeit macht frei* translates to "work sets you free."

Jews in many parts of the world were forced to wear distinctive clothing or a special emblem to distinguish them from the rest of the population. The Nazis chose a yellow six-pointed star for the murderous purposes.

On these rails and through the gate passed train after train bringing two million Jews to their death. Even in April 1944, when the Russian army was already inside Berlin, the Nazi death machine was still dispatching trains to this death factory, Auschwitz.

Isidore Reiniger

We met Paul in Israel during the filming of *Hill 24 Doesn't Answer*. We met again a few years later after he moved to New York. We maintained close contact with him until the day he died. He was my best friend and valued advisor.

for a US visa under the Czech quota in 1940 and was advised that his number would be "considered" in eight years! When this fine and dedicated doctor, father of eight and a learned Jew, starved to death in the Terezin Concentration Camp, he faced six more years of waiting before his application to enter the United States would be "considered"!

Uncle Isidor's lot was not different than the destiny of most of the Jews in Europe. To survive you urgently needed a miracle and miracles were few and far between. Take for example my life-long friend Paul Tyras who spent 3 years in the Terezin concentration camp before he, his little sister, and his parents were sent to Auschwitz. When they arrived there, as was the common practice, they were separated into two columns along the side of the train that had brought them — women, children and old men to the left, the rest to the right. Most of the commands came from members of the *Sonderkomando* (Special Command Forces). These were prisoners — mostly Jews who — for a few months, got better treatment in return for organizing the mass of people that were "processed" each day in this death factory.

The two columns were ordered to move towards a small group of SS men. During this brief march, a member of the *Sonderkomando* recognized Paul's father. They had been school friends many years ago in their hometown. Suddenly this man sneaked up behind Paul and whispered: "When they ask you how old you are, tell them you are sixteen" and then he disappeared. When Paul and his father arrived before the SS men, Paul was asked the anticipated question and the fourteen-year-old answered: "sixteen." He and his father were directed to go to the right and marched to their assigned barracks. Paul never saw his mother and little sister ever again. Other inmates told them: "By the time you reached the barracks, they were already dead." This was how Paul's life was saved — this was Paul's miracle. Paul and his father were sent to a slave labor camp where they spent a brutal year repairing railroad cars. There they were liberated when the Russian army arrived.

The Gestapo arrested my father, Nathan Ticho, in April 1939, a month after the German war machine marched into Czechoslovakia. No rational explanation or reason was given. He was just a prominent Jew. He was sent to the Dachau Concentration Camp. His younger brother and business partner, Baruch Ticho, was arrested on the same day and they were together throughout their incarceration.

Nathan Ticho

When my father returned from Dachau, he looked remarkably younger. Perhaps it was the loss of some 50 pounds or more or the missing small mustache or the long hair that gave that false impression of youth. He looked a little awkward in his old suit that looked like it was several sizes too large. For many years after his return, he would not speak about his ordeal. He rarely and very reluctantly spoke about his brutal treatment and abuse. Only one day, after he learned his brother whom he had left behind in Dachau had been killed, he tearfully told me how "lucky" he was to have survived and how sorry he was that his younger brother had not been so fortunate. Of course, I asked, what did he mean by "having been so lucky?" How could you call anything that happened in the Dachau concentration camp a piece of luck? After a few demands, he began to recall.

"All prisoners in the camp had a color identification on their uniform so that each one's "crime" could be readily identified — communists had a red patch on their shirt, common criminals a brown one, homosexuals a pink one, Jews a yellow one and so forth. Jews were, by far, subjected to the worst treatment. They received the poorest food, slaved the longest hours, and lived in the

Stops Along The Way

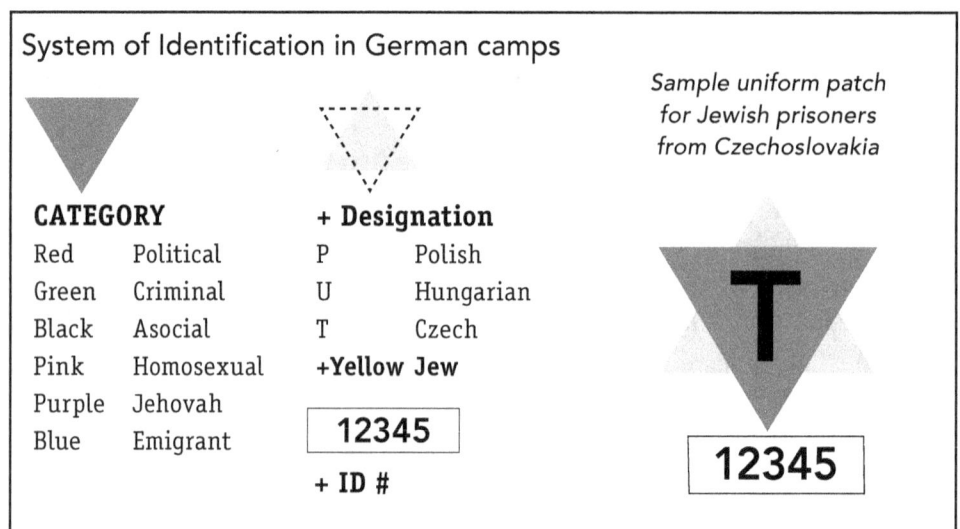

worst barracks. Jews were employed in a stone quarry where they had to move mounds of heavy rocks from one corner of the camp to the next one — and having done that — they were ordered to bring all the rocks back again.

This was beastly work and prisoners simply died of exhaustion and beatings. Others were driven to suicide — some by rushing at the fence hoping to be shot by the guards or to be electrocuted when they reached the electrified fence. In one case, father told me, a prisoner broke a light bulb and started eating the glass. Father confessed that thoughts of suicide had crossed his mind. As he was reaching the end of his endurance he developed a serious rash on both hands. It was very painful. However, Jews were not allowed to seek medical attention at the camp's infirmary. Nevertheless, Father dared to approach the building and was greeted by a guard who demanded that he leave at once. Father had the nerve to show the man his hands and begged for assistance so he could properly fulfill his job. After a few long moments, the attendant relented: "I can't give you any medication but I will assign you to two weeks of 'light work.'" Father left the infirmary with this life-saving permission slip.

For the next two weeks, instead of hauling heavy rocks, he sat on a stool, at a table, hammer in hand, straightening old used nails.

This, he insisted, saved his life — this was his miracle.

A Rosh Hashanah to Remember

It was late afternoon on Wednesday, September 13th, 1939, and, like I had done so often before during the last three years, I took the number 5 streetcar from my home on Dolni Street number 5 to the Divadelni stop on Koliste Street where, as usual, I jumped off the streetcar before it had come to a full stop. In those days, the streetcars in Brno, a town in former Czechoslovakia, that Nazis had now renamed the Protectorate of Bohemia and Moravia, had open doors. It was a matter of pride for a 12-year-old like me not to wait for

This photo features the Brno streetcar in the plaza in front of the Brno train station in the 1930's. It was at this streetcar stop where Charles would change streetcars on the way to and from the gymnasium. Notice that the doors are open.

Brno temple doors.

Temple Interior.

something so mundane as the streetcar coming to a complete halt before jumping off. Besides, I had to walk back about three houses anyway. So each meter I jumped off earlier meant that much less I had to walk back.

I made my way back to a large apartment house behind which our "Small Temple" was located. It was called the "small temple" but it wasn't really a small synagogue — it seated perhaps 500 worshipers — but Brno used to have a "Large Temple" that the Nazis burned down after they invaded our country on March 15th, 1939. I walked through the central hallway of the building to a courtyard in the rear and arrived at our synagogue and its entrances into the sanctuary. The three center doors were for men and led to the ground floor. The side doors were for women and led to the balcony that ringed the ground floor on three sides.

I did not enter any of these doors and instead turned right and then left and went along the side of the building to an entrance at the rear. There I entered and reached the choir room to join my fellow choir members, four men and five more boys, putting on robes, *talitot* and *kippahs,* in preparation for the evening's services. When I was 9-years-old I auditioned for the choir and was accepted. For the past three years, I've been a soprano in the choir and by 1939 had become the principle soprano who sang all the solo parts.

However, this wasn't the usual Friday night or Sabbath morning service, regular weekly events when the choir participated in the ceremonies. This evening we were getting ready to assist the cantor and the congregation in celebrating Rosh Hashanah, the launch of the first day of a New Year in the Jewish calendar. We assumed that Cantor Leo Ast and the Rabbi were already in a small room on the opposite side of the building also getting ready for the services.

Cantor Ast was a small, kind, and gentle man with a pleasant voice who had rehearsed us during the week for this important evening. He and I were already making plans for my Bar Mitzvah the following April. Alas, that event never took place.

Since, as I've been told, Jewish lore teaches that from age 70 you start counting your years anew, I waited 70 years, until I was 83-years-old when, with my dear wife by my side, surrounded by our children, grandchildren, many friends and even visitors from Israel, I rose on the *bimah* of Temple Emanuel of Pascack Valley in Woodcliff Lake, New Jersey, to read from the Torah scroll, recite my *Haphtarah* and have a true heart-warming and meaningful Bar Mitzvah.

But, I digress... back to 1939.

I knew that soon people would start arriving and fill the pews of the synagogue. In the past, there would have been no question about the size of the congregation. All the pews would be filled and people would be standing in the rear as well as in the balcony. However, on this evening we weren't sure who could or who would attend.

Nor was this, by any means, just a usual Rosh Hashanah. There were many things unique even about

> *... my father was arrested by the Nazis and held in the Spielberg prison ...*

this already very special holy day. It has been six months since the Germans invaded Czechoslovakia and many changes had taken place. For the moment, Jewish services in two of our three synagogues were still permitted. We did not know it at the time, but a few months later our "Small Temple" would be closed never ever again to hear the prayers of devout Jews. After the war it became a furniture warehouse, then it was torn down and a medical clinic replaced it. A small unimpressive plastic sign on a wall now testifies where this grand synagogue once stood.

Other things made this evening unique. For the first time in my twelve years, my parents were not with me on this holiday. My father was arrested by the Nazis and was now held in the Spielberg prison in Brno. He would soon be sent to the Dachau Concentration Camp in Germany. My mother had departed for the United States about a year earlier in order to renew her American citizenship. On her return trip she reached as far as Zurich, Switzerland where she remained. My older brother, Harold, was also no longer with us. He was now in Chicago. My little brother and I were now watched over by two elderly uncles, Jacob and David. One day in the future, in August 1940, little 8-year-old Steven and I would travel alone, through war-torn Europe to Switzerland and meet our mother after an eighteen-month separation. On this holiday, our uncles decided that they weren't feeling well enough to come. They and their wives remained at home. Frankly speaking, I was so occupied with what was happening that evening that I did not see whether any of our family members were there. At one time, with my father being one of thirteen siblings, we would easily fill a whole row of seats. But this evening there may have been none — except me.

There was so much tension all around. Things were so different from previous years and throughout the service I became aware that this might just be my last Rosh Hashanah service in Brno. Regrettably, I was right.

There was another matter that made this Rosh Hashanah so special. The Jewish calendar had reached the year 5700. We were celebrating not just the start of a new year, but the start of a new century! We had reached a significant milestone in Jewish history. For me, the fact that I was alive at this point, when we were starting a new century in the Jewish calendar, made a great impression. We were at the eve of the most horrendous period in Jewish history — the Holocaust — yet to me, reaching the year 5700 was proof that we had been around for a long time and a sign that we would survive for many more centuries to come. As a 12-year-old it was also a great source of pride. Just look, I thought, the Christians have reached only the year 1939, but we have them beat by more than 3,700 years!

No matter what the world has thrown against us, despite of the pogroms, the Crusades, the anti-Semitism, the envy and the jealousy of our neighbors, we have survived — we have persisted — we are here and 5,700 years into our history.

Little did I realize, at that time, what horrendous challenges we will have to survive during the next five years. But, miraculously, survive we did.

The Bar Mitzvah That Almost Wasn't

One evening in August 2017, the students, faculty and parents of the Jewish Day School of Allentown, Pennsylvania gathered to welcome a holy survivor of the Holocaust, a Torah scroll that once served the Jews of Prerov, a small town in today's Czech Republic. I was invited to address the gathering on that occasion. I was known to the leaders of the school because, a few years earlier, I succeeded in securing another survivor Torah Scroll for the Brith Sholom synagogue in Bethlehem, Pennsylvania, a neighboring town.

Here is the text of what I said:

"A man of my age — I became 90 last April — spends a lot of time reminiscing. So, please allow me a few minutes to reminisce out loud and tell you a little about one of my experiences. Back in the 1930's, my father would take me to the New Temple of Brno where we sat in a pew that was almost completely occupied by family members — male family members, of course. My Mother, aunts and sundry female cousins were all up in the balcony. My father was one of 13 siblings so there was no shortage of uncles, aunts, cousins and in-laws to occupy a considerable portion of the temple.

Charles at 12 when he was visiting with Dr. Reiniger preparing for his Bar Mitzvah.

For a 10-year-old boy the services were pure agony. My father would hand me a heavy prayer book and I was invited to follow along during the services. Because I

Stops Along The Way

Today, students of the Jewish Day School in Allentown, Pa. are greeted whenever they arrive in the building by one of 1564 Czech Memorial Scrolls saved in Prague from 1939–1945. This scroll was donated in 2017. It originated in Czech city of Prerov and was written in the 19th Century.

was going to the grammar school run by the Jewish Community in Brno, I had started learning Hebrew in kindergarten. But, even when I was 8-years-old and in the third grade, I could not read fast enough to keep up with the cantor. Also, the prayer book, because it was designed to be used for all occasions and holidays, had constant instructions to "add this for Succoth" or "delete this on Shabbat" or "proceed to a particular prayer at this point." And to make these instructions more challenging, they were not in German or Czech, languages that I spoke — they were printed using Hebrew letters but were actually in Yiddish.

The "small" synagogue in Brno sustained some bomb damage during the war.

Each member of the congregation was obliged to bring his own prayer book. So, once I was lost in the Hebrew text, I had to confess that fact to my father who would gently guide me to the right place in my book. I always felt terribly guilty when I had to do this as if I had offended G-d by not paying attention. By the time I was 10-years-old, perhaps in order to make my visits to the temple pleasanter, I volunteered to sing in the temple choir and was happily accepted. Now, I sat, along with my fellow choir members, on a bench directly behind the cantor and only had to read the music pages. Now, I always knew where we were during the service. Alas, that lasted only three years — until right after the High Holiday services in 1939 when the Nazis closed our beautiful and familiar *shul* — never, ever to be opened for Jewish services again.

Charles, the U.S. navy sailor.

At this point followed some 15 years of chaos, turmoil and instability as our family engineered its escape from Europe and the Holocaust, arrived in the United States and moved several times while trying to establish a foothold. Also, during these years, I served in the United States Navy, went to college, and started a career. Not surprisingly I found myself each year in a

The *"bimah"* of the Ticho family synagogue in Brno. The building became a furniture storage place after the war. It was razed and a medical clinic is now in its place. A simple plaque marks the place where this house of worship used to be.

different synagogue, marking the High Holidays in new surroundings, led by a great variety of rabbis and cantors. It wasn't until I was married and settled in New Jersey that I, once again, began to enjoy the warm familiar environment of Temple Emanuel of the Pascack Valley, year after year, from 1960 to this date. This temple also became the place for my Bar Mitzvah.

Does that sound strange? Let me explain.

You see, when April 21, 1940, my thirteenth birthday, was approaching, it had been two years since my older brother suddenly departed for Switzerland and from there to the United States. It's been almost one-and-one-half years since my mother went to the United States in order to renew her American citizenship and was now stuck in Switzerland reluctant to return to Nazi controlled Czechoslovakia. And it was now thirteen months since my father was arrested by the Gestapo and was sent to the Dachau Concentration camp. My 9-year-old brother and I were now alone and living with relatives.

It was also the time when preparations were supposed to start for my Bar Mitzvah. The Nazis had burned down the large synagogue. The smaller synagogue, where our family worshiped and where I had sung in the choir, was closed. We learned that services were still held in the new "Polish" synagogue and preparations were made for me to have my Bar Mitzvah there. Uncle Isidor undertook the task of preparing me for the reading of the blessings and the Haftorah. The Bar Mitzvah was scheduled for Saturday, April 22, 1940. The Torah reading for that Saturday was Mishpatim. After school, I'd take my *chumash* and *kippah* and headed for Uncle David's apartment and my lesson with Uncle Isidor.

Uncle Isidor had always been a very imposing figure for me. I saw him occasionally when I was a small boy since I would sleep in his apartment on my frequent visits to Vienna. Still I did not really have a chance to get to know him well. He was perhaps six feet tall, had a short beard, and always wore a hat, which made him look even taller. He was, apparently, a great humanitarian besides being a very good doctor. He believed that a doctor's task, first and foremost, was to alleviate suffering even if the patient could not afford his fee. Further, he considered circumcising a Jewish baby an honor, a *mitzvah*, and did not charge for this ceremony and his services. It was no big surprise, therefore, that he was kept very busy and that people often took advantage of him. As a result, his large family of eight children was often short of money. The family helped quietly.

Now in 1940 in Brno, after being forced out of Vienna, he was no longer allowed to practice medicine. Now a new chapter in my relationship with this unusual man began. During the many weeks of my lessons he and I became very close. Uncle Isidor was a great storyteller and raconteur, and we spent many hours together while he told me of his experiences and background. Uncle Isidor was in his 70s but, to a 12-year-old boy like me, he seemed much older. I really looked forward to each meeting even though Uncle Isidor was

... it wasn't a good idea to draw attention to the Ticho family by my Bar Mitzvah ...

very strict and would get very upset if I had not done my homework. The lessons went on and I was doing pretty well.

However, as the Bar Mitzvah date neared, my Uncle Jacob and Uncle David decided that, with my father in the Dachau concentration camp, my mother trapped in Switzerland, and with the current serious and dangerous conditions, it wasn't a good idea to draw attention to the Ticho family by my Bar Mitzvah. The Bar Mitzvah was scrapped and, on the Saturday when I should have been reciting my *Haftorah*, I wasn't even in a synagogue. I was bitterly disappointed.

A few days later, before dawn, there was a knock on our apartment door. This was cause for immediate panic. Early morning was the dreaded Gestapo's favorite time to come calling. We prepared for the worst as we opened the door and breathed a sigh of relief when we saw that it was Uncle Isidor. "Get dressed quickly," he said to me. A few minutes later, with his hand firmly holding mine, we left the apartment and started walking through the early morning deserted streets of our town. We did not speak and I had no idea where we were going. I knew, however, that we were violating German rules by breaking the curfew that prohibited Jews to be outside before sunrise. I was frightened.

The sun was just starting to rise when we arrived at a small building on the Krenova Street. We went to the rear of the house and down a few steps and entered a small room. Inside the dimly lit room I could discern a dozen or so men, wrapped in their *talith*, wearing their *tfillim*, and already deeply engrossed in the morning prayer. Uncle Isidor opened a brown paper bag and brought out two sets of *tfillim* and two *talitim* and we joined in this ancient ritual.

The large synagogue in Brno had an organ that was played during services. Some members of the Jewish community were not pleased. They felt that you should not play an instrument on a Sabbath — not even in the service of G-d. The small synagogue in Brno, as I mentioned earlier, had a choir instead. The cantor of the synagogue, Cantor Ast, rehearsed us twice a week and conducted the services on Friday evening, Saturday morning, and of course, on all holidays. Cantor Leo Ast was a little man with a great tenor voice and a very pleasant personality. He treated the boys in the choir with great respect and dignity, always calling us by our last names.

Our synagogue was called the small synagogue only because it was somewhat smaller than the large synagogue. Actually, our synagogue was quite large and probably accommodated over 500 people. At one end of the synagogue was a raised platform surrounded by a brass railing. The choir sat on a long bench in front of this railing. In the center was the reading table where Cantor Ast conducted the services. In the back of this platform was the Aron Kodesh covered by a beautifully embroidered drape where the Torah scrolls were kept.

Above the Aron Kodesh hung a silver lantern on a long chain that reached all the way to the ceiling. The eternal flame always flickered inside this lantern. I often wondered how this was possible since I never saw anyone refilling it with oil. And this entire splendor was presided over by little Cantor Ast bedecked in his black robe, dome-shaped black hat, and beautiful silver-embroidered *talit*.

I had been away from a synagogue for almost a year since the day ours was closed by the Nazis. Now, in this small prayer room in the basement of a house, I was surprised to discern the familiar voice of Cantor Ast, intoning the liturgy from somewhere in the front of the tiny dimly lit room that was serving a few dedicated Jews as their house of worship. For just a while I imagined that I was back at our own synagogue singing with the choir. From the back of the room, hidden from Cantor Ast by the men in front of me, I sang my part as in the old days. When the Torah reading started, I was prodded to the front where, for the first time, my eyes met Cantor Ast's. He smiled at me briefly and then proceeded to sing the regular Bar Mitzvah liturgy — the same one I had heard him sing so often in our glorious synagogue for so many other boys. I was deeply touched by this gesture.

By 7:30 a.m., the services were finished and Uncle Isidor and I were heading home. Uncle David gave me a wristwatch as a Bar Mitzvah present, and Uncle Jacob gave me a fountain pen. Uncle Isidor wrote out a blessing on a small piece of paper in his tiny and very precise script and read it to me very solemnly before he handed it to me. Aunt Emma gave me a kiss and had somehow managed to find a piece of chocolate to give me.

I did not have a Bar Mitzvah, I did not get to read my *haftorah,* or my portion of the torah, and I did not have my family and friends surrounding me but, in that small room, with Cantor Ast next to me and surrounded by a few Jews who were willing to risk their lives to attend morning services, I promised myself that some day, if I survive the war and the Holocaust, and reach my eighty-third birthday, I will have a real Bar Mitzvah, shared by my family, friends and congregation. On April 17th, 2010, I rose to the *bimah* of Temple Emanuel of the Pascack Valley and fulfilled that promise that I made 70 years earlier.

To the young people here today, I hope this is a good example that you should never give up, never lose hope and never doubt the

Charles reading the *haftoarah* during his Bar Mitzvah, April 17, 2010, at Temple Emanuel of Pascack Valley.

Charles celebrating his April 17, 2010 Bar Mitzvah with (L–R) wife Jean, son Ron, grandchildren Connie and Nathan Ticho, Charles, grandchild Hannah Ticho, and Ron's wife, Pam Lott.

power and strength of our Jewish heritage. From now on, as you enter the school, stop for a few seconds in front of the display of this torah and remember the Jews of Prerov who loved and honored this sacred scroll and paid with their lives for this devotion.

Thank you for allowing me to speak this evening and congratulations on becoming the custodians of a sacred Holocaust Torah scroll"

Wounded Hero

The skyline of Brno, the second largest city in the Czech Republic, is dominated by two hills. One is topped by the city's cathedral, an imposing red brick building with two very tall spires. The other hill is called the Spielberg, which in German, rather ironically, means amusement hill. This hill is covered by a very pretty park with lots of walks, paths, and benches and is topped by the Spielberg Fortress.

One of my grammar school's trips in the 1930's, that each class took, was a visit to this old fortress built in the Middle Ages. There were some very scary things to see during this visit that frightened us and gave us nightmares for days thereafter. In one part of the fortress we climbed down into a dungeon that had many little cells where prisoners used to be locked up. There also was an adjoining torture chamber. Here a guide would describe, in greater detail than we wished, how prisoners used to be tortured. We learned about the rack where people were stretched till all their joints broke, the Iron Lady into which prisoners were forced while spikes pierced their body, the Iron Mask which would destroy a man's eyes, the "water torture" where

Brno cathedral.

Spielberg Castle crowns a pleasant hillside park in central Brno but includes medieval torture chambers and secrets.

a prisoner had drops of water fall on his head until he went insane, and many other frightening devices. The lecture was topped off with a visit to the chopping block where prisoners' heads were cut off. Even today, I still remember how frightened we all were and how glad we were when we reached daylight once again.

It was to this fortress, in April 1939, to which our father and Uncle Paul, his younger brother and business partner, were sent after they were arrested by the Gestapo, the Nazi German secret police. Remembering the tiny cells and the torture chamber, we were very concerned what fate awaited a prisoner in the Spielberg Fortress and we imagined all kinds of horrors that our father may be subjected to. Nothing that we imagined was as bad as what actually awaited Jews later under the Nazi regime.

We heard very little from our father. Every once in a while a prisoner, who had been released, would let us know that Father and Uncle Paul were alive, surviving, and getting along as best as they could. One prisoner, when he was released, even smuggled a pencil drawing (opposite page) of our father out of the jail. We were very grateful for this simple but accurate drawing and for the hope it gave us. Our family kept going to the Gestapo offices to see what could be done to get Father and Uncle Paul released. It was suggested that if they would sign away their business, perhaps a release might be arranged. The Ticho Brothers business was signed over to the German authorities and a former salesman, who was a member of the Nazi party, was now made boss of the business. Unfortunately, this did not result in Father's release. We continued to wait and hope but heard the very bad news that they both were sent to the Dachau Concentration Camp in Germany.

Some of our family members managed to emigrate. Aunt Irma (Rivka), father's youngest sister, left with her two sons, Kurt and Fritz, (Yitzchak and Aaron) for the land that became Israel. The Rooz family left for the United

States. My cousin Olga Schick (a daughter of Sara and Isidor Reiniger) and her husband Max departed for the United States with their children. Lisa Weiss (the daughter of Uncle David) and her husband and daughter left for Australia. Suzy (Heinrich's daughter) and husband also departed as did cousin Otto and his family. Cousin Anna departed for Uruguay, Cousin Trude for India. Our family, that once lived all in one small circle, was now scattered all over the world.

Unfortunately, many could not leave and were stuck in Brno. Uncle David and his wife, Uncle Jacob and his wife, the wife and children of Uncle Paul, cousin Lilly Ticho, Uncle and Aunt Reiniger and, of course, my brother and I were all trapped in Brno. Of all those left in the grip of the Nazis at the end of 1940, only Cousin Lilly survived. All the rest were killed in the Holocaust.

The summer of l939 came and there still was no news regarding father's or Uncle Paul's possible release. Our mother would write to us regularly from Switzerland asking us to be good boys and expressing the hope to see us soon. Her letters were full of praise for our governess — calling her loyal, dependable, honest, responsible, caring, etc. We hated to hear all this praise and wondered whether our mother had any idea what a Nazi witch her wonderful governess had turned out to be. What we did not realize at that time was that mother's praise was, most likely, her desperate way of trying to ensure our well-being and to assure that Miss Gusti Miksch would not cause us any harm. Mother's letters would also contain news of what was being done to obtain father's release. Unfortunately, most of the time, these efforts ended in failure.

... All the rest were killed in the Holocaust ...

It was decided that my little brother, Steven, and I would spend the 1939 summer in the well-known health spa, Luhacovice, with my cousins Frantisek and Renatka (Uncle Paul's children). Frantisek was a couple of years younger than I but was in many ways much tougher and self-assured. One did not mess with Frantisek. He was always ready to defend his honor. He also was very good in sports and did not seem frightened of anything. He was always the first to climb over a fence, to climb a tree, or to lead when leadership was needed. Even though he was younger and smaller than I, I always had a lot of respect for him and a little fear.

I don't remember too much about this 1939 summer in Luhacovice except one incident in which Frantisek and I got into a rock-throwing battle with a group of Czech kids who called us dirty and antisemitic names. Frantisek, true to his style, would not take this without a fight even thou there were four of them and just two of us. Fortunately, the fight took place on a slope with us holding the high ground that gave us a distinct tactical advantage. The rock throwing went on for a while when, suddenly, one of Frantisek's rocks found the head of one of the boys at the bottom of the hill. His head promptly started bleeding rather profusely. The injured boy started to cry and ran off. The other three boys also retreated. "We won!" I rejoiced at the victory but, to my great shock, Frantisek burst into tears and ran for home. For the first time I realized that, under his tough exterior, there still was a small boy.

Cousin Frantisek

When summer ended we left Luhacovice and I never saw Frantisek ever again. My cousin Lilly told me that Frantisek was in a slave labor camp up to 1945 and the end of the war. As the Russian army approached the camp, word spread in the camp that the German guards were planning to kill all the Jews before retreating. Ever the leader, Frantisek organized an escape and was shot and killed during the attempt. The Nazi guards fled and disappeared when the Russians arrived.

All of the other prisoners survived.

A Matter Of Life And Death

It is now 75 years since the end of World War II when the Russian, British and American military units were finally able to enter the Nazi death camps, where they discovered the result of the beastly, finely-tuned and unbelievably cruel German plot to eliminate all the Jews of Europe and North Africa.

Today in Israel, the memory of the Holocaust is noted with a very solemn *Yom HaShoah*, the Day of the Holocaust. It is a day nearly as solemn as Yom Kippur, the Jewish Day of Atonement. Ceremonies recall the rich and productive lives of Europe's Jews and honor the millions who died at the hands of the vicious German Nazi death machine.

By the middle of 1944, the Nazi armies had swept through virtually all of Europe, the whole North African region, and a substantial part of Soviet Russia. As a result, virtually all of the Jews of this part of the world were trapped in the Nazi cage — more than 7 million souls. Only Spain, Portugal, Switzerland and Sweden managed to avoid the brutality of the Germans.

Regrettably, we Jews became familiar with the narrative — the expulsions from home, the deprivation of property, the insults and abuse, the gatherings in ghettos, the transport to death factories and the ashes thrown into the river.

But, remarkably, not all Jews died. A small group of Jews tried to avoid the Nazi web by hiding or passing as a non-Jew. Most were exposed, betrayed or denounced and the German spider caught them in his web and sucked the blood out of them. But some succeeded. Some were married to non-Jews and were spared. Some joined partisan groups and fought the Nazis as best as they could with the arms and ammunition they managed to gather.

Aunt Gisela Rooz   Uncle Moritz Rooz   Dr. Karl Egon Ticho

And then there were the very, very few who somehow managed to survive, to escape, to stay alive. All of them, without exception, credited a "miracle' or two that saved their life. Every Jew who in 1945 managed to be still alive, after the Nazis were defeated, and was living within the vast territory that had been under German control, must have had a miracle — all the rest of the Jews, some six million, were murdered.

Our family lost 15 close relatives during the Holocaust — five of my uncles and their spouses and five first cousins — only one first cousin, Lilly, survived. I said that Lilly was the only family member who survived. Well, actually, she was the only one that survived through all six years of the Holocaust. There were four more of us who managed to survive by escaping. Three were my father, my little brother, Steven, and me. The fourth was my cousin, Karl. He is the oldest son of Baruch (Paul) Ticho, my father's brother and business partner. Karl is a year older than I and we have been sharing our lives together for more than 90 years. His survival was the result of a remarkable miracle.

The story of this miracle was related to me by Gisela Rooz, my mother's oldest sister. Aunt Gisella was a remarkable woman who lived just a few weeks short of 100 years. Her mind was as bright when she died as it was over the many years I knew her. Her hands were never idle. She was either cooking, baking or creating wonders with needles and thread.

Aunt Gisella and her husband managed to escape to the United States where I had the honor and pleasure to interview her for my book "Generation to Generation: A Family's Story of Survival." Here is what she told me about Karl's miracle.

It was 1939 — my mother was in Switzerland, my older brother was in the United States, my father and Karl's father were both in the Dachau Concentration

Karl (left) his sister Rene (center) and brother Frantisek in happier days before the Holocaust.

Camp and my little brother, Steven, and I were temporarily living in a small apartment in our building. Two couples shared this space with us — Uncle Isidor Reiniger and wife, Sarah from Vienna, and Uncle Moritz Rooz and wife, Gisella from Berlin. In an effort to escape the Nazis, both couples had fled to Czechoslovakia but were now trapped, once again, after the Germans marched into the Czech lands March 15, 1939.

During this time, while Aunt Gisella and her husband, Moritz Rooz, and Uncle Isidor and Aunt Sara Reiniger were staying at our apartment, Uncle Paul's wife, Marie, visited them on a Friday evening just as they were having their Sabbath dinner. She was very distraught. She had heard that if she placed her oldest son, Karl, on a train the next day, Saturday morning, he might be able to escape. The Zionist Youth Aliyah people were supposed to have arranged for a train that would take a group of Jewish children out of the country and to Palestine. With her husband in a German concentration camp, she was looking for advice from the two older men as to what to do. Should she dare to put this 13-year-old boy alone on a train that may or may not get him to safety? Would it be safer to keep him near? Will she ever see him again? The questions and options were heart wrenching.

... Would it be safer to keep him near? ...

Uncle Isidor, who was a very religious man, said "This is not possible. Tomorrow is the Sabbath, and you are not allowed to travel on the day of rest." "But Dr. Reiniger," said Uncle Moritz, who was at least equally religious but more practical, "this is a matter of life and death. Jewish law permits you to violate the Sabbath to save a life. You can travel on the Sabbath under those circumstances."

"So, do what you wish!" said Uncle Isidor curtly, rose from the table and left the room. Uncle Moritz turned to the confused and bewildered woman, took her hand into his and said, "Put your son on the train tomorrow."

So, the next morning, Aunt Marie kissed her son good-bye. Karl and a group of about 20 youngsters boarded the train. His mother, his younger brother, Frantisek, and his little sister, Renee, waved as the train left the station and disappeared in the distance. They would never ever see each other again.

Six weeks later, Karl landed on the shores of what is now Israel. He knew that an Uncle Alfred lived in Binyamina and somehow managed to make his way there. Suddenly, unexpectedly and completely unannounced, he appeared at his uncle's home to be greeted by a stunned and overjoyed family.

And that is how Karl became Dr. Karl Ticho, the only member of his family to survive the Holocaust, a highly-skilled eye physician and surgeon, the father of five boys and the grandfather of twelve.

The train was Karl's miracle.

Karl became a highly regarded and successful eye surgeon.

On Becoming Ninety

By some strange coincidence, my life has been a series of goals. In 1939, when the Jewish calendar entered a new century, 5700, I decided that I wanted to live to the end of the 20th-century and reach the year 2000 when the Christian calendar would change millennia. Then, in 1940, when the Nazis prevented me from having a Bar Mitzvah, I decided that I wanted to reach my 83rd birthday and have a real Bar Mitzvah based on the rabbinic belief that God gives every one of us 70 years and then every year thereafter is your second life.

Frankly, at that time, since we were living in Nazi occupied Czechoslovakia and staring into the face of World War II and the Holocaust, my chances of making either of these two targets was very questionable. However, thanks to the fact that my mother was born in Chicago, the determination of my uncles Ernest and Julius Klein, the coincidence of Julius Klein becoming a friend of Generalissimo Italo Balbo (the commander of the Italian Air Force), the intercession of Italy's dictator, Benito Mussolini with the Nazi authorities, and the benefits of modern medicine, I was spared the ravages of the Holocaust and the consequences of a heart attack at the age of 50 and lived to reach both of these goals.

This is the lovely lady I fell in love with 65 years ago. Jean Yocheved Ginsburg has been the light of my life ever since.

Yochi and Ruthi, twin sisters who lived many adventures during their 83 years together. The three of us celebrated 250 birthday years in a grand family gathering.

However, once I reached 83 and celebrated my Bar Mitzvah, I decided to stop gambling and I ceased setting future goals. So, I was completely unprepared to reach my 90th birthday. A few weeks later, on June 26, 2017, devoted and loving wife, Jean Yocheved (Yochi), and her twin sister, Ruthi, marked their 80th birthday. To celebrate this combined total of 250 years of birthdays, (80 + 80 + 90) we decided to assemble family and friends in a gathering that attracted more than 100 family members and friends.

So, what changes — what happens — when you reach 90? Well, one thing changes, you are no longer hesitating to tell people how old you are. You are a little proud of achieving this point in your life and look for reasons to let people know about your achievement — like telling a waiter "I've waited 90 years to have a schnitzel at this restaurant." — or "It's been 90 years since I had a taxi ride like this one" — or " Thank you, Madam, that's a nice compliment, but you should have met me before my 90th birthday." It also means that you stop buying year-long subscriptions to magazines or a bunch of green bananas.

So what does living 90 years really mean? — Well, 90 years are 32,850 days — plus 22.5 February 29 for a total of 32,872.5 days — or 788,940 hours or 47,336,400 minutes and, believe it or not, at 60 beats a minute — I've been kept alive for the 90 years by a heart that faithfully supplied the blood my body needs by beating 2,840,184,000 times — so far!

The September 1960 wedding was the culmination of a relationship that stretched over a five-year period and had to reach across the Atlantic and Pacific oceans.

But it means much more than this.

It means having the incredible good fortune to meet and marry a woman who could and would love me. It means being married to that same woman for more than 61 wonderful years — so far! It means raising three delightful children and four great but unpredictable grandchildren. It's also a 70 year career in the visual arts field that provided the means to live a comfortable suburban life.

It means having memories of your father — this heroic figure who was deprived of his fortune three times by the tragic events in his life — the economic panic of 1907, World War I when the Austrian Government failed to repay the bonds it issued to pay for the war and, of course, the scourge of the Nazi regime and the Holocaust that stripped him of everything he ever earned and possessed and nearly cost him his life and the lives of his family. At the age of 56, after nearly 2 years of brutal abuse in Nazi concentration camps, he came to a strange country, with a strange language, with strange customs, with a wife and three children and only about $8,000 to his name to start a new life and to build a new future.

> ... *What does living 90 years really mean?* ...

It took nearly a year for him to just recover and get his bearings. Then, one day he left Chicago for New York, and when he returned he told us of his decision to move to New York where he and a partner will manufacture sportswear. A month later we were in the Anderson Hotel, in a one-bedroom furnished apartment, in new schools and in a new life — that included me going to the office of King Sportswear on the 2nd floor of 23 East 20th Street — every day after high school to pack and deliver orders to stores around town.

My dear mother, Francis Fannie Klein, before the Holocaust.

It also means watching Mother, who had enjoyed the luxury of a cook, a governess and maids during her previous life, now trying to create a home for the family in this one-bedroom furnished apartment where her two sons slept on a fold-out bed in the living room, where she had to make meals on an electric hot plate hidden in a clothes closet and where I washed the dishes in the bathroom sink — because the hotel did not allow cooking in the apartments. And all the time her oldest son was in Chicago to study and was not heard from for months at a time.

Becoming ninety also means an occasional sleepless night reviewing the decisions you've made or were forced to make. Why did you choose to pursue engineering when you really were more interested in medicine? By the time you received your degree you realized the error you made and that you now needed to reinvent your future — to pick a way to utilize the knowledge you have gained toward the arts. Music — I really wanted to do something in this field, but years ago while learning to play the piano, I realized that I would never learn to read music the way I needed to.

But it wasn't my lack of music reading skills that soured my music ambitions. There was the memory and the humiliation during my first public performance. My teacher, in order to impress parents and grandparents, would stage a concert of her pupils. The program was arranged in a progression of skills starting with a little girl playing a simple tune and concluding, after an intermission, by a string quartet playing a Boccarini Quartet. I was slated to be the second performer until my mother announced that I could not go on stage as planned because it was Sabbath and I could not play until after sundown. As a result I was moved to appear after the intermission, after all the more skilled students had performed. The shame and embarrassment I felt makes me cringe even today. Then, of course, came the Nazis, the seizure of our apartment along with its music room and its

We love it when we can get together with our children and grandchildren. Here, we are together for the start of Robin and Dan's wedding celebration on June 20, 2015 — from left are Nathan (Ron's child), Pam (Ron's wife), Ron (our son), Jean, Dan (Robin's husband), Robin (our daughter), Michael (Robin's child), myself (Charles), Hannah (Ron's child), Connie (Ron's child), Richard (our son), and Sharon (Richard's wife).

Boesendorfer Grand Piano and the end of my piano lessons.

The Nazi occupation also meant the end of my schooling in the Reform Gymnasium high school that was run by the local Jewish community. I had attended the Jewish schools since kindergarten and the same group of boys and girls advanced together year after year as we progressed through the various grades.

The High Holiday services in 1939 marked the end of my career as the lead soprano in our Temple choir. All Jewish institutions were ordered closed and all Jewish religious services were prohibited. By then, my little brother and I were living in our uncle Jacob's small apartment. My father, having been arrested, was now in the Dachau Concentration Camp, my mother was in Switzerland and my older brother was in the United States. When the Jewish schools closed for the summer in 1940, my little brother Steven went to live in a village in the home of a former maid of ours and I, along with five classmates, went to work on a farm. There we worked six days a week and received three meals a day. On Sunday, we could rest but had to remain on the farm.

I tried to enjoy life through my 90's.

... I live one day at a time ...

My thoughts today no longer dwell on my desire to live to the year 2000 nor the hope to have my Bar Mitzvah at the age of 83. I reached these goals years ago.

Now, at 94, I live one day at a time.

My Cousin Henry

In Memory of my cousin Henry —

Cousin Henry was a product of chaotic times.

Born Heinrich David Ticho in Vienna, Austria in 1930 he, like most of us of the "third generation" in the Ticho family, became well aware of the fragile nature of the lives of Jews in Central Europe. Like all of us, he learned of the atrocities that were committed against us in the past centuries and the struggles that our forefathers, grandparents, parents, uncles and aunts faced to create a life for themselves and for their families. None of this knowledge prepared us for the things to come.

And then, in March 1938, when Henry was just 8 years old, Austrians voted to join Nazi Germany. Henry lived through the initial Nazi era where he watched as his father's jewelry store was seized by the Nazis, along with all their other property, and the three of them, Father, Mother and Heinrich were scattered to different places. During a three-year period Henry went from German schools to Czech schools, then to French, Hebrew and, finally, to English schools as his family made their way to safety in the United States.

Like many of us in this "third generation," the 35 grandchildren of Yitzchak Zvi Ticho, the history and experiences taught Henry to make decisions deliberately and to treat money with respect. He was a true product of his parents, He had the good nature and love of life that was so typical of his mother, Rosa, and he had the modesty, humility and careful nature of his father, Victor. For his family, regrettably, Israel did not present a haven. Uncle Alfred, who was already overburdened with caring for the many family members, brought over from Austria, could only house Henry and his parents in a small shack in an orange grove. The family earned a small income by harvesting fruit. Neither did the United States present a country whose streets were paved with gold. The family had to live frugally as money was always tight and the future appeared to be a challenge. And then, while Henry was in his teens, his mother passed away and the whole vast Ticho family suffered the loss of this gentle, loving, and bright young woman. Then Henry's first marriage ended in a difficult divorce and resulted in estranged relationships with his two daughters. Henry who loved to be with people was now living a lonely existence. These experiences formed the man.

Nevertheless, he sported a great sense of humor and was a loyal and considerate member of the Ticho family. And then, a miracle occurred and he found Yaffa, a new jewel, in his second marriage. His greatest joy was that, as he grew older, he was able to return to Israel and had the time to be with his wife Yaffa and her family and be near the Ticho family members and their many friends. On several occasions, after Henry married Yaffa, he would confide in me: "At my age, I never thought I would ever again find someone who would love me as I love her." I was so glad he had found such happiness.

Cousin Henry, the ever happy bachelor, after his wedding to Yaffa and a new happy life

Henry was a companion of mine for most of my life. We shared some tumultuous times together and we both were fortunate to survive the Holocaust. I certainly will miss not having him alongside — now and in the future.

In The Footsteps Of History

A working title of a proposed film series concept

Isn't it ironic that one of the most popular tourist attraction in Prague, the capitol of the Czech Republic, is a cemetery dedicated to a people who have been, in effect, wiped off the map of that country? Yet virtually every visitor to Prague makes a point to visit this small plot of land in the center of the old city and wanders around the forest of lopsided tombstones that huddle together in unruly, poetic groupings.

The Old Jewish Cemetery in Josefov, the former Jewish Quarter of Prague, was created in the 15th century when Jews were forbidden to bury their dead outside their own district. Space was scarce, so bodies were buried on top of each other in an estimated twelve layers. In the centuries the level of the cemetery kept rising and today the surface of the cemetery stands some fifteen feet above street level. As each level was added the tombstones were also raised. As a result, today there is a crowded jumble of tombstone that represent centuries of Jewish life in the city.

Throughout the years, Prague, one of the great capitols of Europe, was in the center of the momentous events that formed the history of the continent. Wars, crusades, epidemics, religious upheavals and persecutions were mixed together with scientific discoveries, architectural achievements, literary triumphs, political progress and the constant enlightenment to form the society that essentially shaped the world.

Jewish cemetery in Prague.

Jewish cemetery in Prague.

Maisel Synagogue

In the midst of all these historic events, crowded together in an isolated area, was a tiny minority that belonged nowhere but was found everywhere while playing a disproportionate and effective role in the life of the country. If the existence of the Gentile population, under these circumstances, was exciting, ever changing and dramatic, the days and times of the Jews were doubly so.

Each of the layers in the unique ancient Jewish burial plot represents an era — a page from the history of this city as well as from the history of the Jewish community of Prague. There are times of great joy with tolerance and economic progress only to be reversed by cruel decrees and banishment. There are times of great scholars and marvelous writings and days of book burnings and prohibitions. There are days of despair and anguish followed by rays of hope and expectations.

Yet, through all the waves of good and evil that buffeted the Jews, the community survived holding tight to its history and to its heritage — even to its painful and slow rebirth after the Holocaust. It is the survival, the perseverance, the family ties, the strong faith, the clever wit, the dedication to learning and the very human failings that constitute the threads of the story.

"Footsteps of History" will take the viewer on a dramatized journey through the centuries of Jewish life in Prague and its vicinity. We will progressively visit the community in different ages, in different centuries and under different circumstances yet weaving a continuous tapestry of history. Each episode will be a dramatic vignette — a look at life at various times with the fate of one family forming the essential binding thread as we move from one episode to the next. The films will transport us into the homes and hearts of the people as they fight for survival and progress under ever changing circumstances. And throughout our narrative the cemetery is the key that binds all the vignettes together into one unified continuous story.

Prague is a unique location for the production of this film series. Many houses and whole streets from the 15th century are preserved, as are castles, churches and major buildings. Prague even boasts a bridge from that era and a synagogue that was founded in the year 1270 and is still in use today. Czech filmmakers are particularly skilled in the production of period motion pictures. Their talents and skills are ideal for this endeavor.

"Footsteps of History" is not all dark and somber. There will be periods of gloom and sorrow but mixed in will be stories of achievement, progress, and joy — human-interest tales that will enchant and involve the audience.

Spanish Synagogue

Benito Mussolini Saved My Life

Yes, it's true. Benito Mussolini, the Italian politician, the leader of the Italian National Fascist Party, the dictator who ruled Italy from 1922 to 1943, the man who dragged Italy into World War II alongside Nazi Germany, the tyrant who became so despised by his people that they killed him — yes, it was this Benito Amilcare Andrea Mussolini who rescued me from the Holocaust along with my brother and our father.

But that is the end of the story. Allow me to go back to the beginning.

The German Nazi army marched into Czechoslovakia on the 15th of March 1939 and our life was soon greatly changed. By 1940, my older brother Harold was studying in Chicago, our mother was also in Chicago in order to regain her American citizenship that she had lost when she married our father, our father was arrested and was now in the Dachau Concentration Camp and my little brother Steven, 8-years-old, and I, four years older, were living with relatives. That also did not last very long and, by early 1940, Steven was living in a small village with our former housekeeper and I, along with four other schoolmates, was working on a farm.

My life on the farm lasted for several months when I suddenly received a postcard from my uncle asking me to return to Brno, my hometown, and prepare an escape from the clutches of Nazi Germany.

How did this miracle come about?

World War II was raging in Europe, all borders were closed and Jews were under severe restrictions and brutal laws. How was it possible that we, my little brother, and I, would be able to leave Europe and escape from the Holocaust

On October 25, 1936, an alliance was declared between Italy and Germany, which came to be known as the Rome-Berlin Axis. Here Hitler and Mussolini watch a parade in Germany.

while millions of Jews were trapped and were murdered? For that story we must go back to 1933.

When you look at the city of Chicago today it is hard to believe that this great metropolis was incorporated less than 200 years ago. By the middle of the 20th century Chicago had much to be proud of and, therefore, in 1933 it decided to celebrate the city's centennial, with a great World's Fair. The fair dramatized not only the advances that had taken place in Chicago, but also the progress that the whole world had achieved in the past and the grand future it could anticipate. Unfortunately, one of the things that the planners of the fair did not anticipate was that the Great Depression would be at its height just when the fair's doors were scheduled to open. A huge number of workers were unemployed or working for very low wages. The fair was well received, but fewer people than expected were willing to spend their hard-earned money on entertainment.

"A Century of Progress" World Exhibition was a grand event celebrating 100 years since the founding of America's second largest city.

The sponsors of the fair tried various promotions to get people into the fairgrounds. One such public relations ploy was the overseas arrival of a fleet of five Italian military aircraft. Remember, in l933 flying across the Atlantic was still quite an adventure. So, a great deal of excitement was generated by the announcement that a group of planes from Italy were going to fly across the Atlantic and come to the Chicago World's Fair.

The commander of this group of airplanes was an officer in the Italian Air Force named Italo Balbo. When the planes arrived in Chicago they were grandly welcomed and a parkway on the Chicago waterfront was renamed Balbo Drive.

Balbo's visit made headline news.

Colonel Italo Balbo was welcomed with a grand parade and many ceremonies.

Since this was a military matter, it was appropriate that the welcome should be led by Colonel Keen, the commander of the 33rd Division of the Illinois National Guard. He, in turn, selected his *aide-de-camp*, Captain Julius Klein, as the personal aide to General Balbo during his visit to Chicago. This is how General Balbo befriended Julius Klein, my mother's brother, my uncle. Captain Julius Klein was a newspaper reporter who, in addition, was very active in the local state militia. During World War II, he served on General McArthur's staff in the Pacific and ultimately retired as a two-star general.

After Balbo returned to Italy, the two colleagues lost touch with each other. By 1940, Balbo had become Generalissimo Balbo, the Governor of Libya, a colony in North Africa that the Italian Army had conquered. My uncle Julius Klein was now a colonel in the regular United States Army. It was this chance meeting of my uncle and Balbo in 1933 that played the key role to save my life and the lives of our family.

Of course, back in Brno in 1940, we all were totally unaware what role my uncle and Balbo played in our survival. All Uncle Jacob simply learned from the German authorities was that my little brother Steven and I will be granted exit permits and that father would soon be released from the Dachau concentration camp. It was at this point when Uncle Jacob sent the urgent postcard to the farm asking me to return to Brno and start preparations to arrange our trip. This was by no means a simple task.

In order to get to the United States, we had to cross several other countries. These countries wanted to be sure that we would not stay within their borders. So, before you could get a visa to enter one of the countries you had to have a visa to enter the next country. Our quest, therefore, started with the United States.

Now, that our mother had regained her United States citizenship, Steven and I no longer had to wait for our visa because we were now the children of an American citizen. Uncle Jacob gave us some documents and some money and Steven and I went to Prague to obtain our American visas. I was 13-years-old at that time and Steven was nine. Nevertheless, the trip did not frighten us. Nearly a year of more or less unsupervised living had made us fairly self-reliant and, besides, there really wasn't a choice.

Steven and I went together by night train arriving early in the morning in Prague. We went to the American Consulate where we handed in our documents and were told to sit and wait. The two of us sat for almost half a day. Finally, we were ushered into an office where a rather large man sat behind a big desk smoking one cigarette after the other. I was amazed at the wasteful manner in which he smoked. He would light a cigarette, take a few puffs, and then discard it. Cigarettes were rationed and good quality cigarettes were very hard to find and very expensive. My eyes wandered over to the man's ashtray and I tried to count the number of very large American cigarette butts in it. I wondered how much money I could earn selling these butts if I could just take them with me. I was certain the contents of the ashtray would have brought a neat profit.

The man asked us a few questions in German and kept writing things down. We just sat there wondering whether we would succeed in getting this all-important document. Then suddenly everything was ready. A few signatures and a lot of rubber-stamping and Steven and I were on the night train back to Brno clutching our lifelines — our American visas. It would be 55 years before I would visit Prague again.

With an American visa, additional visas to pass through Portugal, Spain, Unoccupied France, Switzerland and Austria could be arranged. Mother, in Switzerland, bought tickets for a boat ride from Lisbon, Portugal, to New York and the hard-won precious chain was now complete.

While this process was going on, Father arrived from Dachau. I don't remember much about our reunion. Father was staying with some other relatives because there was no more room at Uncle Jacob's small apartment. We did ask him some questions about his experiences, but his answers were very vague and evasive. It was obvious that he did not want to talk about his ordeal. Father was also busy making his own arrangements for departure. Under these circumstances we did not get to see him very often.

Our German exit permits were valid only to August 31, l940. Our papers were ready, but Father's still had a way to go. It was, therefore, decided that Steven and I would leave first without our father in order to be sure we got out before the expiration date of our exit visas. And so, on August 13, 1940, I said my last goodbyes to my friends and family, and Steven and I boarded a train for Vienna and a new life. I expected never to see Brno ever again.

It is hard to describe how you feel when you are closing the door on the only life you have known since birth. The tragedies and disasters that had befallen our family poisoned most of the love I had for my country and my city. When we were departing, the Nazis were at the crest of their success. Hitler's army had conquered Poland and France and was knocking on the front door of England. It seemed to me that, when Hitler said his Third Reich was going to last for 1,000 years, he was probably right. But, mostly, my feelings were of great relief that our nightmare may just be ending. I felt a great anxiety to get out from under the Nazi boot.

Steven had always been a quiet and obedient child. He and I got along very well together. We learned to live with each other, playing games together, eating our meals together and, when we were left alone during the Nazi period, we grew even closer. We had our own secrets, developed our own language and signals, and protected each other with an occasional necessary lie. Steven was 9-years-old when we left Brno. We'd been together on our own for such a long time it never occurred to me that I should be concerned about traveling alone through a war-torn continent along with my little brother. My only worry was the constant unknown menace that being a Jew in a Nazi country represented. Every uniform, every armband, and every insignia were a threat and, even when someone spoke to us in a friendly manner, we were much too suspicious to trust anyone.

By early evening our train arrived in Vienna. The border crossing from the Protectorate into former Austria was uneventful. The German authorities in Brno had sealed our baggage. When the border guards saw the official seals they did not bother to check our luggage. They did, however, study our passports carefully and passed them around to all the other agents. They all seemed very puzzled. Like all official documents issued to Jews, our passport had a big red letter "J" stamped on the front page and, I guess, the guards must have wondered what two little Jewish kids were doing alone on a train bound for Vienna. Both Steven and I stood there afraid that we may not be permitted to cross the border. But they finally handed the passports back to us. A heavy stone fell from our heart. We sat back down as the train proceeded on to Vienna.

Early the next morning we ate a quick simple breakfast and the two of us were marching back to the railroad station. We said a hasty goodbye to the nice lady who had housed us for the night and ran to catch the train that would take us to Switzerland. At each stop, as the train moved towards the Swiss border, people would get off the train. When our train finally arrived at the border at about noontime, only about 20 passengers got off the train along with their baggage. We were in a forest clearing and there wasn't a real station where we stopped. On our side of the tracks was a small shack with some benches in front of it. In back of the shack were, what looked like,

Nathan Ticho's passport with the red "J" stamp.

two outhouses — small shacks used as toilets. Off on the other side, about 500 feet away, stood another train consisting only of a locomotive and one car. We were told that this little train would take us across the border to Switzerland.

A German officer came out of the shack and asked everyone to hand over their passports and exit permits. He took all the papers and disappeared back into the shack. People made themselves comfortable on the benches or, like us, on their luggage. About 10 minutes later, another officer came out and called out a name. The person responded. The officer handed back the passport and told the man to board the little train. This procedure was repeated over and over again. Steven and I waited and waited.

More and more people had received their passports and the number of passengers waiting to board the little train kept getting smaller and smaller. And then, we were the only ones left — just little Steven and I sitting on our luggage. Before departing Brno, my father asked me to take a large overcoat with me. I objected because we were allowed to take only our own clothes and this large coat could not possibly be mine.

When people are desperate and unsure of the future they may do strange things in the hope that they can assure their survival. Now, as the two of us sat all by ourselves at the German border, with the little train making noises like it was ready to depart without us and with panic in my heart my eyes fell on "the" coat. "That's it!" I said to myself, "it's the coat! Because of this stupid coat we are not getting our passports back and will miss the train!" I made a quick decision. Stood up, grabbed the coat, and walked over to one the outhouses in back of the shack and stuffed the coat into the toilet. In retrospect, of course, the coat had nothing to do with our delay of getting our passport, but as far as I was concerned it worked! A few minutes later an officer finally came out of the shack and returned our passports. We got to the train and, as soon as we were on board, the engine blew its whistle and started to move. We plopped down on our seats to catch our breath. The train chugged into the mountain pass to St. Margreten, Switzerland — and our freedom.

Where does Generalissimo Balbo and "El Duce" Benito Mussolini fit into this story? We learned the answer to this question only after we arrived in Chicago and met our uncle Julius Klein.

From the day the Nazis marched into Czechoslovakia our uncle Julius Klein and his brother Ernest Klein endeavored to bring all of us to the United States. In 1940, the USA was not as yet involved in the war and our uncles were able to communicate with any country they wished. They reached out to the US ambassador in Switzerland to get reports regarding the state of our mother's health and well-being. They did the same with the ambassador in Prague to learn about our well-being; information they sent to our mother to quiet her nerves. Both of my uncles were in the business of public relations and during the years they had accumulated many contacts in high places. Now they reached out to many people of influence to seek their aid in obtaining our father's release from prison and our escape from Europe. Nothing brought forth any hope of success.

Benito Mussolini

In desperation, they devised a plan to re-ignite the friendship uncle Julius once had with Italo Balbo. They induced a prominent judge of Italian extraction to write a letter to Balbo asking him whether he would, in honor of their friendship, assist our uncles in the reunion of the Ticho family in the USA. The appeal was successful! Balbo responded with a very friendly letter stating that he would very much like to arrange the exit of the Ticho family to the USA. However, as his relationship with the German government is not very friendly, he will ask his representative in Berlin to carry on.

Unfortunately, a couple of months later, Balbo was killed when his plane crashed. Now, our uncles received a letter from Balbo's representative in Berlin stating that, "with the death of Balbo he is no longer able to attend to the matter of the Ticho family reunion."

Other people might have given up at this point. But not our uncles. They contacted a friend, a journalist, who accompanied Benito Mussolini when he was struggling to become the head of the Italian government in the 1920's. During this era this man wrote some very complimentary world-wide articles about Mussolini. Now, he wrote a lengthy letter to Mussolini asking him whether he might consider granting one of his recently deceased Generalissimo Balbo's last wishes to free the Ticho family. The Italian government reached out to Berlin and Mussolini saw to it that Balbo's wish was granted.

Yes, it was Benito Amilcare Andrea Mussolini who rescued me from the Holocaust along with my brother and our father and, at age 93, I am still around to tell the story.

A Reach Into The Dark

"You cannot see him," the little woman insisted through the small opening of the front door to the apartment. I stared at her and wondered who she was. Whoever she was, she looked determined. I stood frozen by indecision. Should I persist and try to convince the woman with my poor Czech to let me enter or should I give up, turn around, and walk away? I've waited decades for this meeting.

It was Fall 1995. My wife, Jean, and I had just spent three pleasant and relaxing weeks touring Portugal and Spain and landed in Prague. Now, I wanted to take a day and visit Brno, my home town, and fulfill a desire that had nagged at me for more than 55 years. I rented a car and drove to Brno alone. That is how I ended up standing in front of the partially opened door trying to decide what to do next.

Locating this apartment was rather easy. Earlier in the morning, before leaving Prague, I drove to the Ministry of the Interior, and got to the Personal Records Department. After a lengthy discussion with a clerk, I was finally able to convince him that I was not a bill collector, an attorney, or a person with sinister motives. I was simply trying to locate a person, a very, very old friend of mine. I was certain, since the country had only recently been liberated from an oppressive Communist dictatorship, that every citizen's whereabouts were carefully registered. I was not disappointed. After paying for a 20 Czech Crowns tax stamp and waiting for about 20 minutes, the clerk handed me a form with the person's address and all his vital statistics neatly listed.

Lada as a young boy.

Lada and Stephen play

Knowing the address of the apartment was one thing but locating the house at Mendlovo Namesti 13 in Brno was another challenge altogether. During the day, I had to visit Adamov to meet with a business client. Then I decided to tour the beautiful wooded area north of Brno. So, by the time I arrived at the Brno Holiday Inn, it was dark. After registering at the hotel, I set out to search for the address which is located in the oldest part of Brno. Despite the poor lighting, I finally found the building.

A large door, which in the past had been used to admit horse-drawn carriages into a courtyard, seemed to be the only way to enter. After a while, I found a smaller door within the larger one. I pushed it open and found myself in a large dark courtyard. My eyes became adjusted to the darkness, and I was able to make out the open outside staircases and walkways that faced me on all four sides. I located a switch for the lights. I pushed the button and a few lonesome bulbs came to life. Which of the several staircases facing me should I take? Before I could decide, the lights went out. I pushed the button again and tried to locate a directory. No luck, there was none to be found. The lights went out again. I pushed the button and decided to proceed up the nearest staircase. Before I reached the first floor, the lights went out again. I searched and finally located another light switch. During the next period of illumination I knocked on the nearest door. The door opened cautiously and in the best Czech that I could muster I asked for directions. "Two more floors higher and to the right," I was told.

> *... after a long while, the door opened a crack.*

After several pushes of the light switch, I finally arrived at my destination and knocked. Only after my third rather forceful knock, I heard some sound of motion in the apartment and, after a long while, the door opened a crack. In the dim light I made out the shape of a woman, perhaps no more than five feet tall with a pinched face that made her look a bit older than her years. "Is this the home of Ladislav Kellner?" I asked. "Yes," came the curt answer, "but you can't see him." The door started to close. It was time to decide what to do.

What has brought me to this point? I was going back 55 years to the last day before my departure to the United States. That afternoon in August 1940, my childhood friend Lada (as he was called by his family) came to visit me at Uncle Jacob's house to say farewell. Now he was the last and only person who was still

Lada (left) and his parents after WWII.

alive who could bridge for me the gap between today and the life of our family before World War II, before the Holocaust, before its horrible consequences. Could seeing him and speaking with him help me connect the present to the past, fill in the gap that has existed all these years between now and the day I left my birthplace for the United States more than a half-century ago? And if such a bridge could be formed, could it bring back some of the feelings, some sense of the life of my youth that the war and the Holocaust destroyed?

From inside the apartment a man's voice was heard. The little woman turned her head to the side and shouted something back. I stood in front of the door waiting for something to happen. The woman looked back at me. "He's a sick man," she whispered, "he has sugar." Then, slowly and still reluctantly, she opened the door wide enough for me to enter. The door closed behind me and I was standing in the middle of a kitchen. To my right was a small gas stove with some shelves mounted on the wall. Boxes, cans, jars, and cooking utensils were stacked on the shelves above the stove. One shelf held a motley collection of dishes that obviously had come from various sources. In the corner was a stack of cardboard boxes and plastic bags. Against the back wall was a cabinet badly in need of painting. To my left was a doorway and a table with three chairs set under it. The walls and ceiling looked like they had not been painted in decades. The whole scene was lit by a single bare bulb hanging from the ceiling.

The woman walked through the doorway to my left without saying a word. I stood in the room waiting. Suddenly I was flooded by great doubts whether I should have made this visit. When I last saw Lada he was 14-years-old. He was a good-looking teenager, a head taller than I, thin, and with a typical round Slavic face. After the war, we would correspond on and off and I would receive pictures and postcards from him. The pictures showed a handsome young man looking back at me. Then, after a while, we stopped writing and the contact was lost for nearly 50 years. Nevertheless, Lada always occupied a warm spot in my heart. All my Czech friends abandoned me when the Nazis marched into Czechoslovakia. Lada remained a good friend until the day I boarded the train that, ultimately, brought me to the United States. When I decided to make this visit, I wasn't sure what I would find. Now, that I stood in the middle of the kitchen of this ancient apartment, I was filled with anxiety.

Just then I heard shuffling footsteps to my left. I turned left towards the doorway. Will I recognize Lada? Will he recognize me? Will he even remember who I am? The questions were racing through my head. It had been such a long time, so many things had happened; so many years had gone by. In the 55 years since I had last seen Lada a third generation of the Ticho family had been born, matured, and some had already passed away. I looked to my left as the footsteps came closer. Then, through the door, walked a very old man. It shocks me to write this. But that is really the only fair way to describe what I saw. I searched the face desperately to find a trace of the 14-year-old boy I had last seen or the young man that had stared at me in the photographs I had received from him. There was not the slightest resemblance. It was obvious that he had just hastily put on some clothing and slippers neither of which were very clean. I stood there in my London Fog winter coat and the Hermes silk shawl that Jean's cousin Mira had given me in Paris and felt very much out of place.

> *... his mind rolled back to the years before the war ...*

The man looked at me quizzically and not even my name, repeated several times, seemed to explain to him who I was. After several very awkward minutes, Lada asked me to sit down at the table. I believe this gesture was not as a result of politeness, but rather because he could not stand too long at any one time. I reached into my pocket and withdrew an envelope. I had saved the postcards, the photographs, and the letters that I had received from him and brought them along. Slowly, with trembling hands, Lada flipped through the pictures and read his own letters and postcards. I realized that I was really hoping for too much. I should not have expected that this man could have a stranger walk in on him one evening and remember him after 55 years.

Nevertheless, slowly the veil of time was drawn back and there was a spark of recognition in Lada's eyes, his mind rolled back to the years before the war, and our conversation was beginning to flow easier. For the next hour or so, we sat and talked. Lada and his family remained in our building throughout the war. Our apartment, that was seized by the German General Braunau von Trillingen, remained in their hands even after he was killed on the Russian front. Our governess lived for a few months in our apartment on the second floor but disappeared when another German army officer moved into the apartment. Both German families cleared out of the apartments and disappeared a few weeks before the Germans surrendered. The apartment stood empty until the end of the war when the Czech authorities took possession of the building and assigned Czech families to live in them. Our large apartment was subdivided and three families moved in.

After the war, Lada became very ill and he was certain that the penicillin that we sent to him saved his life. When his father died, his mother could no longer handle the janitorial duties in the building and Lada was not interested in such a job. His mother moved back to their hometown, Ivanovice, and Lada lived alone for a while. He lost contact with our building when they moved out. He got married to the woman that was now watching television in the next room. They had two children, but his daughter died at the age of 24. His son had two sons so, he told me proudly, the Kellner name will live after he dies. His life had not been easy. He worked for most of his life at the large plant known locally as Zbrojovka. This company produced a vast array of machine products ranging from cannons to motorcycles. Now that he was suffering from diabetes, he was receiving a small pension.

Then, it also became my turn to answer his questions. He was pleased to hear that my father had lived to a ripe old age. He remembered that I had a brother in America. What happened to him? I told him about Harold and his work at the University of California. I had much greater problems trying to explain what I do. I finally settled the matter by claiming to be an engineer in television. Ultimately we came to the question that I had feared: "You had a little brother. How is he doing?" I struggled with the answer for quite a while. How was I going to explain to this man how and why my wonderful, talented, successful, kind, considerate and generous brother, the father of three wonderful daughters, a highly regarded attorney and a successful real estate developer was murdered in his sleep? Slowly I told the story as best as my poor Czech and my heavy heart would allow. When I mentioned that it had happened in Chicago, Lada understood. "Yes," he said knowingly shaking his head, while pretending to be shooting a machine gun, "Chicago, gangsters." I left it at that. Further explanations were not really necessary.

By then, Lada's wife had wandered back into the kitchen. She stood there behind her husband listening to our conversation. The belligerence had disappeared from her face, and she was obviously very interested in what we were saying. When I started to tell Lada what had happened to some of our relatives in the German concentration camps during the Holocaust, how many had died, and who had survived, she became a little puzzled.

"What," she asked her husband, "are you talking about?"

As I left Lada's apartment, never ever to see him again, I stopped at the top of the stairs and stared into the darkness.

"How could this woman," I asked myself, "know nothing about the Holocaust?"

It had been a very difficult and sad evening in many ways.

Jewish Tears

I never thought that I would cry over trees.

But I did.

For much of my life there's been one thing that I have hardly ever done. I would not cry. I suppose psychologists or psychiatrists could probably discern some deep underlining reasons for this strange behavior but, for me, it was very simple. Crying could be considered a sign of weakness — something I was inclined to avoid.

I do vividly recall the group of boys who chased me through the fields behind our house in Brno, Czechoslovakia back in the mid-1930's, before the *Shoa*, (the Holocaust) when I was about 7-years-old. They were yelling: "Let's get the fat little Jew!" and other similar endearing expressions of their desires. Well, they were right. I was somewhat overweight and I was a Jew, but that did not give them the right to chase me.

They finally caught up with me and the biggest one put my head into his forearm and squeezed and twisted my head. He promised to release me if I cried. Under the circumstances it did not take much more inducement. I was really in pain and I was also furious. So, I cried and, after a few additional twists and squeezes, I was released. The boys stood there laughing at me as I tried to control my tears. I recovered some of my composure and ran off in the direction of my house. Somewhere along this time I must have decided that, in the future, I would learn to control my impulse to cry.

In recent years, I've become more prone to allow myself the luxury of responding to some situations with tears. Back in 1978, when a bullet brutally tore my brother Steven away from us, I was completely distraught, but dry-eyed. But, when his oldest grandchild celebrated her *Bat Mitzvah* 35 years later, that earlier loss overtook my emotions. These days on *Yom Kippur* (the Day of Atonement) I will arrive at the synagogue early for the services so that I can spend a few quiet moments before the memorial plaques in our synagogue. All the memorial lights are burning including the three marking the names of my parents and my brother Steven. Then, when the services reach the Yizkor Memorial Ceremony and my thoughts turn to Steven, my parents, and the fifteen family members who were innocent victims of the Holocaust, I find relief in the tears that mix with my prayers.

In private moments, I will now indulge myself with a tear or two as I contemplate the choices my children have made or the challenges that they will yet have to meet, or as I am overcome by the joy of watching our grandchildren, or as I wonder over the miracle of my wife's love and the 61 years that she has so loyally devoted to me.

But, cry over trees?

These days, as Israelis and Palestinians are trying to find a way to live in some form of harmony in the postage-stamp-sized territory they occupy, there are many elements that distinguish the two parts. When I visit Israel, nothing is more obvious to me than the relationship of each side to the land. In the over 145 years, since the founding of modern Zionism and the 72 years since the founding of the Jewish State, Jews have tended the land with love and care, firm in the knowledge that this little country is all that will ever be ours. For decades, dedicated pioneers came to Palestine from the teaming ghettos and crowded cities of Europe, from the slums of North Africa, from the villages of Poland and Russia, from India, Ethiopia, South Africa, Yemen and even from the United States in order to work on the land. Immense labor and great sums of money

Charles stands in front of a cypress tree in Israel.

have been dedicated in the effort to convert the barren land into a green island. What little water was available was carefully diverted and sent where it would do the most good. Pioneers, such as my Uncle Alfred, would struggle with the land to determine which crop might survive and thrive in this harsh climate. Many attempts failed, but Alfred and his fellow pioneers persisted and slowly the land began to bloom.

One of the major efforts in this endeavor was the planting of trees. Each year the *Tu B'Shwat* holiday is dedicated to the planting of trees. On that day, school rooms empty out as the Jewish children, clutching seedlings in their little hands, march out to the countryside, plant trees, and spend the day singing, dancing, and celebrating the joys of spring. These efforts, combined with the formal reforestation program of the Jewish Agency, started, ever so slowly, to turn vast areas of rocky hills into patches of green. The little seedlings grew and, as years turned into decades, the patches of green met each other and formed a carpet of green trees covering the bare rocks. The forests have become a symbol of the rebirth of the Jewish people and of the Jewish State.

After the 1967 Six Day War, when Israel occupied all of Palestine and Sinai, a new four-lane highway was constructed from Tel Aviv that reaches the Shar Hagai crossroad. Then, as the road starts to rise into the mountains on the way to Jerusalem, the forest on both sides makes a great impact on the driver. By the year 1990, the trees that had been planted decades ago had risen to a substantial 25, 30, or more meters and the forest had become quite impressive as it rose majestically to the hilltops and beyond. When the road reached the top of the mountains, the observant driver could look left or right and see that the forest stretched out past the next valley and beyond the mountaintops to as far as one could see. Each time, I drove this route my heart was filled with joy and pride seeing what decades of hard work and dedication had accomplished.

And then one day, during a visit in 1995, I first got an inkling that something terrible was happening on the road to Jerusalem. The reports were incomplete, but one thing was certain: The road to Jerusalem was closed to all traffic in both directions. In a country that, unfortunately, is used to bad news, this nevertheless sounded very ominous. Slowly more information made it obvious that a major disaster was occurring. It wasn't till the following day that the road was reopened and it was two more days before I was on that road on my way to Jerusalem.

I was completely unprepared for what greeted me when I reached Shar Hagai. What had been the beautiful green forest just two days earlier was now a sea of gray and black. As far as I could see the trees, those magnificent symbols of Jewish rebirth, had been turned into ashen monuments. I was stunned. I stepped on the gas and pushed the car up the hill hoping to reach the end of the devastation. But kilometers passed by and still there was nothing but ruination on both sides of the road. Then, when I reached the top of one of the hills, I could see that the fire had reached well beyond the road and into the valleys on both sides of the highway and up and over the next mountainside. It was all devastation. Those proud beautiful and majestic cypress trees were just blackened stalks standing forlornly on the mountainside. It wasn't until I reached the village of Shoresh, nearly six kilometers from Shar Hagai, that the countryside once again turned green. For me, the disaster was monumental.

I pulled off the road and I wept.

It wasn't just the trees — although that was reason enough to cry — it was what they represented.

> *Each coin was a promise to resurrect the Jewish people by the planting of trees in Palestine.*

My thoughts went back many decades to the time before World War II and the Holocaust and to the thousands and thousands of little blue-and-white metal coin boxes that had been part of nearly every Jewish family's life for generations all over the world. In every country, on every continent, the little metal *pushka* with the coin slot on top, the locked trap door on the bottom and the blue Star of David on its front was as much a symbol of a family's or a business' Jewishness as a *menorah* or *mezuzah*. I thought of the millions of hard-earned and carefully saved coins that were dropped into these containers. Each coin was a promise to resurrect the Jewish people by the planting of trees in Palestine. Each little donation represented a silent prayer for the restoration of a Jewish homeland. Each time the box was shaken to measure the growth of its precious contents, the fulfillment of a dream came nearer. I thought of the many businessmen who had the coin box stationed right on the sales counter or on their office desk and were not embarrassed to urge their customers or visitors to drop a few coins into the slot before leaving.

Our family in Czechoslovakia was not different from the others, and our parents encouraged us to make regular contributions into our *pushka*. A man from *Keren Kayemet l'Israel* (the Jewish National Fund) would visit from time to time with his magic key that would unlock the bottom of the box so that he could collect the contents. I thought of all the other children who proudly brought these boxes to the *Keren Kayemet* offices to have them unlocked and watch the flood of coins spill from the opening.

Then I remembered all the births, *brit milahs*, weddings, *Bar Mitzvahs*, anniversaries, and other happy occasions that were celebrated with generous donations to plant one, two, five, 10, 20, 100, or even several hundred trees on the barren slopes of Palestine. These gifts were honored with a beautifully framed certificate proudly mounted on the wall for everyone to see. A dreadful thought was mixed in with these recollections. I realized that most of these good, hopeful, and faithful souls, whose generosity, dedication, and determination had made these forests possible, had mostly been brutally wiped out during the Holocaust. And now, a substantial portion of their living memorial had just been destroyed in virtually the same fashion as their lives. Each blackened dead tree stood there like a silent witness to the destruction of those whose generosity had created the trees. Here and there, just like in the Holocaust, a tree or a group of trees stood untouched having been, somehow miraculously saved, like our small family. But the vast majority were just ashes.

Yes, I cried over trees, and each time I pass through this area, I am gripped again by the same sadness. To me, that forest represented a small victory in the Jewish struggle for survival. For two millennia, the world has tried to wipe us off the face of the earth. In the last century, it almost succeeded. But we are still here and we remain, despite our small numbers, a major force in the life of the civilized world.

New trees have been planted and some day proud trees may once again cover the mountainside. It is the task of our children and grandchildren to see to it that these young trees survive and thrive. I know they will. This fact is one of the great joys of my life.

Stops Along The Way

Unwelcome Featured Speaker

A man wearing a traditional kufiyah on his head. This is not the "unwelcome featured speaker". Only a representation of how he was dressed.

For decades, Jews in the United States have generously supported Israel, principally with donations. For some, this is a way of easing their conscience for their lack of participation in Jewish religious affairs, or for letting other people do the hard work of creating a Jewish homeland, or for not immigrating to Israel or out sheer love of Judaism. Others, however, donate large sums of money out of their fervent desire to help Jews in need anywhere and everywhere, including Israel, to live a better life. Our United Jewish Appeal federation, which covers only a small part of the State of New Jersey in the United States, raises more than $11.1 million each year to support this activity.

Part of this fund-raising effort includes phone solicitations, direct mail, meetings, social events, and dinners. At times, depending on the level of your family's donation, the Federation would send out an invitation to a dinner with other donors of the same donor caliber. To make these dinners more attractive, the Israel office of United Jewish Appeal would send a *shaliach*, a representative from Israel, to address these social events. He, or she, would report on the accomplishments of the UJA and loosen the purses of the guests at the dinner. At one particular such dinner that I attended, things went quite differently than planned.

In a very ornate dining room of a local golf course, some 500 of the $5,000 to $10,000 category donors were gathered for this type of UJA dinner gathering. When it came time to introduce the celebrity guest speaker for the evening, the chairman rose to the dais and said something like the following: "Ladies and gentlemen. As you know, it is our usual practice to have a speaker from Israel at these dinners with a message about the Jewish people here and in Israel, their needs, their successes, and their appreciation for what you do for them. This evening we have decided that, in fairness, we should also hear from the other side. We have, therefore, invited a Palestinian Arab to tell his side of the story." There was a gasp reaction from the audience. The chairman proceeded to introduce the speaker who then strode to the podium to the amazement and consternation of the audience. The man was tall, had a black beard, wore an Arab cloak, and a *kufiyah* on his head and spoke with a distinct Arabic accent.

He started his presentation in a very friendly manner speaking about the common heritage of Jews and Arabs, the close relationship of the two religions, the similarity of their languages and the need to live together as friends in Palestine. However, as his address moved along, his rhetoric became more and more strident. He started to point out the many ways that money contributed to the United Jewish Appeal was making the life of the Jews better while the Arabs were suffering. Soon he was shouting at the audience telling them that the day would come when the Arabs would chase all the Jews out of Palestine. When he approached the climax of his presentation he suddenly stopped, stood still for a moment, and then collapsed on the stage. There was a moment of stunned silence in the room. Then the chairman came to the microphone and asked a totally unnecessary question: "Is there a doctor in the house?" About 20 people sprang up and rushed for the stage. Some went to their car to bring medications, others performed artificial respiration while others went to the phone to call for an ambulance. About 20 minutes later, the Arab gentleman was wheeled out of the room with three doctors following him to the hospital.

Slowly, the room settled down and the chairman rose to the microphone and said something like this: "Ladies and gentlemen, the man who has just been taken to the hospital is in fact not an Arab but an Israeli Jew who does his presentation in this fashion — pretending to be an Arab — in order to dramatize the need for your contributions. I am sure he appreciates that you

Collection boxes of the Jewish National Fund from before WWII thru today. They all featured a slot on the top and a locked trapped door on the bottom.

sprang to his aid and probably saved his life, despite the fact that he was in the process of berating you."

Two years later this speaker came to our dinner once again. He told us that he no longer travels to make these presentations but wanted to come to our dinner to thank all those who came to his aid when he was in such great danger. He concluded with "If all of us in the world, and in particular in Israel, could act toward each other as you did even though you believed I was an Arab, Israel and the whole world could and would be such a wonderful place for everyone."

Hands Across The Void

Gil Karu, an accomplished chef and restaurant manager in Israel, was 47-years-old when he suddenly collapsed and died without any apparent cause.

The Karu family, good and close friends of ours, is a highly respected and successful family who had four equally respected and successful sons. Now, unexpectedly and tragically, they had just three. Gil was well known to my family, as he had been the chef at my 85th birthday party. His sudden and totally unexpected death was a great shock to us, the Karu family and to their wide array of close friends. Gil died of a brain hemorrhage and, almost immediately, the family decided to donate the organs of this young man so that others may live.

Gil Karu shortly before his sudden and unexpected death.

On Saturday, May 11, 2013, my wife and I departed very early in the morning to join a caravan of seven or eight cars headed north for Ixcel, an Arab-Israeli town near Nazareth. We were invited to meet the man who had received one of Gil Karu's lungs. I remember it as one of the most remarkable days of my life. The recipient of the lung, it turns out, is a member of one of the most influential families in this community. They told the Karu family "bring as many family members and friends you like — we have room for one hundred." So my wife and I were invited and were a part some 45–50 visitors.

When we arrived, we were welcomed by a large group of men who greeted us warmly and ushered us into the second floor of the five-story residence building. We were presented with large bowls of fruits, nuts, and fresh vegetables and, after a few minutes of awkwardness, the barriers came down and we felt at ease in this beautiful home. They made sure that Jean and I were partnered with an English-speaking family member who introduced us to other family members and to some of the foods we were offered. There were welcoming speeches and responses and presentations of gifts. Members of the household and their friends made an obvious and determined effort to make us feel "at home." The patriarch of the family shook my hand whenever I was in his vicinity, gladly posed for pictures and planted a warm kiss on my cheeks. During this time another Arab Israeli arrived to join the event. He was now being kept alive with Gil's heart beating in his chest.

We noticed a film crew hovering around and videotaping just about everything. We learned that they had come to cover a horse show in town but, when they learned that the lung of a Jewish man is saving the life of a prominent member of the town, they decided to also cover this event. The story is scheduled to appear on Israel TV and other outlets.

> *... why can't we learn to live in peace?*

The ground floor, that covered the whole space under the building, was apparently cleared and was now filled with tables and chairs. Some 85 to 90 people joined in a feast — an endless parade of great varieties of meats, salads, vegetables and traditional foods. Our English-speaking host remained with us and described the food and drinks that we were sharing. We were then advised that, before we visit the horse show, we are invited for coffee and desert at a cousin's house.

House? When we reached the top of the mountain we were greeted by a mansion — a truly remarkable building both inside and out. Once again, we were invited to make ourselves at home while sweets and dark coffee was offered to us.

Then we were escorted as honored guests to the horse show — actually the National Competition of the finest Arabian horses in Israel. There were perhaps 4,000 people assembled. We were ushered into the VIP area and were welcomed by the town's mayor. When the top prize was awarded, Gil's

The Karu family set aside a portion of their land to create a public park in memory of their son, Gil.

parents and brothers were invited to join in the ceremony and the awarding of the winner's trophy that was given in Gil's honor by our hosts. It was a truly a moving moment — particularly when the whole crowd stood and applauded.

It was hard to say goodbye — we had — in a few hours — developed a close relationship with the recipient's family and friends. There were many embraces and warm handshakes as we departed. Just a few weeks later a very large crowd gathered at Gil's graveside to mark the first anniversary of his passing. The ceremony was quite moving and when I saw more then ten members of the lung recipient's family among the 200 assembled mourners, my eyes filled with tears.

I, and surely many others who attended these events, walked away asking themselves: "why can't we learn to live in peace?"

About 200 people gathered in the park to hear stories from Gil's parents, Nani and Hannah, and many of his family members on the occasion of his eighth memorial day.

The design of the garden called for a large stone with flowing water in the center. This 2 ½ ton granite stone arrived, with a hole already drilled in the center, a gift from the grateful recipient of Gil's lung.

A Brother's 90th Birthday Wish

Dear Harold —

When Suzy first asked me to "say a few words" on behalf of the Ticho family at your 90th birthday celebration, I readily accepted this honor and made plans to say a few unrehearsed "off the cuff" remarks. However, as I delved deeper into this assignment, I realized that this approach would be inappropriate for such a unique event and for so unique an audience. Besides, how often do you get a chance to speak at your brother's 90th birthday — how often does anyone have a chance to speak at someone's 90th birthday? So, I decided that more serious, more thoughtful, more personal, more truthful and better-prepared remarks are called for.

So speaking of "more truthful" — Let me start by stating that having you as an older brother was not always a bed of roses. When you are 4-years-old and your brother is 10, the difference seems like an eternity. You were already studying in the gymnasium before I even entered grammar school. And by the time I entered the gymnasium, you were already off studying in Switzerland. I managed to placate my feelings with the thought that one day I will catch up — I will make up this age difference. After all, I calculated, when I was born you were 6 times older than I. By the time I was 3 you, at 9, would be only 3 times older than I. By my 18th birthday the difference would be 1/3 and so forth. But soon, as I advanced in my knowledge of mathematics, I realized that if you plot this equation on a graph the two lines would get closer and closer but they would never meet. Even today, you are still 1/15 older than I.

Suzy and Harold Ticho

There were other areas where this age differential played a role. When we moved into our new apartment in 1933, you got your own room complete with a desk, bookshelves and a big bed while little Steven and I were relegated to the *Kinderzimmer*, the children's room, which we were obliged to share with a governess. Then you had a grand *Bar Mitzvah* that attracted relatives and friends from everywhere to the services and to an elaborate reception and lunch in our apartment — a sit down affair with 103 in attendance. How come I remember the exact number? — well — I was assigned to the coat-checkroom where I had hung up 103 coats. But I got even for this wound of my dignity by advising anyone who would listen that you had stuttered three times during your recitation of Uncle Isidor's learned and lengthy dissertation on the significance of that Saturday's Torah portion — a lengthy exposition that you had to learn by heart — and in German.

It was shortly thereafter that an inebriated truck driver knocked you off your bicycle, breaking your hip and causing our mother to decree that henceforward no one in the family will ever get a bicycle. However, all this time, perhaps without really realizing it, you subtly influenced Steven and me and guided us towards higher goals. You introduced us to classical music, to the value of serious studies and to the love of books. When Steven and I were forced from our hometown and the Nazis allowed us to take no more than 20 kilos of our possessions, I loaded our suitcase with your collection of Karel Capek novels and my prized Czech version of Jules Verne's *20,000 Leagues Under the Sea* — a book I still treasure today.

The war and the Holocaust forced us apart for a quite a while, but you and I renewed our close relationship during three wonderful weeks in 12,000 foot high Climax, Colorado while you tried to photograph some very shy and elusive sub-atomic particles and I was recovering from my stint in the U.S. Navy. Our close bond has remained steady, firm and unchanged ever since.

I did not believe that my greetings from the Ticho family would be complete without messages from our Ticho first cousins. One, Karl, has chosen to deliver his message in person. From Jerusalem our cousin Esther Ticho wrote: "Dear Harold. Many, many happy returns of your special birthday. May you continue to enjoy good health and happiness in the coming years. I am with you all in thought at your festivities. From your cousin, Esther."

Our 94-year-old cousin, Laura Rohrlich, who has retained her sharp mind and equally sharp wit, sent a slightly more elaborate message.

Dear cousin Harold, So, you, too, are joining the 90-year-olds? Welcome!

Thinking back over the many years, what strikes me is that, though the distance between Brno and Vienna is really quite minimal, how rarely the Brno Tichos and the Vienna Tichos got together. I remember one time when I was 12-years-old being taken along on a trip to "Brünn" for a family wedding (whose? Maybe Otto's?) I met you and your brothers then. You, Harold, were a good-looking, robust fellow, projecting health and energy; Leo, a lovely, angelic-looking boy who immediately charmed me; When he died it broke my heart; Charlie was full of tricks, an *enfant terrible*; And Steven, still very little and quite skinny. Apparently, your mother's daily cream-of-wheat breakfast routine had not as yet taken hold of him! Then we met again *"am Semmering"* in a kosher hotel, after your brother Leo had died. I heard your mother say that God had punished her with Leo's death because she had not kept a kosher household. Personally I thought that God had other *"tsures"* than whether Tante Fraenze kept a kosher household, but, as usual, I kept my mouth shut. The next time I saw you, was when you visited us, alone already, as a young teenager. You had heard about the artificial big ocean waves that the "Dianabad" featured. You

Cousin Laura Rohrlich, the witty, educated and proud mother of a brilliant family was with us till age 102 with a mind that worked till her passing. Her daughter Susanne Feldman at her side.

wanted to try them out with your cousin Felix. The two of you, both raised in countries far from any ocean, marched off with great anticipation to experience that new sensation.

Well. enough of reminiscing ...

Harold, being ninety has its attractions. When you don't want to do something, you can always mention your age as an excuse. You have reached the age that allows you to do just what you really, really badly, want to do. Also, the doctors these days furnish you with a panoply of pills to keep you well and functioning. And as the Romans already said, 'mens sana in corpore sano.' – a sound mind in a healthy body. People used to say that your creativity vanishes after age thirty. Not so. The other day I read in the *New York Times* that the famous composer Elliot Carter – frankly not a favorite of mine – but anyhow, that he celebrated recently his one-hundred-third birthday and that he had composed in that year many new pieces all of which were played in a concert at the 92nd Street Y to great acclaim. Amazing!

Here, where I live, there are several hundred-year-old residents. They are well and robust, and "with it." One 102-year-old lady still sews, dresses beautifully, and participates in all activities. She made a remark recently worth quoting, "oh," she exclaimed with a sigh, "how wish I could be 90 again!"

So enjoy being 90, Harold, and stay well and chipper! Much love to you and yours, Laura, and all my family.

P.S. I have to report to you that another physicist is sprouting in our family: My grandson, Ben Feldman, Susie's son, hopes to get his PhD. at Harvard in a year or so.

What can I possible add to this message? Yes, Harold, enjoy being 90. Remain the sun around which all of us revolve, the sun that has illuminated our path to higher goals and greater achievements and the sun that generates so much of our love, esteem and admiration. In spite of what I said at the start of my "few words" I have truly loved the 84 years we have shared together and I look forward to many more to come. *Mazel Tov,* Good luck. *Le Chaim.* To life!

On Monday, May 13, 2019, I was obliged to send the following letter to our family.

> *Jean and I have just been notified that our wonderful 102-year old cousin, Laura, has passed away peacefully this morning. This great lady was a pillar of intellect, education and humor. Jean and I attended her*

100th birthday celebration and her grandson's wedding and enjoyed her wit, her charm and her smile. She was truly one of the last examples of the classic Ticho intelligence and brains that was the bedrock of the 35 children of the original 13 Ticho siblings of our grandparents. She set a high standard for all of us to follow.

On, Tuesday, November 3, (Election Day) 2020, I sent the following to our close family members:

This afternoon I said farewell to my dear brother Harold as we shared our last telephone conversation. I had a chance to thank him for a lifetime of companionship and guidance — for the years of inspiration and motivation — for his humor and charm and for the love and affection we shared during some difficult and challenging times. Harold left us just a few weeks before his 99th birthday.

Our grandfather, Yitzchak Zvi Ticho and his wife Esther Ticho had 13 children. All of them married and created a generation of 35 first cousins. Slowly, over the years, the number of these first cousins diminished. During the last year we lost Laura, Karl and now, Harold. As a result, the number has been reduced to just two — Esther Ticho in Jerusalem and Charles Ticho.

A Letter to an Older Brother

Dear Harold —

Today, August 25, 2015, is the 40th anniversary of the passing of our father, Nathan Ticho. I thought the occasion deserves to be noted. His life and his guidance are still influencing me in many ways — today as it has throughout my life.

Nathan Ticho was a man who would make anyone proud to have as a father, grandfather or great grandfather. First of all, he was honest — I never had a reason to believe that he acted in any other way than honorably. He was a wise man who handled challenges intelligently and managed to make a success of his life in spite of the ill winds that blew during his lifetime. He was a clever man who managed to build three successful businesses during his lifetime. He recovered and rebuilt the family's fortune in spite of an economic collapse and two World Wars that destroyed the enterprises he had built and wiped out the investments he had made.

This portrait photo of Nathan Ticho was taken in the late 1930's when he, his family, his business and his standing were at their highest point just before the Nazi horror began in 1939.

Grandfather Nathan enjoying his visit with Robin and Ron, our first two children in our new home in Woodcliff Lake, NJ — our home for 42 years.

He was a patient and compassionate person who managed to handle mother's difficulties as she drifted slowly into dementia. He was a good Jew who patiently did his best to make us be the same. And, he was generous, always looking out for ways to assist people — particularly members of the extensive Ticho family — such as the many cousins who lost their parents in the Holocaust.

He was independent. He never asked anything from anyone. Self-pity was not a trait of his. In the face of unspeakable brutality he never used the Nazi inhumaneness as an excuse. He was a hero who survived the brutal treatment of the Nazi Dachau concentration camp, the loss of five of his siblings in the Holocaust and, at the age of 56, had to recover and make a new life for his family in a strange new country, the United States of America.

When I reached my 56th birthday I was comparatively secure with a profitable and productive business, with a house in Woodcliff Lake, with a wife and three children, with life insurances, two cars, many friends and business associates plus standing in the community and with profitable investments — all circumstances very similar to our father's situation at his age of 56 when the German's marched into Czechoslovakia and launched the Holocaust. On that birthday, I sat down alone in a quiet place and conjectured for some time and at great length — what would I do if some officers were to suddenly burst into my house right now, arrest me and deprive me of all my possessions – the house, the cars, the business — everything and be subjected to almost two years of senseless cruelty in a concentration camp, then be forced to leave everything behind and flee to another country — say, for example, Brazil — where I did not know the culture, the commerce, the people or the language and be responsible to create a new life for a family of five — what would I do? I sat for quite a while and imagined this scene that had actually happened to our father. Frankly, I just could not imagine how I would have or could have survived — how I might have carried on. Yet, this is exactly the situation that our father confronted when we arrived in the United States in 1940. Yes, he was truly a hero.

Harold, I believe our Father's life and his passing deserves a moment of acknowledgment, appreciation and gratitude and, I am sure, that you share my feelings.

I look forward to seeing you and Suzy soon.
Love, Charles

Harold lived to be nearly 99 (Dec. 21, 1921 — Nov. 3, 2020) and I never manage (at the age of 94) to match him in age, wisdom and accomplishments.

An American's Yom Kippur in Israel

A man of my age — I was 94 just a few months ago — does not like changes. We like to be in familiar places, doing familiar things with familiar people. This tendency also applies to how we like to celebrate Jewish holidays. I like to be in a familiar synagogue, hearing the voices of familiar clergy, singing familiar melodies and hearing the sound of a familiar *shofar*, a ram's horn.

Back in the 1930's, when Yom Kippur rolled around, my father would take me to the New Temple of Brno in Czechoslovakia where we sat in a pew that was nearly completely occupied by family members — male family members, of course. Mother, aunts and sundry female cousins were all relegated to the balcony. My father was one of 13 siblings so there was no shortage of uncles, aunts, cousins and in-laws to occupy a considerable portion of the temple.

For a young boy, the services were pure agony. I was handed a heavy prayer book and was invited to follow along during the ceremony. Because I was going to the grammar school run by the Jewish Community of Brno, I started

The shofar, a rams horn in blown during several Jewish holidays particularly during the New Year Day and Day of Atonement.

learning Hebrew in kindergarten. But, even when I was 8-years-old and in the third grade, I could not read fast enough to keep up. Also, the prayer book was designed to be used for many different occasions and holidays, so there were constant instructions to "add this for *Succoth*" or "delete this on *Shabbat*" or "proceed to a particular prayer at this point." And to make these instructions more challenging, they were not in German or Czech, languages I knew — they were printed using Hebrew letters but were actually in Yiddish.

Each member of the congregation was obliged to bring his own *siddur*, prayer book. So, once I was lost in the Hebrew text, I had to confess that fact to my father who would guide me to the right place in my book. I always felt terribly guilty when I had to do this as if I had offended G-d by not paying attention.

By the time I was 10-years-old, perhaps in order to make my visits to the temple pleasanter, I volunteered to sing in the temple choir and was happily accepted. Now, I sat, along with my fellow choir members, on a bench behind the cantor and only had to read the music pages. Now, I always knew where we were during the service. Alas, that lasted only about three years — until right after the High Holiday services in 1940 when the Nazis closed our beautiful and familiar shul — never, ever again to be opened for Jewish services again.

At this point, followed some 15 years of chaos, turmoil and instability as our family engineered its escape from Europe and the Holocaust, arrived in the United States and moved several times while trying to establish a foothold in a strange new country. Also, during these years, I served in the United States Navy, went to college, and started a career. Not surprisingly, I found myself each year in a different synagogue, marking the High Holidays in new surroundings, led by a great variety of rabbis and cantors. It wasn't until I was married and settled in New Jersey that I, once again, began to enjoy the warm familiar environment of the same congregation year after year.

Temple Emanuel of the Pascack Valley, located in Woodcliff Lake, Bergen County, New Jersey, was formally incorporated in 1929 and grew to become one of the largest congregations in New Jersey. By 1966, when we joined this assembly, it was already under the leadership of a rabbi, cantor and school principal triumvirate that guided it for nearly the

For more than 50 years, Rabbi Andre Ungar (left) was the wonderful and learned leader of our temple. Cantor Biddleman (right) was the ideal partner for the more than half-century they conducted the services and guided our Temple Emanuel of the Pascack Valley.

whole next half century. Now, once again, on each *Yom Kippur*, I was surrounded by familiar circumstances. The whole congregation used the same prayer book and, should you lose your place or allowed your mind to wander, the rabbi would gently guide you back to the right page. The book had English text along side the Hebrew so you knew not just *that* you were praying but *what* you were praying. For the next 50 years, Temple Emanuel was my home on *Yom Kippur* — until 2016.

That year, my *sabra* wife convinced me that we should travel to Israel a day or two after *Rosh Hashanah* and spend the Day of Atonement in Israel. I asked Israeli friends and relatives "What does a practicing but non-orthodox Jew do on *Yom Kippur* in Israel?" The first thing they asked: "Will you fast?" "Of course, I will fast! I have done so since I was 12-years-old — every year even while I was in the Navy." "Well, there must be a temple near you in Rishon — although it is most likely orthodox."

Suddenly I had this sinking feeling that, in an orthodox congregation, I will, once again have to revert to the conditions of the Brno temple with my wife hidden away somewhere, everyone reading from a different book and a cantor storming through the Hebrew service under the assumption that everyone knows Hebrew and can follow the text. "No, I don't think we want to do that," I responded. "Well, than, I was told, all you can do is stay at home, read, study, rest, go for a walk or visit neighbors." I was deeply disappointed by this choice. What kind of a way was this to spend *Yom Kippur*?

But, I shouldn't have worried. The day turned out to be rather unique and quite appropriate for the occasion. First, there was the absolute quiet that descended on the country — the streets and highways were virtually empty of all traffic, the television and radio stations were mute, the phones stopped ringing and I faced the prospect of spending the day without touching food, drink and the computer. With this uncommon silence came a chance to converse with your dear wife, to think, to meditate, to reflect and to exercise some much-needed self-examination. In many ways, the day became an unexpected pseudo-religious experience. This had in fact, and to my surprise, become a quite meaningful Day of Atonement.

When the day of fasting ended and things returned to their "normal" state, I realized that I had not pined for the usual synagogue service, or missed the camaraderie of a familiar congregation, or searched for the voices of a familiar cantor or a rabbi.

The only thing I truly missed was the sound of the *shofar*.

The Epshtein family sometime in early 1930's. Hannah Epschtein, circled on the left, before she came to Israel. She was the biological mother of Jean (Yochi) and her twin sister Ruth. She committed suicide when the girls were 4½ years old. The photo and several others in the family album were Jean's first look at her immediate family.

By 1939, the Epschtein family had added several spouses and grandchildren. Missing now were Father Mosses who had passed away by then and Hannah Epschtein had died in Israel. However, son Aaron (front row second one on the left) visited the family just before World War II started and brought back the family photo album that led to the reunification of the family in Israel. Every other member of the family was murdered in the Holocaust.

Lost Generations

"Dora isn't really my mother," said Yocheved as we were mounting the stairs to the third floor of 45 Maccabi Street to reach her parents' apartment, "but, please don't mention it at dinner." We had just walked to what was, in 1954, the North edge of Tel Aviv in order to be formally introduced to Yochi's (as she was called in Israel) parents and sisters. This last sudden remark caught me by surprise. What did this mean and why can't it be mentioned, were questions that immediately arose in my mind. But there was no time to ask them because the apartment door opened and I was welcomed into Yochi's and her family's home. Five years later, we married in Chicago, but that's another story.

Needless to say, the next time we met over tea and cake, I posed the questions that were on my mind since the dinner. Yochi began to explain rather hesitantly: "I really don't know the whole story," she began, "all I know is that Dora is not our mother. Our real mother is dead. She committed suicide when we were about four years old. But we never mention this or discuss it. I think my father believes that we were too young to remember the suicide and that we are willing to accept the fiction that Dora is our mother. But he is wrong — we certainly remember the event." "Why are you saying 'we'?" was my next question. "Well, Ruthi, who you met at the dinner, is my twin sister." Yochi continued, "when Dora became part of the family, our father told us that Dora is our mother and we should call her 'mother,' which we did." Dora became pregnant and a third daughter (Nurith) was added to the family. "We don't have any photographs of our real mother, or birth certificates, or any other papers. The whole thing is just a big fat secret in the family."

It took the next 40 years for the story to slowly unfold and, once again, demonstrated what bitter pain and chaos the Holocaust inflicted on Jews for decades even long after the War had ended and the Nazis had been defeated. It wasn't till a chance meeting in Israel in 1993 that the many blank spaces in the story were filled.

Of course, as the twins became older, the desire to learn more became more urgent. Ruthi did some searching at home and discovered some interesting but unidentified negatives of photographs. She decided on a multi-purpose trip to Paris in order to visit the twins' only first cousin, to heal her broken heart, to assist caring for the cousin's little daughter and to talk to her cousin and learn what she could about the "family secrets."

When she returned from Paris a year later she related to Yochi these facts that she learned: their father, Solomon Ginsburg, born in Grodno, Poland, a graduate in electrical engineering at the Berlin University, came to Tel Aviv in 1935. There he met an Israeli young women and, apparently, fell in love. However, shortly, thereafter, Solomon's mother (Hasha) arrived from Poland and notified her son Solomon that she had arranged his marriage to a lovely young woman from a very prominent Jewish family in the town of Slonim, Poland. Such arranged marriages were, apparently, not so unusual as they enabled the marriage partner to escape from the Nazi threat in Poland and to gain permission to enter the Palestine Mandate despite of the very restrictive British rules.

> ... *it took 40 years for the story to slowly unfold* ...

A few months later, Hannah Epstein, the "lucky bride," arrived in Tel Aviv and met her "husband." Solomon, apparently, acknowledged his mother's decision and obediently accepted Hannah as his wife. In 1937, twin sisters, Yochi and Ruthi, were born. But they were not born in Tel Aviv. As I mentioned earlier, Hannah Epstein came from an important Jewish family in Slonim. Her father was the head of the local Jewish hospital and convinced his daughter to come to Poland and deliver the baby at a modern hospital instead of a who-knows-how-good hospital in the Middle East. So, Hannah traveled to Poland where, "surprise!", twins were born.

Hannah returned to Tel Aviv but only with Yochi. She left Ruthi in Slonim in the care of her sister. Ruthi was left behind because she was deemed to be "not strong enough" to travel. In 1942, Hannah, mother of Yochi and Ruthi, "fell" off a balcony and was killed by the fall. There were two possible causes for her despair that were rumored in the Jewish circles of Tel Aviv. My Uncle Alfred, who was privy to most of the gossip around town, claimed that Hannah learned that her husband may have been unfaithful. The other report that may have caused the despondency was the tragic news that all the Jews of Slonim, including Hannah's complete family, were murdered by the invading German army. Whatever the reason, Hannah was dead and the twins were motherless. However, shortly thereafter, Dora entered the family as the wife of Solomon and became the "mother" of the twins.

All this new information was never brought up in the family as the secrets continued. When the twins' half-sister, Nurith, was slated to be married, her two older sisters finally sat down with her and, for the first time, revealed the fact that Dora was, in fact, Nurith's mother but is not the twins' mother ... that Nurith was not a sister but a half-sister.

All these secrets continued to be "secrets" until 1993. By then, both Dora and Solomon had passed away. My wife and I happened to be visiting Israel when Yochi received a phone call from her sister, Ruthi, with the news that there may be someone in Israel searching for them. In 1993, there was a special department in the Israeli government that "searches for relatives." They advised Ruthi that there is a family that recently arrived from Russia that may be related to her and her twin sister. Yochi broke into tears when she got the news. Ruthi, on the other hand, was much cooler to the situation — she, apparently, never forgave her biological mother for abandoning her in Poland and then, two years later, tearing her away from the only mother she knew.

After a few more phone calls a meeting was arranged for the two of us to drive to Ma'ale Adumim to meet Lev Epstein and his family for what became a five-hour-long heart wrenching exploration, revelation and disclosure of the events that took place in the family during the past 45 years. Slowly the missing pieces in the Yochi/Ruthi story began to fall into place. Lev also, for the first time, learned

The three sisters (l to r) Yochi, Ruthi and Nurith in happy days.

that his Aunt Hannah, his father's sister, had committed suicide, that he was meeting Yochi, his first cousin, that he neither knew existed nor the fact that she had a twin sister. It was all news to him.

We, on the other hand, learned that Lev's father, Aaron, followed the Russian army after World War I, left Poland, and moved to Moscow, Russia. Aaron's son, Lev, became a doctor of mathematics and Aaron's daughter, Mira, became a doctor of philosophy. When the Stalin government started to pursue and execute Jewish doctors, the family searched for some security by moving to Petrozavodsk, a city near the Finnish border. Throughout this time, Lev's family did not dare to reach out to possible family members in Israel. Jews that tried such contacts were considered disloyal Russian citizens and were persecuted, jailed or even murdered.

Lev told us that in the late 1980's and early 1990's, many Soviet Jews seized the opportunity of liberalized emigration policies to emigrate. More than half of the Jewish population packed up and left the miserable conditions of Russia. Many arrived in Israel like Lev's daughter who came to Israel to study. She convinced her father Lev to bring the whole family to join her in Israel. We further learned that Hannah, Yochi's biological mother, visited Slonim in 1939, just as World War II was about to start, to see her family and in order to pick up Ruthi, the second of her twin daughters that she had left behind.

At the end of the memorable afternoon the principals posed for a photo (left to right) Charles, Lev, Jean and Valia (Lev's wife).

Lev, now told us that his father somehow obtained an album of photographs containing pictures of the Slonim family. Lev brought this album to Israel and he offered to show it to us. He walked out of the room. Yochi reached for my hand and gripped it firmly. We both held our breath as Lev returned with an album carefully wrapped in several layers of plastic.

Now at last, as the final act of this monumental and emotional afternoon, was our opportunity to see this album and meet Yochi's family. It was an incredible and heart wrenching experience. Everyone was in tears as we slowly turned the pages of the album and Lev identified the individuals in each picture. We saw photos of Yochi's mother as a young girl, as a young woman as well as all of Yochi's uncles, aunts and grandparents. Everyone in the album had died at the hands of the Nazis, except Hannah, who may have killed herself because of the Nazi's cruelty. We found it hard to take our eyes off each photograph. What an unforgettable experience. Lev allowed us to make copies of many of the photos. At last, we gathered up everything we've learned and started on the way home. We did not talk as we drove home, we were both deep in thought.

> *Everyone was in tears as we slowly turned the pages …*

About two weeks after this memorable afternoon, Yochi (who was, by then, my wife of 35 years) and I attended our town's outdoor remembrance ceremony for the victims of the Holocaust. Yochi cried throughout the whole very moving ceremony.

As we were driving back home, she murmured: "This was the first time I really knew who I was crying for."

A Bus To Jerusalem

"You are NOT taking a train to Jerusalem," was the emphatic decision of my Aunt Ella, "you will take a *sherut*." It was late 1953 and I had recently arrived in Israel and wanted to visit with my uncle Avraham (Albert) Ticho and his wife, Anna. Aunt Ella and her husband, Aaron Ticho, had very kindly invited me to stay in their home in Tel Aviv and, as their guest, politeness dictated that I must accept her decision, "but please tell me, what is a *sherut*?"

I soon learned that a *sherut* was a large, former US taxicab DeSoto that could accommodate eight people — a driver and as many as seven passengers who shared the cost of the trip. It is safer and more comfortable, I was told, though a bit more expensive. Two days later, I was squeezed between two men in the back seat of the *sherut* on my way to Jerusalem. The ride was pleasant, my neighbors spoke rudimentary English and asked a lot of questions about the United States and tried to sell me on the idea to make Aliyah. As the road turned uphill, our car stopped and refused to move. We were invited to exit the car, collect our baggage and find transportation for the balance of the trip. So much for "safer and more comfortable".

A few minutes later, we boarded an Egged bus that mercifully stopped for us and I completed the trip to Jerusalem standing in a crowded bus. Now what? I asked a few people about the Ticho house. A nice man took my hand and lead me out the back of the station, pointed uphill to a large white building and said in Hebrew, what I believed was, "that's the Ticho home." That is how I learned that, in 1953, the Ticho home was a stone's throw away from the Jerusalem bus station, that Ticho was a well-known name in Jerusalem and that Israelis are friendly and welcoming people.

Entrance to the Ticho House

Ticho House garden path.

I hiked up the hill and reached the house to be greeted by Aunt Anna. Anna immediately inquired whether I wanted to eat or drink something. She then ignored my response and personally saw to my assumed needs. Then, with the food and drink set before me, she sat down facing me and inquired about all the news I could bring to her. In 1953, I was the first family member from the United Sates to arrive after the war and the Holocaust, so the questioning was quite extensive and detailed. She looked straight into my eyes, and I got the feeling that every word I uttered was of great interest to her. My interrogation ended when Anna's husband, Dr. Abraham Ticho, arrived to have lunch.

This metal arrow, nailed to a tree, directed visitors to the Ticho apartment.

I met this uncle once before in 1934 when he came to my older brother's *Bar Mitzvah* in Czechoslovakia. But I was only 7-years-old and few of the many guests paid any attention to me. But I was determined to make this second meeting more meaningful. I was in the midst of writing my memoir, "From Generation to Generation," and I had every intention to include material about my "famous" uncle. I brought my cassette audio recorder with me and was determined to interview both my uncle and my aunt.

Here is what I gathered:

Albert (whose Hebrew name was Abraham), the sixth in the line of 13 Ticho siblings, was born in 1883 in Boskovice which was then in the Austro-Hungarian Empire. He followed his two brothers, Joseph and Max, to the University in Vienna. Unlike them, however, he opted to study medicine and decided to specialize in eye diseases. However, when he reached the final examinations in this field, he encountered some difficulties and decided to switch to the Charles University in Prague. There, a year later, he received his diploma in the field of ophthalmology. Albert returned to Vienna where he was offered a position on the staff of one of the professors at the hospital. "However," said the learned doctor, "two of my assistants are Jews, and I can't put another Jew on my staff. You'll just have to convert to Christianity." Albert was very upset by the professor's bigotry but, nevertheless, responded politely: "My father would be deeply hurt. So, I must respectfully refuse the offer." An older doctor and friend, a Dr. Stern, turned to the young man and told Albert: "Leave these *goyim* and these anti-Semites. Why put up with this abuse? The Lemaan Zion eye clinic in

Jerusalem is looking for a doctor to run the clinic. Why don't you apply?" Albert applied for the position and in 1912 found himself on, board a mule, on his way from the port city of Jaffa to Jerusalem. There, near the Madelbaum Gate, just outside of the Mea Shearim Jewish Quarters, he found the clinic. It consisted of a rented house with 40 beds, an assistant doctor, some nurses, and hundreds of people waiting to be treated in a country where nearly every second person was suffering from an eye disease.

The family reluctantly accepted Albert's departure for Palestine secretly hoping that a lengthy separation from his first cousin Anna might break up, what they considered, an undesirable romance that had been flourishing for some months. They were due for a disappointment. In 1912, the family had gathered in Brno to celebrate the *Pidion HaBen* of David's son, Robert. While everyone was there, a telegram arrived that simply stated: "*Mazal Tov* to everyone. Albert and Anna are engaged." This struck the family like a bolt of lightning. The family was deeply disappointed and concerned what a marriage between two first cousins might bring. Unfortunately, the family's worst fears became true as all six of Anna's pregnancies ended in miscarriages.

It is difficult today to get a true picture of the vast influence that Dr. Albert Ticho had during his lifetime. He came into a country where poor sanitation and poor medical attention caused many people to lose their eyesight. Trachoma, an ancient eye disease caused by an invasion of parasites into the eye, was the principal cause of blindness. Dr. Ticho determined that the spread of trachoma could be reduced with improved hygienic conditions and the elimination of flies in households. He devised a clever plan to get his message into the homes by mounting an intense campaign to educate the children in schools regarding proper hygienic care. The children brought the information back home and, after only a few years of this effort, the incidents of trachoma were greatly reduced.

Dr. Ticho's day was an extremely busy one. It wasn't unusual, at times, for a whole Arab village to arrive at the clinic's door. For example, an Arab eye doctor was overwhelmed by an outbreak of a form of gonorrhea that affected the eyes in a village near Rishon Lezion. The whole village was brought to the clinic for examination and treatment. For many Arab patients, the most important part of the treatment was an injection. Albert learned that an Arab patient who did not get an injection as part of the treatment felt that he had not been properly cared for. An injection of plain sugar water would often send the patient home beaming.

World War I greatly disrupted the lives of Albert and Anna. As an Austrian citizen, he was forced to leave Jerusalem and join the Austrian Army. Thus, Albert found himself in Damascus in charge of an eye clinic at an Austrian army hospital. Life for Albert and Anna was very difficult. Prejudice and abuse were rampant. Jews, in particular, were subjected to a great deal of persecution. Albert was forced to witness the execution of a Jew by the name of Nilli who was hanged on a trumped-up charge of treason.

In the meantime, the Turkish army in Palestine was defeated by the British. The British army occupied Jerusalem and Albert's eye clinic was converted into a horse barn for the army's cavalry. When they finally returned home, Albert and Anna were confronted by their ruined clinic. Further, Albert's wallet contained only Turkish money that was worthless. Albert and Anna were penniless. The family came to the aid of the destitute couple, and Albert and Anna proceeded to rebuild their lives.

After a three-year term as head of the eye department at the Rothschild Hospital in Jerusalem, Dr. Ticho decided to open a private clinic and hospital. His reputation grew far and wide, and patients from all over the Middle East came to his door. For 36 years, until he died of a stroke in 1960, Dr. Ticho and his staff performed thousands of operations and treated hundreds of thousands of patients ranging from the royal house of the Hashemite Kingdom to the poorest peasant. No one was turned away. The rich were charged a high fee to offset the cost of treating those who could not afford to pay anything. At first, Anna was Albert's assistant. But soon, nurses were added to the hospital's staff, then doctors, and other technicians. At its busiest time, five doctors were actively assisting Albert in the clinic and the hospital. Early each morning, a line started forming in front of the clinic door. Patients learned to arrive early to secure a spot at the front. This applied to everyone. Not even British Army officers got preferential treatment. The same procedure applied in the operating room.

In 1924, Albert purchased a building called "The Castle of Haj Rashid" and converted it into a hospital. The downstairs housed the surgery, recovery wards, pharmacy, kitchen, laundry, library and reception area. The upstairs was converted into the couple's apartment. The house was located in a beautiful garden just a few feet from Jerusalem's busiest intersection of Jaffa Road and Ben Yehuda Street. However, when the house was originally constructed it was set in a wide open area. Built as a summer castle for the Nashashibi family, it served as an idyllic place in which to spend the hot summer days outside the crowded Old City. The house had several owners before it came on the market and was purchased by Albert and Anna.

Living in Jerusalem in the 1920's was not simple. There were a great number of political pressures affecting everyday life. Two Arab families, the Huseini and the Nashashibi, ruled Jerusalem. They could be bribed at times to allow Jews to make some progress in the city. Nevertheless, they still essentially pursued Arab nationalistic goals. At times the two families competed with each other for control

Albert and Anna Ticho in 1958.

of the city but, when it came to fighting the Jews, they usually managed to present a united front. The British, in order to control the country, played the various factions against each other. One day, in response to the demands from the Arabs, the British suddenly decided to prohibit the blowing of the *shofar* at the end of the Yom Kippur services. A British policeman was stationed in the synagogues to enforce the rule. In Jerusalem's main synagogue, when the services concluded, a turmoil was suddenly created and from the midst of the milling crowd the *shofar* was heard. In the confusion the perpetrator disappeared and could not be arrested. The rule was soon repealed.

In the year 1929, the Arab resentment over the British rule resulted in serious rioting. The major victims of the rioting was the Jewish population in Palestine. Many settlements were attacked and fighting spread throughout the area. The British tried to separate the factions as best as they could. At the height of the rioting, Albert was attacked by a young Arab and was stabbed in the back. The exact reason for the attack was never determined. Some claimed that Albert was one of four prominent Jewish leaders that had been targeted for assassination by the Arab revolutionary group. Albert was rushed to the Hadassah Hospital where Dr. Wundereich attended him. When the knife was removed, Albert collapsed. Fortunately, the knife had missed the heart and Albert survived. A great wave of concern flooded the country. People were asked to pray for Albert's recovery, and letters of concern arrived from all over the world. Alfred Ticho, Albert's youngest brother, decided to send a special letter and gift to his brother. He sent one of his field workers to Jerusalem to deliver the goods. The man rode

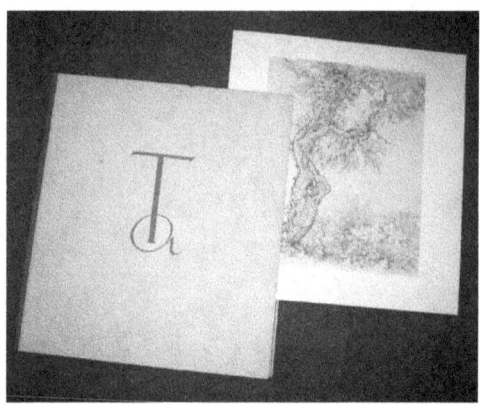

Thousands of these reproductions of Anna Ticho's art were created and sold worldwide

a donkey from Tul Karem and returned a few days later. with a glowing account of the manner in which he was welcomed, fed, and given a place to sleep. From the description of the event, Alfred realized that the man had gone to the wrong eye hospital. Even without Alfred's gift and wishes, Albert recovered from his wound and returned to his tasks.

The home of Albert and Anna became a key element of Jerusalem social life. Everyone of stature residing in Jerusalem or arriving as a visitor was seen at social events at the Ticho house. Writers, poets, philosophers, statesmen, politicians, scientists, artists, musicians, physicians, officers—Arab, Jew, or Christian—all found their way to the Ticho apartment. Quietly in the background, Anna practiced her talent as an artist. For many years, it was considered a hobby of a rich man's wife who had nothing better to do with her time. But as years passed, her works were becoming more and more known and in ever greater demand. Most of her subjects were the faces of Israel and, later on, the hills around Jerusalem. When her husband died, she was able to give her art all of her time. For 20 years, even as arthritis made hand movements painful, she continued working. She spent more time now in the studio working from memory and hardly ever going back to her beloved mountains and villages. When she died in 1980 at the age of 86, she left behind a large portfolio of her art. This, along with the Ticho house, she willed to the Israel Museum.

With the funds made available in her will, the former Abraham Ticho Eye Clinic was converted into an Artists House and is now part of the Israel museum. Today, visitors who come to the house can sit in the garden, view the works of many artists including Anna Ticho's in several large rooms, view a portion of Albert's large collection of Jewish menorahs, examine documents and photographs from the lives of Albert and Anna, purchase souvenirs, attend a concert or recital, and have a wonderful outdoor meal on the veranda.

The Ticho House is now a permanent landmark in the heart of Jerusalem.

Lifescape: The Work Of Anna Ticho

October 25, 2018
Remarks of Charles Ticho at the opening of the Anna Ticho "Lifescape" exhibit in the Ticho House in Jerusalem

I am truly honored to speak on this occasion and say a few words about my dear aunt Anna. I am certain there are many gathered here this evening who can expertly discuss the nature and quality of Anna's art and her influence and impact on the Israeli art scene — so I will limit myself to just Anna, the person that she was — the person that I knew.

My earliest memories of Anna date back to 1934, when I was 7-years-old, when she and her husband Dr. Abraham (Albert) Ticho came to my older brother's *Bar Mitzvah* in Brno, Czechoslovakia. I knew I had two uncles who were living in Palestine. I had already met Uncle Aaron (Alfred)

Anna Ticho, Israel's best known artist.

Ticho, one of the founders of the town of Binyamina, several times, but this was special: my first meeting with Dr. Albert Ticho, the uncle who moved to Palestine in 1912, the ophthalmologist who is credited to have erased trachoma in Jerusalem, and who was now considered to be the best eye doctor in the Middle East. All I knew about Anna was that she was an assistant in her husband's eye surgery and that she was my uncle's first cousin.

From the early 1920's on, this building, this home of Dr. Albert and Anna Ticho, the "Ticho House," became a key element of Jerusalem's social life. Everyone of stature residing in Jerusalem or arriving as a visitor to Jerusalem was seen at social events at the Ticho house. Writers, poets, philosophers, statesmen, politicians, scientists, artists, musicians, physicians, military officers — Arab, Jew, or Christian — all found their way to the Ticho apartment on the second floor of this building. Anna was a gracious hostess and was never too busy to be kind and attentive to her guests.

> *...the "Ticho House", became a key element of Jerusalem's social life.*

Even when she became a widow, became handicapped by arthritis, and was concentrating all her energies on her art, she would, nevertheless, always welcome guests in the same graceful manner.

Dr. Ticho had a comfortable cot in his office that became my resting place whenever I stayed in Jerusalem overnight. The walls were decorated by a collection of old brass candelabras. The room also contained his sizeable library of interesting books. The most fascinating and riveting books I located was a set of German *encyclopaedias* from 1904. These volumes offered an amazing opportunity to learn and study. I was constantly surprised as I discovered how much was already known back at the start of the 20th century.

During my visits, I was not treated differently from anyone else. Anna's charm captivated everyone who came in touch with her. Not even the year-long siege of Jerusalem in 1948, during the Israeli War of Independence, prevented Anna from being a proper hostess. The beds for patients on the

"The Washerwoman" an Anna Ticho pencil drawing. Anna would search for interesting "faces" among her husband's patients and ask them to pose for her.

first floor became the beds for people seeking refuge. Some 20 people found shelter inside this house during the heaviest fighting. The building suffered some damage including, as I recall, bullet holes in a bathroom door. Food and medicines were in very short supply, yet somehow Anna managed to provide for her guests until the siege was finally lifted by the victorious Israeli Army.

Whenever time permitted, Anna would gather up her art supplies, get into her small Ford two-door sedan and have the driver take her somewhere into the hills around the city. There, she would spend the day, translating what she saw onto paper. These were not photographic reproductions. To the reality of the scene, Anna would add the heat, the intensity of the sun, the dryness of the vegetation and the loneliness of the area.

When her husband, Doctor Abraham Ticho died in 1960, she was able to give her art all of her time. For 20 years, even as arthritis made hand movements painful, she continued working. She spent more time in her studio working from memory. She hardly ever went back to her beloved mountains and villages. She died on March 1, 1980. This house, together with its rich art collection, including her own paintings and her husband's extensive gardens and Judaica collection, was bequeathed to the city of Jerusalem. Today, the "Ticho House" serves as a branch of the National Museum of Israel. Downstairs is a gallery with one room dedicated to Anna Ticho and Dr. Abraham Ticho. A further exhibit and a fine restaurant with a café is on the second floor.

Anna's vision for the Ticho House was for it to be a place where the arts and the artists could meet the public and to create a quiet oasis in the midst of

To honor Anna Ticho's memory, I caused a plaque to be placed on the Zeleny Trch,

When visiting Israel, anyone of importance in the art world stopped at the Ticho home in Jerusalem. In 1951, Marc Chagall (center) visited with Anna Ticho (2nd from right) and two other prominent Israeli artists, Moshe Mokady (1st on left), and Ardon Mordechai (far right).

a very busy, noisy and expanding Jerusalem. Her wish and dream has been essentially achieved, particularly after the recent extensive and very successful renovations. Thus this house has, in addition to her art, become an integral part of Anna Ticho's *Lifescape*.

To honor her memory, I caused a plaque to be placed on the Zeleny Trch, the large outdoor produce market in Brno, the second largest city in the Czech Republic, to mark the location of her birth.

Out Of My Will

This event happened sometime around 1970 in the New York City area when Aunt Hilda became a substitute grandmother to our children. Aunt Hilda was a widow of my wonderful and modest Uncle Victor who died in 1959. Both my wife Jean's mother and my mother were no longer with us when the children were very young and they never got to know them. Hilda filled this gap beautifully. Since 1962, when we moved to the New York area from Chicago, she visited our house often, stayed overnight, sometimes for a week at a time, took the children for walks and played games with them. She also disciplined them when that was called for and watched over them when we were away or on a trip. Aunt Hilda was, for almost 15 years, an integral part of our family.

The children really loved her and always looked forward to seeing her. We all had a good relationship with her and enjoyed her visits. One of the great secrets of her life was her age. She refused to tell us how old she was. No matter how many times the children asked, she kept that information a secret. I also got into this game of trying to trick the information out of her. One day, while we were talking about her older

Aunt Hilda

sister, I asked her: "When was your sister born?" Hilda answered that question, and I put this information away in my memory for future use. Many months later, perhaps as much as a year later, we were once again talking about her family and I casually asked: "How much older is your sister than you are?" Hilda smiled and said: "You must think I am stupid. I know what you are doing," and never answered that question. The mystery was only solved when she passed away and I received her passport and her other documents.

At some point, I suggested to Hilda that she should draw up a will. She, at first, was reluctant. "I really have nothing, so why bother spending money on an attorney?" was her reaction. Nevertheless, one day I received a phone call from an attorney advising me that Hilda was in the process of writing a will and wished to name me as the executor and was I willing to accept this position? I readily agreed and, some weeks later, received a signed copy of the document that named me as the executor. I placed the document into our family bank safe-deposit box.

My mother passed away in 1965 and Father was living alone in Chicago at 3600 North Lake Shore Drive. He would complain to me from time to time about living alone. I invited him to come live with us and even rebuilt the garage into a large room with a separate entrance and bathroom that he could use. But he would not hear of it. "I'll let you know when I need you," he insisted. He also did not consider favorably my suggestion to invite Hilda to live with him in Chicago. "She is too old for me," said my 82-year-old father with a twinkle in his eyes, "I am looking for something more my age — four twenties."

Nevertheless, Hilda somehow got the idea that my father was attracted to her and decided that I was responsible for his reluctance to get involved with her. No amount of denying on my part could convince her otherwise. "You are afraid that I'll inherit your father's money!" was her accusation. "I am very angry and I am going to take you out of my will." A few weeks later, I received a letter from the attorney advising me that I was no longer the executor of Hilda's will and that her nephew, Dr. Joseph Kauff of Chicago, has been appointed in my place.

It was 1977 and Hilda was making plans to visit her boyfriend in Florida. For two or three years she had been seeing Jack, a divorced man living near Fort Lauderdale. Jack visited New York several times and we had an opportunity to meet this very quiet, gentle Austrian gentleman who seemed to be quite fond of Hilda. Even though he was divorced, he and his former wife still lived in two separate sections of their one house. This meant that, when Hilda visited him, they had to rent a room in a motel. All the arrangements had been made and

My father Nathan walks with Aunt Hilda during our wedding.

Nathan and Aunt Hilda celebrating after the wedding of Jean and Charles.

Hilda went to the hairdresser prior to this latest trip to Florida. She left the salon and was crossing Broadway at 63rd Street against the light and was struck by a truck. We received a call from the police and rushed to the hospital where we learned that Hilda was in grave danger. She was on a respirator, and the doctors did not expect her to live.

Of course, I immediately called Dr. Kauff in Chicago and Jack in Florida and advised them of what had happened. We visited Hilda every day. On the fifth day, Friday, the doctors took her off the respirator, and she died peacefully shortly thereafter. I called Chicago and gave Dr. Kauff the news. Hilda had long ago made arrangements for her funeral, cremation, and disposal of her ashes over the ocean. I now put the process into motion and told both Jack and Dr. Kauff that the funeral service would be Monday morning, that all arrangements had been made and that there was no need for them to come to New York. Nevertheless, both insisted that they wished to attend the Monday morning ceremony.

On Saturday morning the phone rang. I recognized the distraught voice on the phone to be Mrs. Kauff. "My husband passed away this morning of a heart attack," was her brief message, "could you please take care of all the matters in New York for us?" And thus, I became the executor of Hilda's will after all.

There is a sidelight to this story. We sued the owners of the truck and, I received a check for $9,000. I called Mrs. Kauff and pointed out to her that Hilda had completely ignored our children in her will and that I was anxious to show them that Hilda had cared enough for them to remember them in her will. Mrs. Kauff readily and generously agreed to have me distribute the money among our three children. The $9,000 was split into three equal parts that were invested in the Massachusetts Investment Growth Fund and the money became known to our children as "Hilda's money." We kept the three funds for future use for each of our three children. When Robin and Ron were married, we transferred the funds (each one now worth about $25,000) to each of them. When Richard, our youngest, decided that he was going to live in Israel he asked for his share and I transferred some $27,000 to him.

Thereafter, from time to time and for many years, I would receive letters from the Massachusetts Investment Growth Fund. These were promotional letters that I ignored, did not bother to open and threw into the wastepaper basket. I did this for about twenty-five or more years. One day I decided to open one of these letters and found a statement advising me that the balance in the fund now stood at $86,000!

I had completely forgotten, that instead of cashing in Richard's shares, I simply transferred this investment to my name and sent Richard what was due to him in a check from one of my cash accounts.

In this surprising fashion, "Hilda's money", thanks to the very fortunate performance of our investment, and my failure to follow its remarkable growth, made a substantial mark in our life years after her passing.

Mitzpe Ramon in 1954
65th ANNIVERSARY OF ISRAEL'S FIRST FILM DREAMS AND REALITY

"'ll kill that bloody driver!" echoed over the hills of the Negev Desert, "I swear, I'll kill him!" At the bottom of the hill that is topped by the ancient Nabattian Avdad fortress, stood Thorold Dickenson, all 6 foot, 3 inches tall, white hair flowing wildly around his head, arms outstretched and flailing, looking very much like an irate Moses in the wilderness and shouting his curses towards the chaos that was happening in front of him. Despite all the noise, the explosions, the trucks and jeeps rushing downhill, and the troops firing their guns, I could clearly hear Thorold's voice screaming in my earphones — and he did not really use the word "bloody" … his language was much more colorful.

It was April 1954, and we had arrived here in the middle of the Negev Desert of Israel just three days earlier and were in the second week of shooting scenes for the film "Hill 24 Does Not Answer," the very first real all-Israel motion picture production. The subject was a dramatization of events that took place during Israel's War of Independence in 1948. During the first week of shooting, one of the few helicopters in Israel was damaged. The accident nearly cost some lives. Now, during the second week, things were not going too well either. For two days, we have been filming scenes depicting the attack of Israeli forces trying to dislodge Egyptian soldiers from the Avdad fortress. Now, we were at the point where the Egyptians were abandoning their position and were supposed to rush helter-skelter down the mountain into their vehicles and, as the audience was expected to assume, back to Egypt.

This involved major and complex preparations. Dynamite charges had to be strategically buried and wired so that explosions could be fired at appropriate moments as the Egyptian soldiers ran out of the fortress and climbed onto the two jeeps and the Egyptian Army truck that were supposed to be charging down the hill. There was just one problem. The truck, instead of rushing down the hill, would roll slowly downhill till the clutch was engaged and the motor got started. Only then it would finally get moving, but much too late. The assistant directors climbed up the hill to the truck and painstakingly explained to the driver, who was also the owner of the truck, what he was supposed to do. Now, the second take of this scene was being shot and the truck was, once again, ruining the scene and causing the director, Thorold Dickenson, to bring down his fury upon the poor driver.

The driver's problem was simple. The battery in his truck had gone dead, and he did not want to waste his own precious gasoline keeping the truck idling while the lengthy preparations were taking place between takes. Only a promise to repay him for the wasted gasoline finally convinced the driver to follow the instructions, cooperate with the production, and make the next take of the scene a success.

Charles was the recording engineer on the *Hill 24* film. His job was supplying power to the recorder and to the camera and recording the sound.

When there was no sound to record, Charles happily assisted whenever he could.

What does all this have to do with Mitzpe Ramon? In 1954, this very modest military installation was the nearest civilized location near the Avdat location where the crew and the equipment could be housed.

Producing the first major film in Israel with a mostly Israeli crew, cast, and resources was truly a daunting project. The helicopter and truck incidents were just the first of a string of problems and challenges that had to be overcome. Today a sizable town with hotels, museum, restaurants, and industry is located at Mitzpe Ramon. But, in 1954, there was nothing more than a small fenced-in area (about the size of a soccer field) with a half-dozen wooden military barracks. But there was water, an electric generator, and a chance for civilized living. The male crew members were housed in two of these small barracks and the women in a third. There was a dining room/kitchen house and one shower room where the men and the women took turns cleaning up the day's dust, dirt, and sweat. At the far side, along the fence, were two outhouses. The arrangement made for tight living conditions and occasional frayed nerves — particularly when deciding which gender had the first turn in the showers.

My job at this location was recording engineer. I sat in the sound truck that supplied the power to the camera and the recorder. A bank of batteries in the truck, that I had to recharge every night, would supply the power to a generator that, in turn, would run the camera motor and a Westrex 35 millimeter magnetic recorder located inside the truck. Actually, it was somewhat of a miracle that the truck had arrived at the location altogether.

In addition to being the recording engineer, I was also given the job of driving the truck. On a Thursday evening, I suddenly learned that my American driver's license did not qualify me to drive a truck in Israel and that I had to get an Israeli truck driver's license. Rather naively, I arrived at the licensing bureau on Friday morning and announced that I came to get my truck license. "You must be kidding!" was what I understood the clerk to say in Hebrew when I told him what I wanted to do, "these things take three to four months at least." "No, you don't seem to understand," I insisted, "I've got to be on location in the Negev on Sunday morning or a whole film crew and a cast of hundreds will be sitting around with nothing to do." "Look," said the clerk, "this is Friday. We close at 1 o'clock and there is no way that you can get a license to drive a truck in four hours." I kept insisting and asked to talk to the head of the department. A half hour went by before I was finally ushered into an office to see a man who fortunately spoke enough English to understand what I was trying to do.

I pleaded my case forcefully. He seemed sympathetic and, at last, I convinced the man of the urgency of my request. The director took me under his wing and proceeded to process me through the various steps of the procedure.

Like many people involved in the *Hill 24* film. Charles had to tackle many different jobs like driving the sound truck, acting when needed, and providing lighting and record keeping.

In quick succession, the application forms were filled out, I took the eye test, passed the physical examination, and took the written examination, which the director kindly translated for me. Each of these steps was taken in front of the startled faces of the clerks and the envious and outraged eyes of the poor other applicants who were standing in long lines at each station waiting for their turn. "Where are your photographs?" asked the director. "Photographs! God! I should have thought of that! What do we do now?" It was almost 12 o'clock, time was running out, and I was getting desperate.

Fortunately, there was a photo store for just this purpose across the street. After a brief argument I convinced the owner to stay open past noon and 15 minutes later I was rushing back with pictures in hand. "Okay," said the director, "now for the driving test." "Driving test! Where do I get a truck?" I looked around bewildered. Things were looking dark. I rushed out of the building just as a truck owned by a driving school was pulling out of the parking lot. I ran after him. "Please, please can I use your truck? I have to take a test," I pleaded. The driver hesitated. "First you've got to take at least one lesson," he insisted. "There is no time for that. I've got to take the test." The driver insisted that I, at least, must show him that I knew what I was doing. So, I hopped into the cab. The man explained the gears to me quickly, and we were off on a quick spin around the block.

It was a good thing that I had this preliminary ride, because the gearbox had apparently been ruined by previous learners and was very difficult to operate. It was 15 minutes before closing time when an examiner joined me in the truck to test my driving skills. As luck would have it, his daughter lives in Chicago and, when I told him some complimentary details about the area where his daughter was living, he saw no reason to make this examination too thoroughly. Five minutes later I was back in the director's office having passed the driving test. A few minutes later, as the offices were being locked up for the day, I walked out of the building with my brand new and hard-won Israeli truck driver's license in my pocket. As I was walking over to the bus station to go home, the clerks, who were leaving the building and were gathered in the parking lot, applauded as I passed by. I had, apparently, made history.

Ben Brightwell was one of four British crew members brought over to head up the sound department. Ben was chief sound engineer and my boss on this project. The others were the chief cameraman, the script clerk and, of course, Thorold Dickenson, the director. Ben was not all that bright — despite of his name — a fact that he would often demonstrate. Here in the desert, after hearing that Arabs at times attacked Jewish settlers; he was extremely upset that we were usually the last ones to leave the location. We had to gather up all the cables we had run to the camera and to the microphones before we could leave. So, regardless how fast we moved, everyone was long gone before we were ready. Night falls quickly in the desert and we often traveled in the dark. "Stick your guns out the windows," Ben would order as we departed for the half-hour drive back to Mitzpe Ramon, "so people will see that we are armed." The truck was hard enough to drive on the unpaved desert road. Now I had to do it with a gun butt clutched between my thighs. However, the chance of being attacked was a real possibility in 1954 and we had to be prepared. This is why the police in Beer Sheva insisted that anyone traveling south from the city had to have a rifle or a handgun.

Ben was not the only one who was concerned. Mildred Solomon, an American visitor in Israel who was acting as a secretary on the production, felt a certain kinship towards me, a fellow American. Unfortunately, this affinity caused her to feel free to wake me in the middle of the night so that I could escort her, rifle in hand, while she marched out to the fence line to use the outhouse. I would then stand there on guard while she relieved herself and marched her back to her quarters when she was done. I made it my business, after a few of these nightly sojourns, to remind Mildred not to drink too much water at dinner and to be sure to use the toilet before going to sleep.

After Mitzpe Ramon, the crew went to Haifa, Naharia, Acco, and several other locations and there were several other sundry mishaps, but nothing was as memorable as the two weeks in Mitzpe Ramon.

As for the movie, in 1955 it became the first entry produced in Israel in the Cannes Film Festival.

The 75-Year-Long Secret

"Who is Dr. Ryshavy and why would he make me the heir of his house in the Czech Republic?" was the question posed to me by the man sitting across from me one day. I opened my mouth to answer, but I stopped. I knew the answer — as a matter of fact — I've known the answer for nearly 65 years, however I asked myself, am I the person to reveal to the questioner a decades long secret — a secret that was well known in our big family but had, apparently, been kept from him all these years?

This man turned to me with this question because I am the last living first cousin in our family, a family that at one time, had no less than 34 other first cousins — sons and daughters of the 13 Ticho siblings, my grandfather's grandchildren. Itzchak Zvi Ticho, was a true-believing Jew living in Boskovice, a small town in the Czech Republic. He was the head of a family that I traced back in this town to the late 1600's and that, very likely, resided in Boskovice

Suze and Lily Ticho as children

for centuries before. All those hundreds of years the many Ticho family members lived within a small circle in what is today the Czech Republic — until 1939, that is, when the German army marched into Czechoslovakia. Six years later, after World War II and after the brutal and heartless Holocaust ended, the remaining family members were scattered in Australia, India, Argentina, Uruguay, England, in several locations in the United States and spread all over the area that later became Israel. There wasn't a Jew left living in Boskovice.

I was 91-years-old when I was confronted by this question. The answer was on the tip of my tongue but I still hesitated. Do I have the right to answer the question truthfully? As far as I knew, everybody in our big family, at one time or another, became familiar with the story but, for all these years, they apparently maintained the family secret. Should I be the one to violate their trust?

Fifteen members of our immediate family died in the Holocaust. Five of my father's siblings and their spouses and five first cousins. An additional five family members were trapped by the Nazis in 1939 when Czechoslovakia became a victim of German aggression. Four of us managed to escape — one cousin, my father, my brother and I. The fifth cousin, Lilly, miraculously survived three years in the Terezin Concentration Camp, a stop at the Auschwitz genocide factory and bitter years in a Nazi slave labor camp.

A stop at the Terezin Concentration Camp was part of the itinerary on a family trip to the Czech Republic. My son Ron, his children Connie (l-r), Hannah and Nathan, and I are standing at the gate of the camp.

Lilly's trials during the Holocaust began first when she was scheduled to be deported to the Terezin Concentration Camp. Despite of their young age, she and her boyfriend, Herbert, decided to get married in the hope that this would keep them together. Terezin served the Nazis as the first in a long list of other ghettos, jails and concentration camps designated specifically for Jews. Upon arrival at this unique fortified city, men and women were separated and lived in different buildings. For three years, Lilly and Herbert saw each other only for brief moments and hardly ever privately. Lilly had studied nursing for two years and her skills were in great demand in Terezin. Among the tens of thousands of women that arrived at the camp, there were always a few who were pregnant. Many women asked to have an abortion because they did not wish to be burdened by a baby or they did not wish to bring a child into the miserable living conditions of the camp. Others wanted to have the baby in the hope that they will be given special consideration to care for the child. Lilly, with the assistance of a physician, granted the mother's wish — one way or the other — as best as they could.

For nearly three years that was Lilly's job. Her husband, Herbert, also had a very fortunate job in the camp bakery. He regularly risked his life to smuggle pieces of bread to Lilly or to other family members who were in the camp. During these years, at regular intervals, transports "to the East" were organized and thousands of camp inmates disappeared. Constant new arrivals kept the camp overcrowded. Ultimately, it became Lilly's and Herbert's time to leave Terezin in a transport. However, they were assigned to different transports and, thereafter, completely lost touch with each other.

Lilly was just 21-years-old and well-built. She must have looked strong and healthy and, in the usual selection process in Auschwitz, she was sent to the right. A few days later, she and a group of Jewish women were sent to a slave labor camp in Poland. This was a miserable camp with sadistic female guards making the life of the prisoners as difficult as possible. The smallest infraction was punished by lengthy line-ups in front of the barracks. This was in the miserable winter between 1944 and 1945 and the prisoners had to stand at attention for hours, dressed in the only clothing they had, — a coat, a dress and shoes. Prisoners that collapsed were beaten and many would die.

One day, a German man came to such a line-up and asked whether there was anyone who spoke German and knew anything about electricity. Lilly volunteered, in spite of the fact that she had no education in this subject — but she did speak German fluently. The man picked her out of the line-up and made her his assistant. Her job was, essentially, to carry the man's ladder and toolbox as he went around the camp making repairs. Lilly and this man had a cold

Lily Sobotka and her child reunited with her husband, Herbert, after a five-year separation during which neither one knew the other had survived the Holocaust.

and distant relationship with the man speaking to Lilly only to give her an order. If she did not respond fast enough or to his satisfaction, he was quick to remind her that he could send her back at any time.

On one occasion, the man ordered Lilly to climb up the ladder to do something up high. "I am sorry, she responded, I cannot do that." The man was shocked and furious and demanded to know why. "I am very sorry, sir," Lilly replied, but I don't have any underwear." This brief sign of pride and modesty apparently made an impression on the man because the next day, he brought her a pair of long underwear.

The relationship between the man and Lilly now changed and, whenever the prisoners were ordered to stand at attention out in the freezing cold, he made sure that Lilly was providing him some essential services and could not be spared. Instead of standing in the bitter cold, she was working in the heated electrician's workshop. As a result Lilly survived, and, in her videotaped testimony, she credited this German man for her survival when the Russian army liberated the camp.

Lilly returned to Brno, her hometown, and slowly recovered from her horrible four years. She zealously and intensely searched for her husband but encountered only death and dead ends. Millions and millions of people were displaced in Europe — families were torn apart — millions died. It took years for a modicum of normalcy to return. During this time, Lilly happened to meet the doctor she worked with in Terezin. He also survived but lost his wife in the gas chambers of Auschwitz.

Five years went by. By then, Lilly had accepted the fact that her Herbert was one of the six million Jews who did not survive the Holocaust. Slowly, she began to rebuild her life and her nursing skills. And then, one day, as she was walking on one of the main streets of Brno she ran into Herbert, her husband! He had miraculously survived and had spent years wandering while searching for his beloved Lilly.

The reunion was difficult. They really did not have a "married" life during the three years in Terezin and then they had been apart for years after the war ended. In addition, Lilly was raising a son. Nevertheless, they seized the opportunity to emigrate to Israel where Lilly could, once again, rejoin her sister and the few other members of the Ticho family who escaped the Holocaust.

To gather material for my book *M'Dor L'Dor: From Generation to Generation*, I tape-recorded detailed interviews with several family members and friends who were familiar with our family's history. It was during these interviews that I became aware of the fact that Lilly's "secret" was known throughout the family. However, in Lilly's videotaped testimony that is on file at the United States Holocaust Memorial Museum she simply states that she met her husband and they had a son.

Dr. Ryshavy died December 29, 1955, and in his testimonies there is no mention of Lilly or her son — until it came to his last will and testament. In his testament, he declared the heir of his house to be a minor born April 2, 1948 and, should he not be able to file a claim, the inheritance should go to his mother, Lilly Sobotkova, *nee* Ticho. On September 10, 1958, the People's Court in Ostrava, Czech Republic declared the minor child, represented by his mother, as the owner of the house.

The minor child was just 7-years-old when all of this was taking place and, apparently, his mother was determined to keep the information from him. It was not until he, many years later, by some round-about manner, received word that he once inherited a house in the Czech Republic, that he decided to turn to his old cousin with the question: "Who is Dr. Ryshavy and why would he make me the heir of his house in the Czech Republic?"

The question caused a bitter rage to rise in me. All the hatred, all the loathing, all the revulsion I felt for the Nazis that I had, at last, learned to control, came back with a vengeance. Here, once again, even after the Nazis were destroyed, the bloody hands of the heartless mass murderers were reaching across seven decades causing such intense pain and distress to me and to this poor innocent man sitting before me. My heart was also aching as I recalled the pain of a father who gave up his son, the ache of the son who never knew his father, the sting of the husband who was forced to live with a secret indiscretion, the torture of a mother who had to live with a lie and the stress and anxiety of a family that had to maintain a decades long lie — the truth behind the question. I resented that I was now forced to make a choice to tell the truth or continue the lie the Nazis foisted on all of us.

With my eyes filling with tears and with my voice abandoning me, I decided for the truth and with great difficulty managed to say: "Because he was your father."

Director's Recollections

The Steven Spielberg Jewish Film Archive is located in the Jack Valenti Pavilion, of the Hebrew University in Jerusalem. In mid-2019 the Archive contacted me and asked whether I would be willing to describe my experiences in the production of two of my films that I directed and that are stored in their archive. I jumped at the chance and here are my recollections of two particularly memorable films:

"FROM DESTRUCTION TO REDEMPTION"
A Director's Recollections

For about fifteen years, in the 1980's, I had the privilege to design, produce and direct fundraising films for the Jewish National Fund. These were important annual short film productions that were used, before the advent of the general use of computers and social media, to send visuals and videos to raise funds. Most of the films revolved around the essential work that the Jewish Agency was doing and dramatized its accomplishments in Israel that were made possible by the funds the Jewish Agency was able to provide. These were, essentially, documentary films, appeals to Jewish audiences for generous donations. After several years of these films, I felt that it was, perhaps, time to consider making the appeal in a different form – from a different point of view, from a different direction.

At a 1977 meeting with the Jewish Agency staff I suggested that the next film ought to be off the beaten track that we have followed for so many years and,

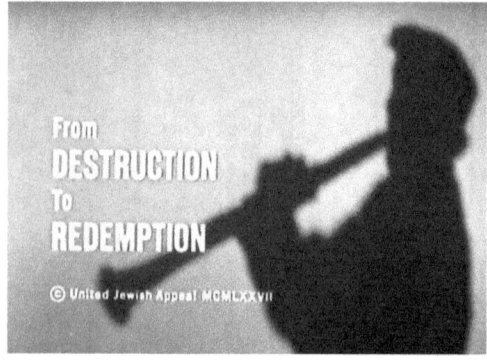

instead, dramatize how Israel has become the symbol of the recovery of the Jewish people after the Holocaust. In response, we hoped, that the audience would be inclined to make more generous contributions in order to support the further recovery of Jewish values and the continued growth of the State of Israel. After some discussion, (there were several strong voices in favor of the old format) my suggestion was accepted, and I was invited to prepare a proposal and a budget with a maximum expenditure of $10,000. That does not sound like a lot of money but around 1990 it was a reasonable budget and, besides, I did not make these films to make a profit.

Okay — now that you have painted yourself into a corner how do you proceed? Several fortuitous events came about to show me the path. First, I learned that the Jewish Agency was going to sponsor a group of "young Jewish professionals" on a visit to Eastern Europe (Poland, Romania, and Soviet Union) and Israel. I asked the client to add me and an assistant to this group. The request was granted. The next piece of good research was a discussion with an Israeli friend, an expert in the Israel music field. He promised to send me a copy of a recording session he just produced with an Israeli clarinetist by the name of Giora Feidman. (The session was issued in 1990 on a CD entitled "The Magic of Klezmer.")

The tape simply blew me away! Here was this magician on the clarinet who could, in one moment, make the instrument sound like the pleading voices from the Auschwitz crematoria and then, in the next, produce a melody of joyful celebrations, songs and dance. Here was the "from destruction to redemption" I was looking for! I contacted the Agency and asked them to see whether the participation of Mr. Feidman and his music could be added to the project. Permission to use the music from his CD and a couple of days of filming in Israel was all that was needed. Two or three weeks later I had the confirmation that Mr. Feidman would be happy to participate in the project.

▶ Watch the film on YouTube at youtu.be/hvEDJJ8QAmo

To conserve funds, I only engaged one freelance film photographer to assist me. He was a talented and highly regarded documentary cameraman. A few days before our departure I was surprised to learn that the Communist controlled government of Poland requires a visa even for a citizen of the USA. I rushed to get the application papers, filled them out, and dropped them off at the Polish consulate in New York.

I supplied the photographer with the same papers and asked him to attend to this urgent matter. He asked: "What do I write where they ask for my profession?" I advised him to do what I did — write "businessman" in that space, a safe non-committal description my father often used as we were attempting to flee the Holocaust. Shortly before departure, I received my visa. I called the cameraman who told me his visa was denied — he wrote "cameraman" on the application and the ever-vigilant and suspicious Communist regime turned him down. I was upset and asked him to make arrangements to meet me in Romania and I will have to shoot the footage in Poland.

I now had to rush out to rent a good 16mm camera, buy film stock, and become familiar with the equipment. I also added two props, a useless old clarinet and a Russian style cap. Those were the only props I required. In the East European "destruction" portion of the film, Giora Feidman would appear only as a shadow. This decision was necessary because, first of all, Giora was not available to travel with us. I also felt, that having the clarinetist appear only as a shadow in the "destruction" portion of the film would be an appropriate symbol and dramatization that fits into the message of the film — his sad music would be performed by a clarinetist, a shadow, who was no longer with us.

The trip started in Warsaw, Poland, and visits to several sites in the infamous Nazi-created Warsaw Ghetto area. When we encountered a memorial or a particularly poignant location, I would ask one of the men in our group to don the 'Russian" hat and pretend to be playing the clarinet. I then placed him in a position where he would cast the sun's shadow that enabled me to compose a scene of his shadow and the object of interest. In this fashion, Giora and his music would be "with us" as we moved from place to place and from country to country.

We visited the large Jewish Cemetery in Warsaw and I was truly moved as I filmed the graves of some of the greatest Jewish minds that I studied in the Jewish Gymnasium (High School) in my hometown of Brno, Czechoslovakia in the late 1930's. Then, our bus drove to Krakow and we visited the beautiful, small and ancient synagogue where the retaining walls were made up of broken Jewish gravestones. The sites offered many opportunities to film pertinent scenes with the "Giora" shadow. On the way we encountered a small Jewish village cemetery where more poignant scenes were captured. We ended the day with a visit to Auschwitz, the dreaded Nazi death factory. Here the challenge was to select the two or three scenes that would best summarize something that was, essentially, impossible to depict.

The following day we landed in Bucharest, the capital of Romania, where I was supposed to meet up with the cameraman that I hired. The hotel advised me that the cameraman had registered the day before but had not slept in the room the previous night. When he finally showed up, he explained that he had been arrested while filming some severely earthquake-damaged buildings in the city. He was doing this as a favor for a friend. You just don't do such things in a paranoid Communist-ruled country! The police arrested him, wanted to seize his camera, but finally relented and agreed to release him if he surrendered his film supply. Thereafter he used the film I brought. I made a note not to engage this naïve man ever again.

In Bucharest, we were invited to attend Saturday morning services led by the famous Rabbi Moses Rosen, the Chief Rabbi of Romanian Jewry between 1948 to 1994. He delivered his sermon alternatively in fluent English and native Romanian. After the services we were invited to meet the congregation in a festive joyful ceremony.

From Bucharest, we flew to Kiev that is now the capital of Ukraine but was then a part of the Soviet Union. The object of this brief trip was to visit Babi Yar, the site of the horrible massacres of Jews carried out by German forces and by local Ukrainian collaborators during their campaign in World War II. The massacres took place in September 1941, killing about 33,771 Jews. The location remained unmarked for decades but, in response to international pressure, an impressive monument was finally erected. However, the memorial was without any mention of Jews. Our group decided to make a point by donning skullcaps and reciting the Kaddish, a confirmation of the Jewish faith. This threw our government-assigned "guide" into a frenzy to stop the proceedings. We completed the prayer, removed the skullcaps and boarded the bus for the airport to return to Bucharest.

From Romania, we departed for Israel and I, at last, met with the "star" of the film, Giora Feidman. We had a very pleasant conversation in which I thanked him for his participation and explained that we had two days in which to capture the scenes in which he was to appear and play. I expressed my desire to film one day in the Jerusalem area and one day in the vicinity of Tel Aviv. We also discussed costume and he kindly agreed to wear our prop "Russian" hat. His cooperation and eagerness to make the film a success almost moved me to tears.

In anticipation of the very tight two days with Giora, we had made advance arrangements at all locations where Giora was involved such as, for example, the top of Jerusalem's ancient walls. Here I encountered a severe problem because Mr. Feidman, I learned to my surprise, suffered from a severe case of acrophobia, the fear of heights. He refused to walk up to the top of the wall until we found a spot where the wall was wide and had a set of stairs. Nevertheless, I had to hide behind him during the filming with a firm grip of his belt.

I feared that the "Wedding Scene" would be another severe problem. Who would agree to allow us to invade their wedding to film a part of the film? Here, I learned, that I had grossly underestimated the popularity of Giora Feidman. Wedding planners fell over each other to secure his appearance at one of their weddings. Now my problem was to make a choice among all the offers. Giora got into the spirit of the scene and played nonstop for over an hour as the wedding party joyfully sang and danced. I suspect that, these days, there is a couple somewhere in Israel that is telling their grandchildren that the great Giora Feidman had played at their wedding — and for free!

And then there was the challenge of the closing scene.

Ah "the closing scene"! That was, perhaps, the most difficult creative challenge. How do I summarize what we had presented so far? How do I depict, symbolize and sum up our hope and desire for the continued growth and survival of the Jewish nation and of Israel? Suppose, I mused, we turn Giora into a modern day "piper of Hamelin" and have his music attract a horde of children and cause them to celebrate, to have fun? And then I recalled my visit to the Knesset, the Israeli parliament, some years earlier where a king-sized menorah candelabra is the center of an out-door plaza and, at last, I had my closing scene... why not have Giora play as children come running from all over, surround the menorah and spontaneously start a happy dance around the plaza to Giora's optimistic music? Problem solved.

When it came to the soundtrack, Lou Jacobi was the only person I wanted to narrate the film. Lou Jacobi (born Louis Harold Jacobovitch) was a prolific character actor who garnered critical acclaim in dramatic and comedic roles in films, on Broadway and on television. I knew his talents having directed him in a couple TV commercials. He spoke with a distinct accent — not the typical Jewish accent featured in comedies — his was just different. I contacted his agent and just a few days later I had his participation. I sent him a copy of the script and a CD of a guide track I had recorded. When it came time to record his voice we did it all in one take and only one take — and we were done. In his usual professional manner, Lou did it perfectly the first time around.

Editing was a challenge — do we use the guide track I recorded, use selections from the CD of Giora's recordings or try to use both? My feelings were clear — the music and some added sound effects must guide the edit. This was the more difficult way to do it and there were several episodes where we backed up and did alternate versions of a section. The work took a little more time than expected but it was worth it. In the final review, the editor decided to leave my voice reciting the Biblical segments at the start and the end of the film. That is how the track ended up.

One more item needed to be decided — titles — if any. I wanted to give Giora Feidman and Lou Jacobi a credit line but, when I brought this up at a meeting, a young know-it-all attendee stated firmly: "If you give Jacobi and Feidman a credit line you have to do it for everyone who contributed to the film." I was asked to prepare such a list. I sat down and made a list of every individual or organization that I could truthfully state had assisted us in the project and presented the list to our client. The reaction, understandably, was: "we can't put all those names on the film" and a few minutes later it was decided that the film will have one credit at the start (Producer/Director) and one at the end (the logo of my company.)

Months later, I was gratified to learn about the fine response the film has received and today I am pleased that several decades later the Steven Spielberg Jewish Film Archive still has requests for copies.

"PEACE WHEN THERE IS NO PEACE"
A Producer's Recollections

To tell the truth, it took me a while to recognize the film and remember my role in its production.

The Israel Motion Picture Studios was established in Herzlia, Israel (yes, "was" established not "were" established because the so called "Studios" was just one studio) in 1953 by the married couple of Margot Klausner and Yehoshua Brandstatter. Margot was the guiding light and supplier of funds while Yehoshua was the dreamer with high goals. While their aim was to facilitate the production of feature films, they were sustained primarily by a long list of sponsored short films paid for by various Jewish fund-raising organizations, political entities and government agencies. I was involved with IMPS (as the Israel Motion Picture Studios was called) during my first visit to Israel 1953-1956. I started as a sound/recording engineer and then as producer/director.

My principle role in this film, "Peace When There Is No Peace" was as a production manager. As I recall, it was a typical low budget film for a department of the Israeli government. Previously I had produced and directed a film called "Give Them Arms" which consisted principally of a montage of scenes where barehanded Israeli soldiers were suddenly provided with weapons of many different kinds. I brought this film back with me when I returned to the States and sold the rights to the Jewish Agency who used it for fundraising. The closing segment of "Peace When There Is No Peace" is made up of a few scenes from this earlier "Give Them Arms" film. The rest of "Peace When There Is No Peace" is made up of stock footage that I harvested from many different sources.

Israel had no television between 1948 (when Israel was born) and 1966. David Ben Gurion, the first prime minister of the country, believed that television was a luxury that a country starting out could not afford. So, there existed just one theatrical company (Habimah) and a few local amateur theaters. As a result, motion pictures became an obsession. Israelis went to the cinema once or twice a week and saw films from all over the world. In most theaters, foreign language films were accompanied on a separate vertical screen where the hand-written Hebrew translation of the dialog was projected. The person in the projection booth had the task of moving this filmstrip along keeping the translation more or less in synch with the action on the screen.

Because of the popularity of cinemas in Israel, government agencies used these theaters as their information outlets. Therefore, each contract for such a government film included the delivery of 50 prints that will be used in theaters to reach the public with its message. "Peace When There Is No Peace" was such a film that also served as a fundraising film principally in the United States.

Unfortunately, these films had a history at IMPS of exceeding their production budget. When I was assigned to produce these films for IMPS, I promised Mrs. Klausner that I will bring them in within the budget. On my first assignment, I met with the director and laid out a series of draconian rules for the production such as: "The government provides, us tax-free, 5,000 meters of 35mm black and white negative film. Once this supply is exposed, filming stops" or "our contract calls for a ten minute film. If the final edited film is longer than 10 minutes, you will need to specify which 10 minutes we should use for the 50 prints — the first 10 minutes or the last 10 minutes — because we will print just 10 minutes." There were a few other similar rules I stated.

The director rushed to Mrs. Klausner's office to protest. I was invited to join the discussion. "But Mr. Ticho, Mrs. Klausner explained, the director is an artist — he can't create art under these rules." I responded firmly: "What do you wish to make — art or a profit?" The conflict was settled with a few minor modifications of my rules.

By the time I was assigned to produce "Peace When There Is No Peace" my rules were well-known to all directors in Israel and I was able to produce a steady stream of profitable documentary films for IMPS and the Israeli cinemas.

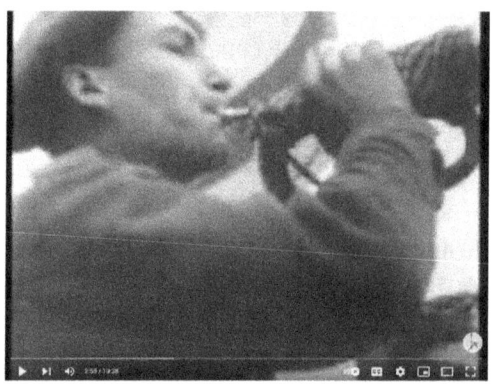

Watch "Peace When There is No Peace" on YouTube at youtu.be/aZvAFKDF1Vc

Before the establishment of Israel, there were two film production companies (Geva Films and Carmel Films) that issued newsreels on a somewhat irregular schedule. I turned to these two companies and several government agencies to produce "Peace When There Is No Peace." They had, fortunately, saved some of the negatives of the early footage of pre-Israel newsreels as well as the newsreels during the Israel War of Independence. These negatives were in 16mm reels and I made fine-grain 35mm black and white copies of the selected segments I needed.

I always owned a film camera and used it in many ways during my producer/director career. The skill came in handy when I had to assume the cameraman's job on the trip to Poland.

We recorded the narration recited by a well-known Israeli actor, Yosi Meelo, and used it to guide the editing. The voice track was supported by a very limited music library. As a matter of fact, there was no music library — there was a man who had a collection of 78 rpm discs of classical music who would review the film and then supply some obscure classical music compositions to support the audio message. This was not very high quality but we did what we could on the budget provided by the government.

The credit titles on this film include the name of Ivan Lengyel, a young man from Hungary, who was involved in the film and who became an assistant director on the feature motion picture *Hill 24 Does Not Answer*, the very first film that was completely produced and completed in Israel. I was the recording engineer on this film that was produced in 1954-55.

If you wish to see "From Destruction To Redemption" or "Peace When There Is No Peace," please visit the Steven Spielberg Jewish Film Archive and search for the films by their names.

Being Jewish

I can't tell you when it happened nor can I point to any special event that may have made the survival of the Jewish people such an important desire in my life. It could have been the prejudice and persecution that I felt in my early years in Czechoslovakia before World War II and during the Holocaust. All those who had tried to wipe out my family, or those who called me a *"smradlavy zid"* (a stinking Jew), or who chased after me and beat me up if they caught me, or who would not allow their children to play with me, or who printed and distributed obscene flyers maligning the Jewish faith, or who were too cowardly to attack the living and instead took out their venom on gravestones and, later on, who would hide their bigotry on the Internet, or those who wrote anti-Semitic slogans on walls, or even those who tell Jewish jokes when they are certain that only the "right" people are around — yes, all of them should know that their miserable efforts have failed. Let them gnash their teeth in frustration. We are still here, and we will certainly remain here.

Perhaps my militancy stems from a deep resentment that there were people who felt that they had to improve on, what was, in my eyes, the first great religion. At a time when most of the people of the world were worshiping statues, the moon, the sun, the stars, fire, volcanoes, or a sundry collection other odd objects, Jews were developing a religion based on one God, the magnificence of man's soul, and the ethical precepts that have become the base of all civilized life. While tribes in South America were sacrificing human beings on the altars of their gods and African natives ate the flesh of their enemies, Jews were preaching the sanctity of the life of each and every being. While the clans of Europe were raiding each other's towns and enslaving their enemies, Jews prescribed laws that demanded the release of bondsmen and while the world stood by as multitudes starved in poverty, Jews were taught that every man's survival is our responsibility and established specific rules as to the manner in which the needy must be helped. Why would anyone wish to improve on what seemed already so perfect?

But wish they did. They felt the need to replace a religion which demands of each Jew to worry what *mitzvah* (good deed) he is to fulfill next. A faith that demands of each Jew to ask such questions as: "am I going to be kind and deal honestly with those I come in contact with today? Or when and how much time am I going to spend studying the Torah? Or what am I going to do to honor the Sabbath properly?" and replaced it with a doctrine that has Christians asking, "What must I do for my soul to be saved?" They de-emphasized, if not altogether changed, the Jewish messianic message of universal redemption into a concern for individual salvation after one dies.

And those who would not and could not leave well enough alone were now consumed by an overwhelming urge to prove continuously that they were right and justified. And so they made it a tenet of their new religion that all mankind must conform to this new religion they devised. They would organize missions that infiltrated into every corner of the earth and, in the name of this new religion, either to convert the populace or slaughter it. And then they would pressure the rich as well as the poor to pour wealth into their treasuries and build magnificent edifices to create visible proofs and monuments of their efforts. No wonder that, when you travel throughout Europe, South America, and many parts of Africa and Asia, you will find that wherever there is a village or a town with a rise or a hill, it is more than likely dominated by a church or a monastery.

And then, after all this effort, there still remained the constant presence of the Jews. As long as they existed, the missionary's work was not done. Jews became a constant and permanent target for all these concentrated efforts. In 1999, the Southern Baptists Convention specifically announced that their future efforts would be directed to bring all the Jews to Christianity. I can live with the thought that Christians want to be Christians, but I deeply resent their constant and pathological desire to convert us, the Jews.

For two years, during my 21-year-long employ by Fred Niles, I was production manager of the Oral Roberts Evangelical Program. One day while Roberts, a Protestant evangelical preacher, was taking a brief rest before a sermon, another local preacher took over the microphone to tell the attentive flock of listeners about his recent experiences while visiting Israel. "Everywhere I went in the Holy Land," shouted this inspired preacher as he was reaching the climax of his message, "people came rushing over to hear me preach. And I told them, it took one World War to make you into a nation, the Second World War to create your country and, if it takes another World War to bring you to Christ, I say, let World War III begin!" The audience appreciatively applauded this incredible pronouncement. The members of the film crew (two of whom were Jewish) and I were so incensed by what this preacher had wished for that we insisted that Oral Roberts make a public retraction. This he did. But, in my mind, the damage had been done. If there are people around who are ready to preach in favor of a nuclear holocaust just to convert us, I will fight more than ever to keep the Jew alive.

Without a doubt, my experiences during the Holocaust and the results of this human tragedy, have caused me to dig in my heels and refuse to allow others to complete the work that Hitler and his cohorts started. Even in the early days of Nazi occupation, I already felt this urge to fight back. Jews who tried to take the easy way out by converting to Christianity were traitors in my eyes, and the cross they wore on a chain on the front of their blouses caused me to turn away from them. Alas, ultimately, it did not do any of them any good and their ashes were mixed together with those who remained loyal to their faith and heritage.

As I grow older my dedication to the survival of Judaism grows stronger every day.

This is not necessarily a matter of pure religion. In my mind I can easily separate fervent Jewish Orthodox religious practices from Jewish ethics and differentiate between the Jewish heritage from Jewish teachings. There are those who insist that you cannot be a Jew unless you are an Orthodox Jew. This is a premise with which I do not agree. It is each one of our unique Jewish qualities, our religious ceremonies, our religious beliefs, our ethical tenets, the knowledge of our history, and the acknowledgment of our heritage that makes a person a Jew and distinguishes us.

It is any one of these qualities — or any combination of them that make a person into a Jew — in the past, today, and I am certain, in the future.

Will The Holocaust Ever End?

A Look at Today's Remembrance, an introduction to a panel

On this Holocaust Remembrance Day, we have been asked to discuss the question: "Will the Holocaust Ever End?" Let me say a few words before I open the discussion by our four distinguished panel members.

Well, the simple answer to that question is: "yes, it will." Yes, the Holocaust will end on the day when we will forget to remember — when the world no longer recalls the horrors that had befallen our brethren. There are certainly sufficient forces around who insist that the Holocaust never happened:

— that it is all a story made up to trick the world into creating Israel, or

— that the number killed was a fraction of the 6 million, and similar theories and stories.

Then there are others who say: "Enough, already. We've heard all about this long enough. Forget it, and let's move on."

But, then there are the voices who say: "These were our fathers, our mothers, grandparents, uncles and aunts that died. This was our heritage, our history that was destroyed. This was our legacy that was attacked. How can we ever forget to honor these losses?"

Here before you, awaiting you each time you enter this sanctuary, is a stark reminder of what we had lost — a piece of parchment that has once served the Jewish men and women of a small town in the Czech Republic. All 547 Jews of this town were murdered. Today, it's a Jewish community that no longer exists. You know, we speak of the Holocaust as the loss of 6 million souls. But that is such an enormous sum — that is such an immense concept — that we really have difficulties grasping the significance of these words. For me, the enormity of the disaster is brought home when I visit my country of birth, when I visit the Czech Republic and the towns and villages that once housed Jewish communities. That is when I get a sense of what we lost.

My friend, engineer, Jaroslav Klenovsky, who has made the search for Jewish remnants his life-long career, was able to locate more than 600 towns and villages in what is now the Czech Republic where traces of Jewish life could be found. In some places it might be a cemetery, in others a former synagogue that is now serving as a meeting place or a museum, or it might be a former *mikve* or a room that had served as a *cheder*, a place of learning. In some villages it may just be a few narrow streets that typically served as the Jewish quarter, or in some places it may be just a depression in the ground marking a mass grave.

To me, these are the remnants that truly drive our losses home, because each one represents a living, active, thriving group of fellow believers who had made their lives in these places. They were born there, loved there, married, raised children, died there, and were buried there. And now they are all gone. What a loss!

Well, not everything was lost. The Nazis in their hysterical madness had determined that, once their war is won, they would build a museum "to an extinct race" and ordered that each of these 600-plus communities send all their treasures to Prague where they will be cataloged and stored awaiting the construction of this museum.

That's how in the early 1960's, Mr. Eric Estorick, a well-known London art dealer, learned of a large collection of Sifrei Torahs that were stored in an abandoned synagogue outside of the capital city, Prague. After a few years of negotiations and a substantial financial outlay, the Czech Communist authorities agreed to release these holy scrolls.

On February 7, 1964, no less than 1,564 Torah scrolls were transferred to the Westminster Synagogue in London. Rather than storing them away, where they will be forgotten, it was decided, that, after lovingly restoring as many as possible, these scrolls will be placed into the care and custody of synagogues and responsible organizations throughout the world.

And that is how our temple now cares for one of these survivors, a Holocaust Torah Scroll that once served the Jewish Community of Pribram in the Czech Republic and which serves us today and each day as a reminder of the tragedy that befell us 75 years ago. As long as these sixteen hundred treasured survivors are spread around the world, the Holocaust will not be forgotten.

Another reminder, whether the world likes it or not, is Israel. Its very existence serves as a reminder of the Holocaust. And on the Day of Remembrance, at eleven o'clock sharp, air raid sirens sound throughout the country. The country comes to a halt for two minutes. Trains stop, machines stop, and traffic stops on the streets and roads, drivers and passengers step out their cars, trucks and buses and stand at attention. People who are in their homes step out on a balcony or the roof to stand at attention. In Israel the Holocaust is not forgotten.

Don't we owe our victims a similar measure of respect?

There is another reminder that is still active around the world. It is the men and women who, like me, were touched by the Holocaust and managed through a miracle to survive. But we are getting old and our ranks are thinning every day. Soon it will be up to the children, the grandchildren or the great-grandchildren to tell the story. But that is not as easy as it may seem. Unfortunately, many of the survivors are reluctant to speak about their experiences. For some it is too difficult — for others too humiliating.

We will learn more about this aspect later when we hear from the temple members who are second or third generation removed from a survivor. Some, like myself, have fortunately taken up the challenge to write down their recollections — to record their experiences and to relate how deeply the Holocaust has influenced their lives.

But the question before us is "Will the Holocaust Ever End?" So, let's assemble our group of descendants of Holocaust survivors and let them tell us their answer to the question before us.

I am pleased to call on and introduce Esther Feldman, Betty Pardes, Steve Berger and Sam Rak.

The Man On the Piano and the Cooked Goose

Not all experiences around the Holocaust involve cruelty, violence, death, and destruction. Some are just heart-wrenching stories of callousness, nastiness, and malice. But they are equally painful.

"His name is Lux; he is my fiancée, and he is in Amerika" is how Miss Badeux explained the large photo on the piano in her heavily accented and somewhat primitive English. There were several more similar photographs of the same man displayed in the Zurich apartment where we were staying while we (my mother, my brother and I) were waiting for our father to arrive having been released from the Dachau Concentration Camp.

It was August 1940 and Steven and I had just arrived in the Switzerland and met our mother who had frantically waited for us for almost two years. Our father was released from the Dachau Concentration Camp and was scheduled to join us in a few weeks so that the four of us could escape to the United States and a new life.

Miss Badeux generously rented two rooms in her large apartment where our mother waited for the day when the four of us would be together again. I was 13-years-old and Steven was nine and we questioned Miss Badeux extensively about Lux, this mysterious fellow who was honored by such an impressive photographic display. The very charming Miss Badeux explained that Lux was in Amerika studying medicine, that she was supporting him and that he would return to Zurich after his graduation to marry her. It all sounded very romantic — almost like a fairy tale.

In today's cholesterol-aware and nutrition-conscious society, it would be unthinkable to consider a piece of toasted rye bread smothered with goose fat and liberally salted a delicacy. Yet, when we were children, that was exactly what it was. Chicken fat was okay and duck fat was acceptable, but goose fat was not only golden in color, it was pure gold to our palate. Americans are not big goose eaters and finding a goose to cook was not an easy task. But, after we arrived in America, and when mother invited, Lux, Miss Badeux's legendary boyfriend to visit us for dinner, nothing less than a goose would do. Father did not understand what the whole fuss was about. He hadn't stayed at Miss Badeux's apartment in Zurich as we had. He couldn't possibly understand how eager we were to make a good impression on Lux and to tell him what a great lady he was engaged to and about the wonderful friendship we developed with his fiancée in Zurich.

On the appointed evening we were ready. The kitchenette table (our apartment had no dining room) was set as festively as we could manage. It was always a little tight for the four of us, but we managed to squeeze in the extra setting for Lux. The goose, which was way out of our budget, had been dutifully cooked and had delivered, as we so eagerly anticipated, a small bowlful of glorious golden goose fat. We checked all the preparation and waited for the arrival of the guest of honor.

A domestic goose which is used for cooking.

The appointed time arrived and passed and still no Lux. Finally, some 30 minutes late, the apartment buzzer buzzed and I went to open the door. Having seen so many pictures of Lux in Miss Badeux's apartment in Zurich, I had no trouble recognizing him at once. He was mid-sized, very thin, in his mid-30s, with graying hair, a very narrow face, and a rather pronounced chin. As he entered we were subjected to our first shock of the evening — he was not alone. Coming in behind him was a rather handsome woman in her mid-20s and about four inches taller than he.

After some preliminary chitchat we went to the kitchenette and dinner. Mother announced that she wasn't hungry and did not plan to eat and gracefully gave up her place at the dinner table to the woman who had arrived uninvited and unexpected with Lux. During the dinner conversation, we were subjected to shock number two when Lux announced that the young lady, who was seated next to him, was his fiancée. Due to our upbringing, neither Steven nor I was tactless enough to ask the questions on our minds: "What about Miss Badeux? Hadn't you promised to marry her? Isn't she waiting in Zurich to hear from you?" As shocked as we were, we were not prepared for shock number three. Mother served the appetizers that included the treasured goose fat.

"Oh! My goodness, goose fat!" exclaimed Lux and carefully selected the biggest piece of toast from the basket and proceeded to pile the entire bowlful of goose fat onto it. Our whole family sat totally still, staring at what was happening but not believing our own eyes. How could anyone have such incredible bad manners and be so selfish and greedy?! After that, we could not bring the evening to a close fast enough.

After Lux and his "friend" left, we sat in stunned silence for a while and then, all together, started to discuss what we should do next. Do we write to Miss Badeux and tell her the truth, do we lie to her, do we simply forget the event—what to do? We were furious. Miss Badeux was such a nice lady and she was, obviously, in love with this man and he was such a rat! All these years she has been supporting his studies and he had been promising to marry her while he was running around with other women. We finally decided that to be fair, we had to write a nice letter to Zurich and report the events of the evening as best we could and let Miss Badeux decide what conclusions to draw from what we experienced. A few weeks later we received a nice note from Zurich thanking us for the news and wishing us well in the future. We did not ever hear from Miss Badeux again.

Lux went on to marry this woman, apparently just long enough to get his U.S. citizenship. Then he divorced her and married a rich widow, and that is the last news we had about him.

The Wonders Of America

There were many surprises that awaited us in 1940 when we arrived in the United States having escaped from the dreaded Holocaust. There was ketchup, hamburgers, Coca Cola, and the complete absence of football – not American football, but what Americans call soccer. We were brought up on soccer and its total absence in the USA was remarkable.

Of course, there were many more things we had to learn and absorb. Eggs came in a box of twelve, bread was white not brown and you can have it whole or have it sliced, milk came in a carton not a bottle. There was the pound instead of a kilo, inches in place of centimeters and milk came in a quart. We had to learn the value of a penny, nickel, dime and quarter and all the paper bills were the same size no matter what denomination! The subway cost a nickel no matter how far you traveled, a nickel also bought a ride on a bus, street car, even on the Staten Island Ferry. A phone

Goudy Grammar School on the north side of Chicago where I was first exposed to the mysteries of our new country.

The Somerset Hotel at Argyle and Sheridan Road, our first home in the United States. Our American in-laws arranged a two bedroom furnished apartment for us that cost way too much for our budget. We left for New York as soon as the lease was over.

The temple of the North Shore Hebrew Congregation where I conducted Junior Services on Saturday morning.

call on a public phone was also a nickel but you had to get a slug to put into the slot. The knickers you wore to school identified you immediately as a refugee and, it wasn't until Aunt Lene (Ernest Klein's wife) took you and Steven to a store and bought two pairs of pants for each of us, that we were finally relieved of the looks, snickers and comments generated by our knickers.

There were so many things to learn! One of the greatest mysteries was baseball, a sport unheard of in Europe. I stood around for hours watching boys play this strange game in the neighborhood playground and trying to figure out what they were doing and why. Near the hotel, I was introduced to a game called "ledgeball." You threw a tennis ball hard against a curved ledge on the outside of the building. The opponent tried to catch it for an "out." However, if the ball fell on the sidewalk you got a "single," if it hit in the car parking area it was a "double," in the roadway was a "triple," and, the ball landing on the sidewalk across the street was a "home run." Three outs and you were out and switched positions to the "field." From this game I learned some of baseball's fundamentals and also to carefully watch out for cars.

Slowly, what the boys were doing on the playground started to make sense. I tried to augment my knowledge of the game by listening to Bob Elson describing the White Sox and Cubs games on the radio. There was no television in the 1940's. (Little did I suspect that I'd be working with Bob Elson just 10 years later.) My admiration for professional baseball players in the Major Leagues became immense. I heard Bob describe a pitch as: "...a curve ball right around his knees..." and I wondered what skill it must take to pitch a ball that would actually go right around the batter's knees. The boys in the playground had a hard time just getting the ball over the plate and here I was hearing about pitchers that could make the ball go around in circles! No wonder the pitcher was in the Major Leagues! And, of course, I pitied the poor batters who not only had to hit those very difficult pitches but, according to Bob Elson's radio report, had to do it while confined in a "batter's box"!

A sandlot program run by the Chicago Cubs slowly dispelled these misconceptions and many more. I learned that if you showed up early at the school playground on Addison Street just east of Wrigley Field, you could get into the Chicago Cubs ballpark for free. The rumor was true and I made sure to be in the playground every Sunday afternoon. A nice man in a

Hyde Park High School where I played soccer and attracted fans. I graduated in 1944.

suit would come, gather us up and walk us into the ball park. In the summer of 1941, I was cheering the mighty Cubs from way out in the left field bleachers. I became a Cubs fan for a while and Bill Nicholson, Clyde McCullough, Andy Pafko, Claude Passeau, Phil Cavaretta, Stan Hack, the mad Russian Novikoff, and the rest of the Cubs became my heroes.

In high school we were offered basketball. What a strange sport — you could not run with the ball, you had to dribble, and then you had to put that big ball into that small basket way above your head. It made much better sense to be able to kick the ball and have a large goal as the target. As far as American football was concerned, I was completely uninformed until I was almost through high school. That sport was a total mystery to me then and, in many ways, is still today.

We had to learn the Pledge of Allegiance and the National Anthem "Oh say can you see …" but, at the assemblies, that we had to attend each morning in school, we sang "God Bless America." That was followed by a blessing that always seemed to include Jesus Christ. As far as I was concerned that was a violation of one of the Ten Commandments and, I later learned, it was also a violation of the U. S. Constitution. I volunteered to come to the stage each morning early and hold the flag for the Pledge and thereby avoided the benediction. And then the strangest thing of all was graduation where we had to wear a gown and a silly looking hat with a tassel. But it was nice to have your name called, walk up to the stage and get a fancy diploma.

Yes, slowly, as times went by, we learned all these little quirks of our new country. We were sworn in to be a U.S. citizen, got to join the United States Navy and serve during the war. We learned about the G.I. Bill of Rights that paid for your college tuition, books and a $50 monthly allowance for living expenses.

Wow! What a country!

In the United States Navy just long enough to qualify for the G.I. Bill.

WQXR and the Bohemian Payment Plan

Dear WQXR — thank you for your invitation to tell "My Story" on this special day — your 80th anniversary.

So, here it is:

Back in the 1930's when we lived in Czechoslovakia, our very large black Telefunken radio played either classical music or the news. That big radio, a large Gramophone and a fine collection of 78rpm discs featuring Enrico Caruso, Beniamino Gigli, Richard Tauber, Joseph Schmidt, etc., turned me into a great fan of classical music.

We managed to escape from the Holocaust and landed in a classical music radio wasteland, the United States of America. In Chicago, where we settled, there was just one lonely classical music radio program — just one hour long — 7 a.m. to 8 a.m. — interrupted regularly by commercials for Talman Federal Savings and Loan. Each morning at 7 a.m., my little wooden clock-radio would wake me with the waltz from Tchaikovsky's *Nutcracker Suite*. I loved that one hour of music but that was all there was.

Then we moved to New York, and I discovered WQXR! It was an AM station tucked away somewhere at the top of the AM dial — at around 1600, I believe. There was no FM in those days so it wasn't HiFi, but it was classical music all day. It was an

WQXR: the source of never ending good music in the USA classical musical desert.

avalanche of great music, great orchestras and great musicians. Wow! When midnight arrived, the station played the National Anthem and went off the air. But I did not turn the radio off hoping that the program would somehow resume. But it didn't — not until 6 a.m.

I remember how excited and frightened I was when WQXR announced it was switching from 5,000 kilowatt to 50,000! Will this added power explode my little radio? Is it safe to turn the radio on? I finally mustered the courage to turn on the radio and was relieved that it sounded pretty much the same as before and that my radio was safe. Today, you are a FM station and can be heard all over the world. My wife and I were marooned in Israel during the pandemic year of 2020 but had WQXR as our companion throughout the year. Wow!

So, I must confess. I've been in love with a radio station for nearly 79 years. It has been my educator, entertainer, informer and faithful companion and one of my joys in life. So, I congratulate you on your 80th anniversary, thank you for all the joy you have brought me and I wish you many more years of continued success.

Incidentally, Talman Federal Savings and Loan, the sponsor of the lonely one-hour classical music program in Chicago, taught me a life-changing manner to guide my finances that I successfully applied all my life.

For a few months they aired a radio commercial that featured the "Bohemian Payment Plan." In the 1940's Chicago and its suburbs was, after Prague, the capitol of Czechoslovakia, the second largest Bohemian city in the world. Bohemians were reputed to be very frugal and the Bohemian Payment Plan appealed to their inclination to be thrifty.

The Bohemian Payment Plan was, stated simply, "100% down and no payments the rest of your life." The announcer went on to explain: If you want to buy something, save up the money by making regular contributions into a savings account. Talman will add interest to this account reducing the amount you need to save. On the other hand, if you borrow the money first, you will need to pay interest. As a result, the item will cost you quite a bit more.

My wife and I followed this principal throughout our life and I am 94 as I am writing this. We never borrowed any money. Not when we bought cars, invested money, took trips, sent the children to college and provided for retirement. The only exception was when we bought our first house and we paid off that mortgage early.

Classical music enabled us to provide a comfortable and worry-free life for our whole family. We never once had to worry whether we had enough money.

Going Up In Smoke

During World War II, the tobacco companies were doing their "patriotic duty" by generously supplying free cigarettes to the members of the armed forces. I guess, on one hand, they were pretending to be doing their share to aid the war effort, while all the time they were developing a generation of smokers. I, like so many others at that time, started to smoke and, like so many others, after I was discharged from the U.S. Navy, found myself consuming about 30 cigarettes a day. There was always a suspicion in my heart that what I was doing was wrong but, like so many others, I really was not sufficiently motivated to quit smoking. The tobacco companies used all sorts of devious methods to convince the public that smoking was relatively harmless.

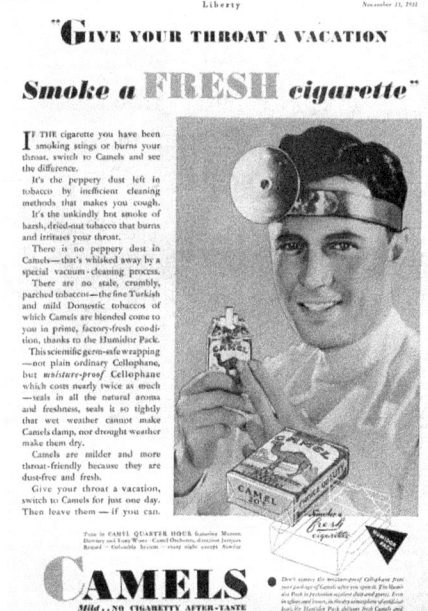

I recall a series of radio (and later television) commercials boasting that doctors who smoke prefer Camel cigarettes. "With doctors who know tobacco best, it's Camels two to one" was one of their slogans. While working for the Fred A. Niles Communication Center as a film director, I am sorry to say, I actually directed Tareyton cigarette commercials with a

I am truly ashamed that, at one time, I actually supported the lies of the tobacco industry.

man dressed in a white laboratory coat. We did not say that he was a doctor, but it certainly looked like he was one.

I struggled with my addiction — trying out pipes and cigars — but always returned to cigarettes. At a meeting of the board of directors of the Midwest branch of the Directors Guild of America one of the members announced that his wife had just delivered a boy and he proudly passed out cigars to everyone. Not wishing to offend the gentlemen, I unwrapped the cigar and kept it unlit in my mouth for the balance of the meeting. By the time I was ready to drive home I was deathly sick. I had no idea that chewing on the cigar would harm me. When I somehow managed to get home I wanted to die I felt so awful. It took two days for me to recover and the pain turned me into a non-smoker. I stopped smoking for about ten years.

Then, in 1968, I was in Slough, England, making a film about the construction of the famous Ford GT racing car. Sometime during that visit, I lit a cigarette and, before I knew it, I was back smoking a pack-and-a-half a day. When I came back home to the United States I was so ashamed that I had resumed smoking, that I only smoked in the office but not at home. Once in a while, however, when I was sure everyone was asleep, I would light a cigarette at home at my desk in the basement. One day, as I was working and secretly smoking, I happened to look up and see my 8-year-old daughter, Robin, standing at the top of the stairs. There were tears running down her cheeks as she stood there silently. Believing that this must be the result of a bad dream, I asked: "Robin, what's wrong?" Looking straight at my lit cigarette, Robin sobbed: "Daddy, I don't want you to die."

I put out that cigarette, threw the rest of the pack into the wastepaper basket, gave my daughter a warm kiss and have never smoked a cigarette or anything else again.

A Student's Life in IIT in the 1940'S

There was great significance in the fact that I had served in World War II in the U.S. Navy. This service entitled me to the full privileges of a war veteran. The United States was very generous to its veterans. The G.I. Bill of Rights, which was enacted in Congress, enabled many of us to go to college. The government paid much of the tuition and also provided a monthly cash allowance. Unfortunately, it wasn't really enough money to live on campus. So, in 1945, I opted to go to the Illinois Institute of Technology that was located on Chicago's near south side. I could continue living at home and go to college without burdening our family's finances. To make use of the training in electronics that I had received in the Navy, I decided to pursue a bachelor's degree in electrical engineering.

IIT extended me some credits for the courses I had taken in the Navy, and I plotted how I could catch up with the time I had lost and graduate in three years. This, I determined, would only be possible if I could take substantially more than the 16 credit hours per semester that the school allowed. Just as I had done in high school, I devised a plan to take substantially heavier schedules and cut a year off my college program and regain the time I had lost in the service.

IIT had a somewhat primitive method of registering for classes. On the specified registration day each department would set up a table in the gymnasium. If you wanted to sign up for an English class, you got in line in front

These are the original buildings dating back to the original Armour Institute.

The new campus was designed by the famous architect Mies van de Rohe.

of the English department table and hoped that, by the time you got to the head of the line, the class that you wanted was still available. You would then rush to the next line to sign up for the next course and so on and so on until your schedule was complete. This system did not present a big problem for those signing up for the normal 16 credit hours per semester. If one of your preferred classes was already full, you nearly always managed to find an alternate class that would fit into your schedule. However, when you were trying to squeeze 22 or 24 credit hours into your program, as I was, a careful strategy had to be prepared. A complex schedule like mine was, usually, possible in just one specific arrangement. If you missed registering for one of the classes that this arrangement required, the whole house of cards would collapse.

Every semester, no matter how well I planned, there would always be one or two classes that were already filled by the time I got to the table. To solve this dilemma I developed a bit of subterfuge. I'd go up to the professor who was teaching one of the closed classes and say: "I spoke to the head of your department and he said that, if it is all right with you were I to join your closed class, it would be OK with him." What could the professor say? I had already received the department head's approval so he could hardly object. He always agreed. I would then rush over to the department head and say: "Professor so-and-so said if it is OK with you it's OK with him if I join his closed class." Invariably the department head approved, and I had the class I needed. Of course, the secret to this system was to get to both people before they had a chance to talk to each other.

IIT was located in the heart of a dilapidated neighborhood of Chicago around 33rd Street and State Street. The campus consisted of four red brick buildings that once served the Armour Technical School. The main building shook whenever a train passed by on the railroad tracks that ran along the west side of the campus.

The famous architect Mies van der Rohe joined the faculty as the head of the architecture department and designed the starkly modern buildings of a new campus. These buildings were being built while I was at IIT. The exterior of the new buildings in the utilitarian style that made van der Rohe famous — had exposed steel beams and exposed brick that made up the outside walls. The design of the new buildings was in great contrast to the older ones, built more than a century before. I actually got to use some of these new classrooms.

During my last year at IIT, the first of van der Rohe's new campus buildings opened. Along with the grand opening ceremony, there was also a photographic exhibit of some of his most famous designs. The large photographs and design drawings were hanging in the halls of the building. Suddenly, while walking to class one day, I was dumbstruck. There, hanging on the wall, was a photograph of a house that I passed many times as young boy on the Dolni Ulice, the street where our apartment house was located in Brno, Czechoslovakia. Our house was on a street that had a steep incline. At the top of the hill the street turned right and ran along the crest of the hill. From this vantage point you could see a pretty view of the city of Brno. Unfortunately houses blocked much of this view. As children we often took walks along this street.

One of the houses on this street was very intriguing to us. Facing the street the house consisted of a rectangular one-story high wall with just one small window. Unlike all the other houses in the neighborhood that had red tile roofs, this house had a flat roof. There was a small lawn in front and a tall fence that was always locked. The rest of the house wasn't visible since it faced away from us downhill. We often wondered what this strange structure, that appeared to have no windows, could be. Using our vivid imagination we came up with all kinds of ideas and, finally, concluded that it must be a military observation point or a secret scientific laboratory of some kind. We did a

The side of the villa that faced the street consisted of walls and a small window.

The rear of the villa, consisting of floor to ceiling windows, a wide terrace and views of the city was located down the hill and invisible from the street.

lot of speculation as to what was going on in this building and behind that mysterious wall.

Here now, in the IIT hallway, in a different country, half a globe away, some ten years later and having escaped the Holocaust, was a photograph of that house the way I remembered it when our governess would take us for walks! Here was the strange square wall with the single small window, the unusual flat roof, and the high fence. I stood and stared. The class bell rang, but I was still glued to the floor. It had been years since I'd seen this structure. Having it rise up before me in a different country and in a different age was quite a shock.

Our mystery house turned out to be one of Mies van der Rohe's early designs, the Tugenhat House. This was a unique and revolutionary design of a villa that actually had two floors that were built into the side of the hill. On the downhill side, which was not visible from the street, the floors face the city and consist of floor-to-ceiling windows giving each room a breathtaking view of the city. For the year 1934, when this villa was built, the design was truly extraordinary and indicated a great future for the young architect. Van der Rohe went on to develop the spare curtain-wall style that became the principal design of skyscrapers throughout the second half of the 20th century. The Tugenhat family, being Jewish, became undoubtedly victims of the Nazi persecution.

Lack of Social Life

IIT had no athletic fields and, therefore, no athletic program. Being an engineering school, which was considered mostly a male occupation, there was also hardly any social life. You went to classes, did your laboratory experiments, conducted your research, studied in the library, took your tests, and got your grades — and that was that. There were two major breaks in this routine. One was the activities of Professor Hayakawa who taught semantics in the English department and was a jazz enthusiast. Every once in a while he would stage a jazz concert on campus. We also started an amateur theatrical group that staged original musicals satirizing life at IIT. A few years later, Professor Hayakawa made a mark for himself by quelling a student riot on a college campus in California by wrestling the microphone away from the student leaders. This was captured on film and was broadcast over television all over the country. There weren't too many school administrators willing to stand up against the upheavals taking place on campuses in the 1960's during the Vietnam War era so Professor Hayakawa was big news. A few years later he ran as a Republican for the senate seat in California and won!

Professor Hayakawa, lover of semantics and jazz — a bright light in the halls of IIT.

Switch to Quicker Pace

In order to enable veterans to complete their studies faster, some universities switched to a three semester per year schedule. IIT did not, but the University of Illinois did. To take advantage of this opportunity I switched to the campus at Urbana-Champaign for Summer 1947. One semester at the University of Illinois was all I could afford; I returned to IIT for my final year and graduation in June 1948. I had achieved my goal of graduating in three years. For a while, I entertained the thought of going on with my studies. Actually I had already accumulated some credits towards my master's degree. But my G.I. benefits had run out and there wasn't any way I was going to ask my parents for money.

It was time to go to work.

The Show Must Go On

One of my great pleasures is good music. Of course, that includes most classical music, operas, operettas, oratorios, and songs. There is also a great deal of so-called "popular music" that I can listen to with great pleasure. However, much of the latest popular music sounds like noise to me and very annoying noise at that. The kind of music, however, that really drives me up the wall is loud background music — music in an elevator or a restaurant that is so loud and intrusive as to interfere with normal conversation and thought. I have walked out of many restaurants because someone in the management is deaf or is under the very mistaken impression that loud music will make the food taste better.

Since my high school days, attendance at concerts has been a regular part of my leisure activities. I must admit that, when I attended some of those early concerts, I was not fully aware of their significance. However, today I treasure the music I heard back then played by such performers as Vladimir Horowitz, Arthur Schnabel, Wanda Landowka, Jasha Heifetz, and Yehudi Menuhin and orchestras conducted by legends such as Bruno Walter, Sir Thomas Beacham, Fritz Reiner, Serge Koussevitzky, Georg Solti, and Leonard Bernstein. Under these circumstances, it is no surprise that our subscriptions to the New Jersey Symphony Orchestra and the New York City Opera Company date back over 40 years. We also exposed our children at an early age to this type of music. There were times when it took a great deal of arm-twisting to get them to go along. But, we hope that today, as a result, they have an appreciation for this type of entertainment. Of course, going to so many performances, sooner or later you are bound to run into some memorable situations when the old adage that "the show must go on" is badly strained.

I recall a time when we all sat around for nearly two hours while the management of the New York Metropolitan Opera Company desperately sought a replacement in a minor role who could not continue and complete the performance. But, find one they did and, after milling around for quite a while, the audience got a chance to hear the balance of the opera.

On one occasion, a group of high school friends of mine and I went to a concert of the Cincinnati Symphony Orchestra. The concert was not too well attended and just before the concert was supposed to begin, the six of us sneaked down from the cheap seats to the better seats up front. At this point, a man in a tuxedo walked onto the stage to announce that the conductor of the orchestra was ill and the concert would be conducted by a replacement. Unfortunately, the replacement conductor was unfamiliar with the recently completed work by Aaron Copland and the orchestra would play something else instead. Our whole group was very disappointed and made our feeling known with a groan. A man sitting in front of us turned around and asked why we were making all this noise. We told him we had come to hear "Appalachian Spring" and now we were going to be disappointed.

We, more or less, enjoyed the first half of the concert. When the audience quieted down after the intermission, the man in the tuxedo came out again and happily announced that Aaron Copland, who happened to be in the audience, had graciously agreed to conduct his own composition that was originally on the program. We were glad to hear this news and applauded loudly. We will enjoy the composition we came to hear after all! Our boisterousness, however, was shocked into silence when the man who strode out onto the stage to conduct the orchestra was none other than the man who sat in front of us earlier. As he took his bow, he looked in our direction and, I think, he smiled at us.

Once, I attended a performance of the Lyric Opera in Chicago. They were performing Wagner's "Die Meistersinger." At one point Franz Sachs, the shoemaker, sang a trio along with the soprano and the bass, who sang the part of the soprano's father. The father finished his part and walked towards the side of the stage where his "home" was located. He reached for the door to open it, but it would not open. He pulled and pushed harder. The whole set shook but the door did not open. The audience gasped. The bass finally solved the problem by simply walking off the side of the stage. All this was happening behind the soprano's back who was still busy communicating with Mr. Sachs. Now she finished her aria and also headed for her home and the same door. The audience, expecting another embarrassment, held its breath as she reached for the door handle. She pushed and, surprise, the door opened without any difficulties. The audience burst into laughter and applause as the soprano sailed through the open doorway. I have always wondered what thoughts raced through the poor soprano's mind as she made this riotous exit.

There was a rather amusing incident once at the start of a performance by the New York City Opera Company when Miss Beverly Sills, who by that time had retired from her highly successful singing career and was now the director of the opera company, came on the stage and made an announcement which went about as follows: "Ladies and gentlemen. A few days ago Soprano A, who was scheduled to sing the lead in this evening's performance, slipped on some ice and broke her ankle. We were fortunate to secure the services of Soprano B. Unfortunately, Soprano B developed a bad throat and is unable to sing this evening. So, what we are going to do is, Soprano B will be on stage acting out her part while Soprano A will be in the orchestra pit singing the part." Miss Sills concluded her remarks with: "Which proves that it is a lot easier to sing in an opera than to run one." The audience received her remarks with applause and after about five minutes of the performance forgot the double-soprano arrangement and enjoyed the opera. This was just another outstanding example of the "the show must go on" adage.

One time my wife and I attended a performance in Tel Aviv, Israel, where the show did *not* go on — well not completely. It was a performance of George Frederic Handel's *Messiah* with the Israel Philharmonic Orchestra and the Prague Opera Chorus conducted by Zubin Mehta. At the start of the performance there was a brief announcement in Hebrew that I did not fully understand or pay much attention to. But, based on the audience's reaction, I sensed it was not good news. When the oratorio reached the intermission right after the "Hallelujah Chorus," I noticed that people were getting up and leaving! "What is going on?" I asked puzzled. It was then that my dear wife, who speaks fluent Hebrew, explained the significance of the opening announcement to me. It seems that Mr. Mehta had to catch a plane to New York and, because it was Friday evening, he had to reach the airport before sundown when the Jewish Sabbaths begins. I could

By 1961 Zubin Mehta had already conducted the Vienna, Berlin and Israel Philharmonic Orchestras..

not believe my ears. Whatever happened to all that "the show must go on?" business?

To this day I insist that Zubin Mehta owes me half a concert — and now he has retired — so good luck.

What a Bargain

My career in "show business" began as a recording and maintenance engineer at United Broadcasting. United was owned by my uncle William (Bill) Klein and Egmont Sonderling. Bill Klein inaugurated a German language radio program in Chicago called the Germania Broadcast in 1927. The program became quite popular among the German speaking population and was a financial success. In its best years the programs included the participation of German movie, opera and literature personalities. Bill also conducted tours of groups of listeners back to Europe. On two occasions, he arrived in Europe along with his American car, a LaSalle, in 1937 and a Cadillac a year later. Both cars were huge compared to European models and, of course, attracted a great deal of attention wherever they would wander.

With the rise of Hitler in Germany in 1933, there were elements in Chicago who resented that the one and only German radio program was led by an

Left: The huge LaSalle car that Bill Klein brought to Europe. It was twice the size of most European vehicles and, for kids like us, was a thrill to ride in. Right: The following year Bill arrived with an equally impressive Cadillac automobile.

opponent of the National Socialist (Nazi) movement and, horrors, by a Jew. Bill had a hard time keeping the program out of politics and withstand the pressures of the Nazi elements in Chicago. The Germania Broadcast remained on the air for many years and is believed to be the longest active foreign language radio program on the air in the United States.

At United Broadcasting, in charge of the very important Lutheran Laymen's League account was a tall, blondish, heavy-set and jolly man named Hutchings. To everyone in the office he was simply Hutch. Around 1948, when it was still a dangerous and unusual adventure to visit war-torn Europe, Hutch announced that he and his wife were going to go on a vacation to Europe and that, in order to record this momentous trip, he had invested $250 in a beautiful new 8mm Bell and Howell film camera. In those days that was quite a lot of money. A few days later he approached me and, to my surprise, offered to sell me his brand new camera. It seems, he told me, his wife had bought him a camera as a going away present and he had no need for two cameras.

There wasn't any way I could afford to spend my money on such a luxury item. The cost represented about two weeks salary for me, money I could hardly afford to waste. From time to time thereafter, until I left United in 1952, Hutch would urge me to buy the camera. Each time the price came down a little.

This precisely made 8mm Bell & Howell camera was the object of many years of intense bargaining.

In 1956, after I returned from a two-year visit to Israel, I went to work for Fred Niles Communications Centers. About three years later, I was surprised to run into Hutch in the hallway. He advised me that he was now also working for Niles as a salesman and promptly reminded me that his 8mm camera was still for sale. "You know," he urged me, "the camera is brand new. I never used it. The test film is still inside the camera unexposed." Once again, Hutch would come around from time to time and urge me to buy the camera. I usually turned him down with a smile. I really had no need for such a camera.

I was earning a much better salary now so, one day, when Hutch once again went into his good-natured sales pitch, I reached into my pocket, took out a $50 bill and said: "OK, Hutch. Here it is, $50, that is my best and last offer." Hutch hesitated for a moment then picked up the money and handed me the camera. We shook hands and had a good laugh about this matter that had stretched over a decade.

A few weeks later, Hutch did not come to work and that day, before we left to go home, the staff was advised that Hutch had died of a heart attack. Needless to say, I have held on to that camera ever since. I firmly believe it has kept me alive for over 94 years.

Watch What You Say

I began my 21-year long career at Fred Niles Communications Centers as the assistant production manager, a rather low position. As an assistant production manager my job was to prepare the schedule for each day, maintain a calendar of the studio usage, maintain an inventory of studio supplies and assist Bill Harder, the production manager, as much as I could. After two years on this job, I was assigned to be the production manager of the Oral Roberts Evangelistic Television Program.

That was quite a step up. First, it got me out of the studio and the offices as I brought the film crew and the equipment to the various locations all over the United States where the Oral Roberts program was staged. I then saw to it that all preparation were made to assure that the four cameras would do an outstanding job filming Oral's sermon and the all-important "healings" that he miraculously accomplished during his presentations. We did this once a month and we brought back enough material for four programs. Unfortunately, after two years, Oral decided to develop his own "Christian" production company and my assignment ended. Well, not quite. Oral decided he wanted to visit the Holy Land and do some preaching there and, when I told him that I spent three years producing films in Israel, he hired me.

Of course I was constantly hoping for an assignment that would give me an opportunity do more than to produce, but to direct. One day, perhaps in my third year at Niles, I was entrusted to take a small crew to Madison, Wisconsin, to shoot a few scenes for a film that the company was producing. The assignment was fairly simple. "Fly early in the morning to Madison, shoot some

The capitol building in Madison, Wisconsin.

scenes of the city and of the capitol building, and then be at the governor's office promptly at 4 p.m. in order to film a statement by the governor. Then fly back to Chicago." Nothing could be simpler. I was very excited and pleased to get this "directorial" assignment.

All went smoothly during the day and we were sitting in the governor's reception room promptly at 4 p.m. waiting to shoot the scene with the governor. We waited and it was getting late and I was beginning to worry whether we would make the flight back to Chicago. At about 5:30 the governor's secretary announced that the governor was very sorry, but he was too busy to be filmed today. "Please come back first thing tomorrow morning. The governor will be available then," she promised curtly obviously unaware what problems this was causing.

What to do? Here was my opportunity to make an executive decision and I wanted to be sure to make the right one. We could fly back to Chicago and then bring everyone back the next day to film the governor. But the crew would not get eight hours sleep time so we would have to pay them double time for the second day. Or we could stay overnight and be there early in the morning to film the governor as requested. I made a quick calculation of the expenses and decided to stay overnight. I changed the airline reservation and checked the crew into a nice motel for the night. I was very pleased with the way I had handled the situation.

I was about to go to sleep when I had a sudden dreadful thought. In all the excitement I had forgotten to notify the office that we were staying in Madison overnight. Tomorrow morning people would be looking for us and worry when we didn't show up for work. It was close to midnight and too late to phone anyone. Then I had a brilliant idea! I decided to send a telegram.

Please remember this was 1957 and long before computers, emails, faxes, telephone answering machines, or any of the new communications channels that we have today existed. But there was Western Union, the company that had a virtual monopoly for sending telegrams within the United States. You could phone one of their offices at any time of the day or night and send a message that would be delivered the following day and the service would be charged to your phone bill. That was my solution to the problem. I picked up the hotel phone, reached Western Union, dictated the message to the friendly female operator, and told her to call at 9 a.m. and relay the message to my boss. I was happy with what I had done and laid down and went to sleep.

There was a sudden knocking on my door. I dragged myself out of bed and opened the motel room door. Two very imposing state policemen were standing there. "Please get dressed and come with us," was their brief request. Of course, I asked what this was all about, but received no answer. I was hustled into the police car and we took off. A few minutes later I was at the Wisconsin State Patrol Headquarters facing a group of five or six officers who started questioning me. "Who are you?" "Where do you live?" "What are you doing in Madison?" "Who do you work for?" The questions did not seem to end. Almost an hour went by when all the officers left the room. About 10 minutes later one of them came back and said: "Come with me, I'll drive you back to the motel."

When we arrived back at our motel and I was getting out of the car, I turned to the officer and said firmly: "Is someone going to tell me what all this was about? What did I do?" The officer looked at me with a strange smile on his face and said: "Next time be more careful about your telegrams," and drove off. I was walking up the steps to the motel when I suddenly realized what my mistake was. In order to save money (telegrams were charged by the word) I had made the telegram as brief as possible.

It read: "Could not shoot governor today, will try again tomorrow."

You Played It Too Loud

It is kind of strange that a Jewish refugee from the Holocaust, and a new arrival in the United States like me, would have so many Christian organizations as loyal clients. During my career as a film producer/director I counted the New York Bible Society, the Oral Roberts Evangelistic Program, the Lutheran Layman's League, and several others among my clients.

Shortly after receiving my bachelor's degree in electrical engineering from the Illinois Institute of Technology in 1948, I went to work for the United Broadcasting Company that was partially owned by my uncle, William L. Klein. His partner was a man named Egmont Sonderling. The biggest client that United had at that time was the Lutheran Hour Program sponsored by the Missouri Synod of the Lutheran Laymen's League. To serve this client, United would produce a half hour recorded program every week. Copies of the program were sent to radio stations all over the country who would play the program usually on Sunday morning.

From time to time, Dr. Karl Mayer would arrive at the studio and record a series of powerful sermons that we would then

Bill Klein (left) with his brother, Julius.

combine with recordings of choruses to make up half-hour programs. Of course, to finance the program, there were also appeals for contributions or opportunities to buy religious articles or publications.

Dr. Mayer was a gregarious man who loved to slap people on the back. "How are you!" he would shout and hit you so hard you staggered. When he learned that I was Jewish, he would test my Hebrew and my knowledge of the Hebrew Bible. Other clerics also arrived to record sermons in German, Slovak, Swedish, and, at times, two or three other languages.

When the 20th anniversary of this nation-wide radio program arrived, a grand celebration was planned for the Chicago Stadium. I had developed a unique skill in a brand new recording method. The late 1940's saw the introduction of tape recorders, a much more economical and flexible recording device than the established method using a disc and a scribe. The other recording engineers that were employed at United scoffed at this new method of sound recording and left the field open to me. I developed the skill of recording on tape and, more importantly, the art of editing this tape — removing unwanted material, like pauses, noise, errors, etc., and selecting the best recording of a particular subject.

With my skill in tape editing, I was put in charge of developing the soundtrack that will be played during a 90-minute grand pageant. For almost an hour and a half, my soundtrack would be the only sound heard by the guests in the stadium audience while this grand pageant unfolded in front of them. This was going to be a spectacular presentation with over 300 people in costume and three large choruses located in the top balcony of the Chicago Stadium. Emmling Flowers supplied tons of decorative plants and a stage was constructed that reached from the ground floor to the second balcony of this huge indoor stadium that could seat as many as 20,000 people for such an event.

I worked extremely hard for over six months preparing the all-important soundtrack that would accompany and guide the action on the stage. The bosses of United, as well as the other staff, left me alone to do my stuff in the little studio space that was set aside for me. The director of the pageant and I worked very closely to develop the needed musical and spoken segments of the track. I did a great deal of research, found some rare recordings to use, and mixed all of this together into a sound track that received praise from the director and from the client.

On the day of the pageant I arrived at the Chicago Stadium early and set up not one, but two tape recorders side by side. Tape and tape recorders were still somewhat unreliable and I was not going to take a chance that the tape might

The old Chicago Stadium was the huge stage for the grand presentation during the 20th Anniversary celebrations of the Lutheran Laymen's League radio program.

break or something else would go wrong. The stadium would then suddenly be in total silence with thousands of people waiting while I made repairs or spliced the torn tape. Therefore, I made a copy of the whole program tape for the second machine and, during the performance; I kept the two machines running together so that, at any moment, I could switch from one machine to the other. Fortunately, this never became necessary. The sound from the tape was fed to the stadium sound system that played it over the existing stadium speakers.

All went gloriously well. The pageant, with all the music, actors, costumes, lighting, and choruses was just magnificent. At the end the whole cast started to climb stairs towards a lighted cross on the second balcony to the sound of the conclusion of Sibelius' Second Symphony. When the last grand chords of this magnificent symphony brought the pageant to a conclusion, the audience stood up as a group and applauded and cheered. I was overcome with joy and a sense of accomplishment. This was the very first "grand" production of what, turned out to be, a life time of creativity.

As I was wrapping up, I was surrounded by the client's staff, people congratulating me and slapping me on the back. I felt just immensely elated and pleased with myself. Dr. Mayer came by, as did Dr. Berterman, his assistant, and several other leaders of the Lutheran Laymen's League to thank me and congratulate my efforts. The little director came rushing at me and hugged me with tears in his eyes and presented me with a tie. Things quieted down and I returned to packing up my equipment. After a few minutes, Uncle Bill came by. He stood there looking at me for a moment. I was anxious to hear what my boss had to say.

"You played it too loud," said he and walked away. I felt that, perhaps, it was time for me to look for another job. Which I did.

A Lesson In Economy

"Whenever you step on the brakes, you are wasting fuel".

Of all the pronouncements that Captain O'Conner of the Chicago Police Department made during his classes, this one got his audience's immediate attention.

I was one of about two dozen hapless souls who had been condemned to attend a four-part "Safe Driving" course because we had accumulated 12 or more "points" on our driving licenses during the past three years. It was either do this or an automatic suspension of you drivers' license for six months. And you had to attend all four classes in a row. Miss one and you had to start all over again. Miss two and your drivers' license was suspended.

I earned my points for speeding (less then 10 miles per hour over the limit), 3 points; making a left turn without signaling, 3 points; and 6 points for passing a stalled vehicle by using the shoulder of the road. Of course, I felt that 6 points for a perfectly safe and reasonable maneuver to avoid the car that was standing in my highway lane, was completely arbitrary and unreasonable.

During the first of the four lessons, it quickly became obvious that I was not the only attendee who felt that he or she was the victim of irrational and perverse laws and were ready to argue their position with the good Captain. As a matter of fact, the first one hour or so was taken up by my classmates' spirited pleading of their case.

However, it soon became obvious that Captain O'Conner had neither the authority nor the inclination to change the dire verdicts and the attendees lapsed into a sullen and grim attitude. There was no test or examination after the 8 hours of listening to the Captain. So we were just prepared to sit there, try to stay awake and wait for the session to end.

So, the pronouncement "Whenever you step on the brakes, you are wasting fuel" landed in the middle of this sullen crowd like a bombshell. Shrill voices were heard to challenge the Captain: "What do you expect me to do, run into the wall of the garage when I get home?" "Am I just supposed run into the back of the car ahead of me?" "What do the car's brakes have to do with fuel consumption?" "You can't be serious!" Our class was suddenly awake.

Captain O'Conner, with a slight smile on his rugged face, waited patiently for the shouting to stop and then proceeded to explain the physics principle known as "Conservation of Energy" that states that the total energy of an isolated system cannot change — it is said to be *conserved* over time. Energy can be neither created nor destroyed, but can only change form. For instance, chemical energy in gasoline can be converted to kinetic energy by the explosions inside the car motor's cylinders and when the driver steps on the brakes this energy is converted into heat by the brakes of the car. The heat is then given up to the air around the car.

Simply put, when you step on the brakes you convert all the fuel you used to get the car moving into wasted heat. So the Captain was right — you *do* waste fuel when you step on the brakes. The Captain continued: "Now, I don't expect you to run into things just to conserve fuel, but when you know that you must stop, take your foot off the accelerator and brake to a gentle halt."

All this happened when I was about 21-years-old. Now, some 73 years later, I still apply this lesson to my driving. Whenever I see a red light ahead of me, or stalled traffic, or a speed bump in the pavement or anything that will impede my progress, I remove my foot from the gas pedal and proceed slowly towards the obstruction.

This is a lesson Israeli drivers, apparently, have yet to learn. Over and over again, I sit in wonderment and amusement as I watch drivers speed past me and then have to slam on the brakes to stop. Cars behind me have blown their horn because I was not going fast enough towards a red traffic light or they have changed lanes in order to pass me and get to the red light ahead of me.

I realize I am not saving a lot of fuel, but with a tankful costing 350 shekels or more, why not try — and your brakes will last longer.

Gil's Funeral

Dear Children, grandchildren and friends;

Mom and I just returned from Gil Karu's funeral. It was scheduled to start at 2:15 p.m. and ended now — at 6:45. We were warned to come early because there will be problems getting to the cemetery and parking. So, we left the house at 12 noon and arrived at the cemetery at 1 p.m., parked and found a shady bench to await the arrival of others. We talked about Gil and reminisced about this wonderful man and great father to his children. We recalled that just a few weeks earlier Gil used his remarkable skills to make my 85th birthday party a great celebration. We knew that all of you could remember how Gil went out of his way to make our dinner party such a very special event and the wonderful manner in which he hosted the festivities. We wondered about the cruel blow that would suddenly cut down a young man's life like his, without any warning, with no chance to say goodbye, or time to be prepared.

Gil's grave.

We soon realized that we had done the right thing as people and more people were arriving. My guess is that there must have been at least 2,000 people when the preliminary services started. And people continued arriving throughout the afternoon. After a brief benediction various family members spoke —the father, Nani, each of Gil's three brothers, Gil's oldest daughter, Gil's wife, and Gil's mother, in-laws and others. It was all very moving and sad. Nani, in his message, spoke of the host of people whose life was renewed by Gil's organs — one lung to a 55-year-old man, the second one to a 53-year-old, one kidney there, the second there, the pancreas to another, the eyes, the liver and when he said: "and his heart is now beating in the chest of a 33-year-old man" many of those in attendance, including Mom, dissolved into tears. It was also noted that several recipients of Gil's organs were Arab Israelis. Unfortunately, my poor Hebrew prevented me from understanding all these heartfelt messages.

Gil's father, Nani Karu, and three of the organ recipients at the grave.

Then the big crowd moved to the burial site but only a few could get close enough to hear and participate in the ceremony. It was quite a while before the crowd slowly moved to leave after the ceremony. Mom and I and a small crowd stayed behind to hear Tal (Gil's youngest brother) take his guitar and sing a song he wrote and composed for the occasion. All who heard his voice and his words had tears in their eyes. Mom went to place the plant, that we brought, among the large mound of flowers that marked the grave. We stayed until most people had left and then departed for the home of the Karu family. Actually, the major problem developed after the funeral when so many cars needed to get to the main highway. We really did not feel that we wanted to rush away — we waited.

At the large Karu house and garden, we found food and drink (every event in Israel includes food and drink somewhere along the line) as well as the 50 or so other guests that were invited to the home. We sat and chatted, hugged each other and ate, chatted some more and hugged again. And neighbors were arriving all afternoon bringing food, gifts and memories. Gil had four children and delegations in each of the age groups arrived, the children's classmates and a large group of Scouts in full uniform. The whole town knew the Karus. Most of the children of the town, at one time or another had been cared for by the highly regarded Karu nursery school. Now, their parents arrived with those children, many much older, some in army uniforms, bringing food or flowers and often tears. Others were already married and brought their own children.

By 8 p.m., it was time to go home and rest up after the difficult day. We promised to come back and help each afternoon and evening during the seven days of *Shivah*. It took quite a while to say goodbye, but we finally did, and here I am now writing this letter to you. I wanted you to feel like you too attended the funeral.

Shalom and much love. Dad

You Would Never Guess What I Did

The most important thing I ever did in my life was marrying Yocheved Jean Ginsburg. I just cannot imagine what my life would have been without her, and I am forever grateful for the magical coincidence that brought us together. There is just one minor problem. Yochi (as she is called when we are in Israel) or Jean (as she is known outside Israel) was raised in Israel, and, throughout our years together, she has had one foot in the United States and one foot in Israel. As a result, nearly every year since our marriage in 1960, Jean has insisted on visiting Israel at least twice a year. At times she suggested that we would save a lot of money if we "only had our own apartment in Israel." I resisted this idea lest having an apartment in Israel might increase the number of visits and the length of the stays.

Nevertheless, despite of my often-repeated objections, one day in 1991, I received a phone call from Jean from Israel that began with: "You'll never

Tirat Zvi 1 under construction.

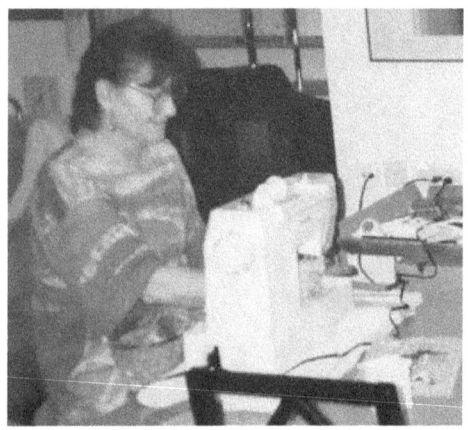
Yochi unpacked her brand new sewing machine and started making drapes.

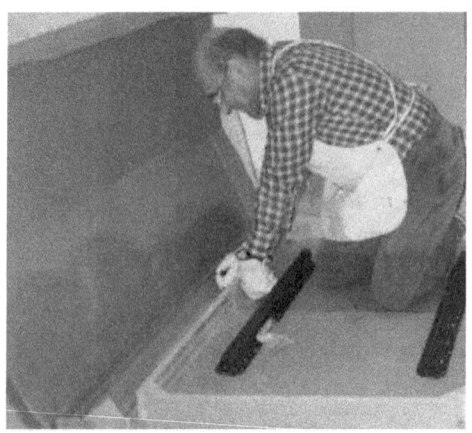
I needed a work place so, the first piece of furniture I assembled was the dining room table.

The dining room was the first 100% completed space, even before the bedroom.

We made a great team.

guess what I just did." I held my breath. "I bought an apartment." She then proceeded to describe the beauty of the location, the size of the rooms, the design of the building, the decor of the public areas, and the park in front and in the back of the building. "Why don't you take some photographs and send them to me?" I suggested. "Well, there is this problem. The place hasn't been built yet. All we have is a brochure and a floor plan."

When I joined Jean in Israel a few days later, she was eager to show me her accomplishment. We drove to Rishon Lezion where she escorted me to a location in the middle of sand dunes with only a few piles of building materials indicating what we were promised. For the next four visits, spanning two years, we visited the site regularly and watched the housing project take shape. Ours was one of nine buildings comprising an enclosed community that, as it was growing, promised to be a very nice place to live in. I did a little redesigning of the floor plan in order to include a second bathroom and I took the kitchen out of the living room space and moved it into the third bedroom. During the last visit, I took careful and detailed measurements of all the dimensions of the apartment. With these dimensions in hand we visited the IKEA furniture store in Newark and selected the apartment's furnishings using the very adaptable and flexible IKEA furniture designs.

When the next visit rolled around, as usual, Jean preceded me. We sent a 1/3 shipping van load of "stuff" to Israel that included dishes, cutlery, glassware, pots and pans, carpets, curtains and the furniture bought at IKEA. From other sources we assembled a washing machine, dryer, vacuum cleaner, sewing machine, even paints and paint brushes as well as all kitchen appliances. The only things we did not ship from the United States were the kitchen cabinets and the bed for the master bedroom.

When I next arrived in Israel, some 50 cartons awaited me in the apartment including about 40 boxes of unassembled furniture. For the next two weeks we were assembling furniture, painting walls, finishing shelving, installing wiring, mounting bathroom fixtures, caulking spaces until the place was done. We found a wonderful company that took our kitchen dimensions and the dimensions of all of our appliances and custom designed the kitchen. We then unpacked all the other stuff and did all the other chores to make the place into a home. We also bought a car that a good friend of ours watches for us when we are away and brings to the airport when we arrive. Since then, when we arrive in Israel, we drive to the apartment, unlock the front door, turn on the gas, electricity, and water, and we are home. Most of the time I arrive in Israel with only a carry-on suitcase. Everything we need is already in the apartment.

Perhaps the most important thing we found in the apartment house were wonderful neighbors. We became very close with several of the families and some became part of our extended family in Israel. We also watched as the family of an orthodox rabbi, who lived in the other first-floor apartment, grew from one son to three boys and three girls in seven years. There were some "difficult" owners, but they did not seem to last very long. Among the tenants we learned to trust each other and we felt that our apartment was perfectly safe when we were in the United States.

We were, therefore, quite shocked one day when the telephone rang at 6 o'clock in the morning with Jean's twin sister, Ruthi, calling from Israel. "I came to the apartment today just to check and I don't understand what happened," I heard her say through my sleep, "but someone stole all your carpets."

I had Ruthi repeat what she said. "Is the TV still there? How about the other valuable items—are they missing?" "No, nothing else is missing," said Ruthi, "it's just your carpets. They are all gone." My mind was clearing up, but I was really puzzled. This was a strange situation. "Please check with our neighbors and see what they say and call us back," I asked Ruthi.

A half-hour later Ruthi called back to tell us that some water was observed leaking out from under our apartment's front door and flowing down the stairs. Our neighbor, who had keys to the apartment, opened the door and found that rainwater had seeped into the apartment from the flooded balcony. Like a good neighbor, he collected all our wet carpets and brought them down to the backyard to dry. He also took steps to stem the tide that caused the flood in the first place. When we next visited Israel, our carpets were all back in their places.

When we bought our apartment in Israel at 1 Tirat Zvi, in Kiriat Ganim, Rishon Lezion we were not aware that we were actually buying something much more valuable, the heart-warming friendship of a young boy. He was only 8-years-old, but he showed a sensitivity, warmth, thoughtfulness and understanding of a person much older. He was special.

He adopted us and called us *Savtush* and *Sabush* (grandmother and grandfather) and we, in turn, adopted him. Each time we came to Israel (as we did twice each year) we looked forward to seeing him and his family who were living in the same building. The summer he spent with us in the United States was a time of adventure, exploits, education and exploration. The people he met on this visit remember him to this day.

The apartment today.

Charles stands near his favorite Royal Poinciana, or flame tree.

We watched him grow to become a serious young man who had a mind of his own. Not all his decisions were wise, but they were his own and he had a plan. We danced at his wedding, celebrated the opening of his ingeniously and cleverly designed restaurant, and drank to the health of his beautiful daughter.

And, when he reached his 27th year and the dreaded news came, a bright light was dimmed in our life. And when the light was finally extinguished, after his heroic battle against overwhelming odds, we felt like we had lost a member of our family.

Life is not always fair but, in Shai's case, it was particularly cruel, painful and harsh.

When we built our "vacation" home in Israel we never thought that one day it might become our long-term home. We arrived in Israel in January 2020 for our usual two months visit. By the time March rolled around the Covid virus pandemic had hit and our doctors suggested to remain in Israel and wait for the pandemic to pass. It has now been six months and we are still waiting for the opportunity to safely return to the U.S.A. Thanks to our careful planning and design, our Israel apartment has become our home away from home. It is a very pleasant place to spend our time with a beautiful large park in the rear of our building for vigorous walks, with neighbors who worry about us, with food delivered to us, with our car available for errands and visits and with a secure and safe place to spend our time. With so much time available, I have, at last, been able to make serious progress on the book I am trying to assemble and also to prepare biographical stories that the *Jerusalem Post* publishes from time to time.

The Frozen Heart Attack

My career in films enabled me to work with many well-known and many, many more not-so-well-known performers. It also provided me with the opportunity to travel and visit many far away places. You cannot be in the audio-visual production and presentation business for over 65 years without several memorable events happening to you. Here is one of the most remarkable.

It's 1967 and we are in Stowe, Vermont, in the dead of winter to shoot a Shell gasoline commercial. Stowe is the premier ski resort in Vermont, and it was covered under a thick blanket of snow. It was an ideal location for the commercial we were producing that I was directing. The script involved parking eight different makes and sizes of cars outside in the freezing weather, covering them with artificially-made snow and then, the next morning, show that all eight cars started without any difficulty thus proving the quality of Shell gasoline. There was just one problem: How could we prove to the audience that the cars had actually started? Of course, there were moving parts under the hood, but we wanted the hood covered by snow — so we had to find something else. Then, of course, there is the sound that the motor makes — but we needed something more dramatic, more visual. We solved the problem by putting some talcum powder into the exhaust pipe of each car. Now, when each car started, every car gave off a beautiful little cloud of white smoke. Problem solved.

The shooting was successfully completed and all that we needed to do was to clean up and go home. Late that night, I was working in my hotel room going over accounts and papers when there was a knock at my door. It was just after midnight and I was surprised by the noise. I opened the door and came face to face with the assistant director, Hal Schwartz, who was in obvious pain. "I think I am having a heart attack," said Hal as he laid down on the couch in my room. "But you are a young man," I protested, "You can't be having a heart attack. It must be something you ate or drank."

I first met Hal two years earlier when he showed up as a last minute substitute assistant director on a monstrous production job on the Salt Flats in Utah. It all started when Bruce Stauderman, a producer at the Ogilvy and Mather advertising agency and an account executive on the Shell account, asked me one day: "Charlie, you are an engineer. Tell me, can two cars go along side by side, at about 60 miles an hour, for about 10 miles without drivers in them?" I foolishly said: "Yes, of course." Little did I suspect that shortly after making this hasty assertion, I would be asked to come up with a way to do it in order to make a Shell television

Hal's first assignment as my assistant director was during the monumental and innovative Shell Driverless Cars commercial which started with two cars launched to go 12 miles down an electronic track without drivers. Car #1 used gasoline without the Platformate additive.

Car #2 used gasoline with the Shell Platformate additive.

Car #2 drove through the smoke marker where Car #1 ran out of gas proving that you get more mileage from Shell gasoline. In 1965, at its cost of $260,000, this was considered to be the most expensive television commercial to date.

▶ Watch the commercial on YouTube at youtu.be/7ULDHdKh3rE .

commercial possible. My original response was not made without a solution in mind. I visualized using a laser to keep the cars in a straight line. However, I soon learned that this idea would not work because the laser beam travels in a dead straight line and, therefore, would not follow the curvature of the earth — thus loosing contact with the car that had to follow the curvature of the earth or learn to fly!

It took about a year, but I finally arrived at an engineering concept that would work. The plan was that we would bury two 12-mile long copper cables in parallel lines into the salt of the Wendower Salt Flats in Utah. The cars would then follow the signal sent out by the wires. Hal became my assistant director and was given the job of supervising the installation of the 24 miles of cable in the salt flats and getting the area ready.

"... there is nothing we can do for him here ..."

A year later the project was ready and some 70 people gathered for three days of filming. The commercial was sensational as was the cost of the project. The "Shell Driverless Car" commercial earned the title of the most expensive television advertisement made up to that time at a cost of over $300,000. By then Hal and I had formed a very close friendship which lasted for over 30 years until his death in his early 60's.

Hal wasn't yet 30-years-old as he lay moaning on the couch in my room. But his suffering was such that I knew I had to take some prompt action. I picked up the phone and asked the hotel to call a doctor. They, at first, refused because it was well past midnight. But, I insisted and they finally connected me with a sleepy voice that listened to what I was relating to him. "Stowe is a ski resort, and we can't help you here. Go to the next town where there is a hospital. I'll call them and tell them you are coming." I bundled Hal in some blankets, and we got into my car and drove off into the night and the heavy snow that was falling. Hal sat in the front seat next to me moaning and groaning. I finally found the hospital. They were ready and waiting for us at the door with a wheelchair. Hal was wheeled into the small hospital where a doctor examined him hurriedly. "Yes, I believe your friend is having a heart attack," the doctor told me, "but there is nothing we can do for him here. We are only equipped to repair broken bones due to ski accidents. I suggest you take him to the hospital in Burlington." "But Burlington is more than an hour away from here!" I protested. "You must be able to do something!" All the doctor did was shake his head. Hal was wheeled back into my car and we took off again.

I turned the car around and headed back South into the darkness towards Burlington. Suddenly, I had a terrible thought. Just this afternoon the production manager on the project had told me that the gas gauge on my car was broken. I looked at the gauge and it showed empty! It was now about 2 o'clock in the morning, everything was closed, there wasn't a gas station in sight, and I was about to drive a very sick man, who could die any minute, through a snowstorm to a hospital some 95 miles away on what may be an empty gas tank!

I got on the four-lane highway and started to drive as fast as I could. I was hoping that my speeding down the snowy highway might cause a police car to catch up with me before I ran out gas. All along Hal suffered in the seat next to me. I did not know what would die first—Hal, the car, or both of us if the car were to slide off the road in the snow. Of course, I was praying that nothing would happen before we got to the hospital. I kept looking for a police car. "There is never a policeman around when you need one," I kept repeating to myself.

Finally, I saw the Burlington city lights over the horizon and 10 minutes later I pulled into the emergency entrance of the hospital. Hal was wheeled into the intensive care unit and a team of people attended to him. "Yes, it was definitely a heart attack, but your friend will be all right," I was told. I stayed at the hospital until early morning and until I was sure that Hal was out of danger. I then headed back to Stowe.

By that time, gas stations had opened. I stopped at the first one and asked the attendant to fill the tank. "You only needed about three gallons," said the puzzled attendant as he handed me the change for my $20 bill. When I got back to Stowe, the production assistant handed me a receipt for gas. "Last night I thought, with the gauge broken, I best fill up your car."

"Thank you, young man, I only wish you had told me last night," was my rueful and tired response.

Take One – Cut!

In the early 1960's it wasn't unusual for an advertising agency to ask a production company to produce a whole series of television commercials for the same product — such as three 60-second announcements, three 30s, three 20s, and three 10s. We were shooting black-and-white film, talent was cheap, residual-use payments to the actors had not yet been invented, nor had we heard much regarding testing promotional concepts. The advertising agency came up with an idea, they wrote the scripts, prepared storyboards, got the client's okay and brought everything to the production company to execute.

It was in this time period that I was assigned to produce and direct three sets of commercial announcements for Holsum Bakers, a nationwide chain of bakeries. Two sets of commercials were for normal ordinary white bread and one was for a strange looking concoction called "Wagon Train Bread." On the photographs, it looked like something halfway between a pumpernickel and a challah.

This "Wagon Train" commercial also had a very difficult opening scene that called for three cowboys sitting around a

Holsum white bread was on the menu in many households. For many years, early every morning, delivery vans such as this one traveled all over the towns and cities bringing freshly baked bread.

campfire with a burro in the background. One cowboy is playing a guitar, the second one is pouring coffee, and the third one walks towards the camera as the camera moves back to reveal a tree stump with a knife and a loaf of Wagon Train bread on top of the tree stump. The cowboy was now supposed to cut one slice as the camera moves in for a close-up. As he was halfway through cutting a second slice, the scene needed to dissolve to the identical close-up scene with the same loaf of bread, the same knife and a woman's hand in the identical position completing the cutting action on a table in a kitchen setting.

As I remember the announcer was saying something like this during this opening scene: "Now you can bring the hardy out door taste of Wagon Train Bread right into you own kitchen … " etc. Now, please remember, this was before computers, green screens, video recording and many of the special effects devices available today.

The shooting schedule was set for Monday, Tuesday, and Wednesday. Since the Wagon Train bread commercial was the most difficult, we decided to shoot them first. We constructed the cowboy set, built the campfire location, brought in the tree stump, confirmed the arrival of the burro, and laid out the tracks for the camera dolly and tested everything. We were ready for Monday and the shoot. As the client was leaving the studio, we asked him to be sure to come in on Monday with at least two dozen fresh loaves of Wagon Train Bread. He assured us that this was no problem, and we went home to enjoy the weekend.

Monday morning the client arrived. We looked around. "Where is the bread?" we asked. "Here" was the answer and the gentleman handed me a shopping bag with two loaves of white bread and two loaves of Wagon Train Bread. Unbelieving, I sat down hard in my director's chair. I was stunned. "How are we supposed to make all three commercials with just four loaves of bread? Nobody around here bakes this Wagon Train Bread." "I requested two dozen loafs of bread," I protested. "I thought you were kidding when you said two dozen loaves," the client said in a subdued voice, as we stood there half laughing and half crying. "I'll call the bakery in Steamboat Springs, Colorado, right away, and we'll have the bread here Wednesday."

We made a quick switch in the schedule, sent the prop man out to buy two dozen loaves of ordinary Tip Top bread that looked a lot like the Holsum white bread so we could shoot the white bread commercials, sent the cowboys and the burro home, and rescheduled the Wagon Train shoot for Wednesday. Then, we sent the client to the phone to call the bakery and order two dozen loaves of Wagon Train bread to arrive tomorrow Tuesday in time for the Wednesday shoot.

Tuesday morning we were greeted by the news that Steamboat Springs had a snowstorm and nothing could be air-freighted out. "Not to worry," our client

Wagon Train bread looked very much like this with a hard crust on the outside and soft inside. It was designed to appeal to customers by combining this bread with the hearty and tough life on the trail as the country spread westward.

assured us, the bakery had called the Kansas City bakery and explained to them how to bake this mysterious loaf of bread and they would ship it to us to arrive no later than Wednesday morning. Wednesday morning the crew, cowboys, burro, and cast eagerly awaited the two dozen loaves of bread that were arriving from Kansas City. Unfortunately, this Kansas City version of Wagon Train Bread had only a slight resemblance to the original. So we were now confronted with the challenge of shooting a 60-, a 30-, and a 15-second Wagon Train Bread commercial announcement with just two loaves of the real bread.

I sat down in a corner of the studio with the key crew people and reworked the shooting schedule. After a few minutes we had a plan. First we will shoot all the glamour shots with the bread inside the wrapper. Then we will shoot all the scenes where the loaf was whole — uncut. Finally, it will come down to the critical opening cowboy scene. I assumed I had four possible chances to make this shot. One for each end of the two loaves of bread.

Of course, we rehearsed until I finally felt it was time for the real thing. We started filming. Take one: n.g. — bad camera dolly. Take two: n.g. — when the bread was cut crumbs fell out of an air pocket in the bread. We dipped the ends of the bread pieces in a bit of water and glued them back together as best as we could. The cowboy was now instructed to grasp the bread at the end in order to hide the place where the loaf was previously cut. Take three: not bad, but the final frame was not great. Take four: was, at last, a perfect take. We all breathed a sigh of relief.

The film magazine was now removed from the camera and taken into the dark room. There a piece of film from the end of the scene was cut off and the assistant cameraman did a quick developing job on the negative film so we could place a precision clip into the Mitchell camera (remember, we were shooting black-and-white 35 millimeter film).

In the meantime, the crew switched over to the kitchen set and I took my "housewife" aside to explain to her the importance of this next scene and the fact that we had one — and only one — chance to get this scene in the can. Painstakingly, I took her step by step through the procedure, told her the whole sad story about why we were down to our last loaf of bread, explained that we would have a clip of the cowboy scene in the camera gate so we could perfectly match the position of the loaf of bread, the knife, and her hand to the preceding cowboy scene, and that we had just one chance to do this right. Finally, I pointed out that all I wanted her to do was to complete the slice which the cowboy had started, then start a new slice, but stop before she was halfway through this second slice because I needed the rest of that cutting action for the next scene. After going over these points several times, I felt we were ready to do the filming.

The camera was properly positioned. The bread was placed to match the clip in the camera. My housewife inserted the knife into the half-cut slice, the hand and knife were positioned to match the cowboy's hand and knife, everyone was ordered to freeze, the camera was racked over, and I said — almost in a whisper — "roll camera, OK, action." The knife sliced through the bread beautifully and, in accordance with my earlier direction, the housewife started on the next slice. "We made it!" I exulted in my heart as I said: "OK, cut."

"I AM CUTTING!"

But what's this? My housewife is still slicing. "Cut, cut," I now shouted, my voice rising with each cry, "God damn it, CUT!" I screamed. "I AM CUTTING!" my housewife screamed back at me, with tears in her eyes as she blissfully completed slicing through my precious loaf of bread.

About a half-hour later, when the crew finally stopped laughing, after my housewife stopped crying, and after I stopped fuming, we resumed the shooting to a slightly altered script.

Kind And Gentle Lloyd

After three years as assistant production manager at Fred A. Niles Productions in Chicago (which included two years as producer/manager of the Oral Roberts Revival Hour program), I was ready for new adventures. My luck was that I was assigned to be the assistant director to Lloyd Bethune who was a staff director at Niles. Lloyd was a kind and gentle man although he could, at rare times, flash a devastating anger. He also tended to be a little distracted.

Once Lloyd and I were having lunch together. When the time came to pay the check, Lloyd reached into his pocket and came up with a package of Christmas cards. "God! I should have mailed these last week!" he said, shaking his head. As we walked out of the restaurant Lloyd paid the check and bought a package of cigarettes. Walking back to the studio, Lloyd walked right past a mailbox. I stopped, looked at Lloyd disapprovingly, and pointed at a mailbox. "I almost forgot again," mumbled Lloyd shaking his head, as he went over to the mailbox and dropped in his new pack of cigarettes into the mail box.

Another time we were filming the international president of Lions International. (Little did I suspect at the time that one day I'd be a member of this organization for over 55 years and be the president of the New York club.) The Lion president was seated in back of a large desk with the usual props on it including a dummy telephone. Just then, Lloyd was paged over the loudspeaker. Without giving it much thought, I handed Lloyd the headset of the dummy phone. "Hello! Hello!" Lloyd shouted into the phone, "God damn it. First they page me and then they cut me off!" Lloyd angrily slammed the phone back down. At that point nobody on the set was about to tell Lloyd what I had done to him.

The 7½ pound large-mouth bass I caught with my bare hands that caused Lloyd such great anguish.

Lloyd was very kind and loyal to me. He was quick to praise me and was just as fast to forgive my mistakes. He tried to hide his very sensitive nature, but it showed up on occasion, particularly if he had had a few drinks. One day he was visiting our house when he spotted the 7-pound, 10-ounce large-mouth bass mounted on the wall. He peered at the brass plaque and then, drink in hand, wandered over to me. "Come here," he ordered, dragging me over to the fish and pointing at the plaque, "what does this mean 'Caught by Charles Ticho with his bare hands?'" I proceeded to tell Lloyd about the film I was shooting on Lake Chickamauga near Chattanooga, Tennessee. We were there for over a week filming a boat safety film. On the last day, we had a little time before we had to leave for the airport, so we all went water skiing. While I was on the skis, I thought that I might have hit something. When I got back into the boat I saw something moving on top of the water. We maneuvered the boat into the vicinity and I spotted a large fish flopping near the surface. I had apparently stunned it with my ski. I slipped a towel under the fish and flipped it into the boat.

I've never been involved in fishing so I was very surprised by the reception I got at the hotel when we landed with the fish. Everyone was ooohing and aaahing and telling me what a great fish I had caught. We had little time to spend on the fish, so I just left it at the hotel and we headed for the airport. About three months later I was surprised by the arrival of a package containing the neatly mounted remains of my "catch." As Lloyd listened to my story his eyes grew wider and wider. When I finished, his face flushed with anger, and his eyes filled with tears. "How dare you display this fish? Caught with bare hands!" he shouted at me, "I've been fishing for 30 years and I have never caught a fish half this size. Take it down! You have no right to display this fish," he insisted with tears running down his cheeks. His anger and dismay was not satisfied till I climbed up and removed the fish from the wall.

And then, one day to everyone's surprise, Lloyd announced that he had accepted a job at Ted Bates Advertising and was leaving for New York. On one hand, I was very unhappy to lose this close association. On the other hand, this gave me an opportunity to seek directorial assignments. A few years later, I followed Lloyd to New York. My family moved into apartment 10G at 5700 Skyview in Riverdale, New

The house in Woodcliff Lake, N.J.

York in the fancy part of the Bronx. Skyview consisted of three huge apartment houses; each 24 floors high with 12 apartments on each floor — that's more than 800 apartments! It also had a nursery school, swimming pool, tennis courts, a playground, a skating ring, a large garage, several physician's offices and many other conveniences. Nevertheless, after Ron was born, it was time to look for larger quarters.

I asked Lloyd how he found his house when he moved to New York. He told me that he used Homerica, Inc., a house-finding service. I went to see them and, even though they usually only served commercial clients and not individuals, they agreed to help me. After an hour-long interview, they arranged for us to see some houses in Woodcliff Lake and Teaneck. The very first house we saw on the very first Sunday we went house hunting was 16 Allen Drive, Woodcliff Lake, New Jersey. We saw it on Sunday and bought it on Monday and we lived there for 42 wonderful years, 1966 to 2008. To our pleasant surprise, we discovered that we were just about a mile away from Lloyd's house. We remained neighbors until Lloyd moved to Los Angeles some 12 years later.

The most memorable moment with Lloyd came when I was producing a series of commercials for Argo Corn Products. These commercials were supposed to dramatize the contribution that sugar, a corn product, makes in various industries. In the plan were commercials about baking, candy making, ice cream production, fruit canning, jam and jelly production — altogether 13 different commercials for 13 different industries to be produced in 13 weeks. Argo was sponsoring a weekly television series, and we were supposed to supply one completed announcement each week. I engaged Lloyd to assist me directing these announcements.

As a rule, we had no trouble locating places to do the filming. However, when it came to the fruit-canning announcement, I ran into a stone wall. No one wanted to give us permission to film on their premises. For weeks I made phone calls all around the Chicago area. Everywhere I turned to I was refused admission. In desperation I started calling various state canning associations. At last, the Michigan Fruit Canners Association agreed to give me a list of their members so that I could contact them directly. I went back to working the phones and hearing one refusal after another until I called a small canning firm in Muskegon, Michigan. There I was told that I must speak to a Mrs. Hayes. To my surprise, Mrs. Hayes called me back almost at once and listened as I gently and gingerly explained what we wanted to do. This must have been the 100th time I have made this call and I was ready for another refusal. "Well," said Mrs. Hayes after I was finished with my request, "my husband died recently and I am now trying to run the company. I am sure he would not object to you coming for a visit, so I don't see why I should. How much will this cost?" My heart leaped for joy. "No, no! We will gladly pay you," I insisted. "Oh, that won't be necessary," Mrs. Hayes replied, and the deal was done. We were already three weeks behind schedule producing this announcement and I was overwhelmed to have, at last, found a place to do the filming.

Several phone calls later, we had made arrangements for the Niles truck to drive to Muskegon on Monday with the equipment and the rest of the crew would fly over on Tuesday for the one day of shooting. When we arrived at the plant Tuesday morning, our electrician, Frank Oleksy, who had driven the truck over to the plant the day before, greeted us with: "You won't believe what's been happening here," Frank blurted out, "when I arrived, they asked me what parts of our equipment will touch the floor of the plant or any part of their equipment. After I showed them, four guys came over and washed all the wheels on the lights, all the cables and extensions, the tripod — almost everything that was on the truck. They arranged a great hotel room for me and treated me to a fancy dinner. And when I told them that no food was served on your flight this morning from

The fruit canning operations offered some exciting and interesting opportunities for visual scenes.

Chicago, they arranged for a fancy breakfast for all of you in the company dining room." Frank went on and on about the wonderful treatment he encountered.

After all the problems I had with this project, I could hardly believe my ears. We were ushered into the company dining room where a large breakfast buffet awaited us. We were knee-deep in the food when Mrs. Hayes walked in to greet us and to check whether we had enough to eat. Mrs. Hayes was a little gray-haired lady with a kindly smile and a twinkle in her eyes. She wanted to know whether everything was in order and assigned four men to help us. Frank was in heaven. He did not have to lift a finger throughout the whole day. At lunchtime, Mrs. Hayes insisted on taking all of us to a restaurant in Muskegon and, of course, paying for the meal.

With all this help we were done well before our scheduled flight back to Chicago. As we were loading up our truck, a skid containing perhaps 30 boxes was brought over to the truck. "You boys were so nice to come over and visit with us," said Mrs. Hayes with the usual smile playing over her grandmotherly face, "that I thought you might like to take a few cases of our products home to your wives and families." Her men proceeded to load the cases onto our truck and all of us fell over each other thanking Mrs. Hayes for her kindness and generosity.

Just as we were about to leave, Lloyd turned to Mrs. Hayes and asked: "You have been so wonderful — is there anything that we can do for you?" There was a long pause and it was obvious that Mrs. Hayes was struggling with her decision whether she could ask for something. Finally, very slowly and hesitatingly she said: "Well, I don't know whether this is asking for too much. But, would it be possible for you to send us a copy of the material you filmed here today? I would like to show it to the boys in the plant." I felt as if I could put my arms around this kind lady and hug her. I was certain that all of the crew members standing around in a circle felt exactly the same way. "Of course! No problem at all," Lloyd said with feeling, "I'll personally see to it that a copy is sent to you as soon as possible. Here, let me give you my business card so you know how to reach me." Having said that, Lloyd opened his wallet, took out one of his business cards and, as he did that, a condom slipped out and fell on the ground. Mrs. Hayes looked like she never noticed it, and Lloyd quickly stepped on it. The crew and I had just enough time to rush over and hide behind the truck as we all exploded in hysterical laughter.

The next day I sent Mrs. Hayes a long and hearty thank you letter and a week later we sent a carefully edited version of every foot of film we exposed at her plant.

Organizing The Chicago Directors Was Risky Business

"It just doesn't make good sense for you to risk your job and career for a union that can't possibly do anything for you," was the way Fred Niles, the President of Fred Niles Productions, greeted my news that I was organizing the film directors in the Chicago area. It was 1960 and I was in the sixth year of what, ultimately, turned out to be a 21-year-long career with the recently renamed Fred A. Niles Communications Centers, Inc., the Chicago-based film production company.

There I was, face-to-face with the founder and president of what, in those days, was the largest film production company in Chicago and one of the largest in the country. I had just invited him to attend a meeting between the officers of our fledgling new directors' guild and the owners of the production companies in the Chicago area. Such a meeting seemed like the next logical step in the process of establishing our directors' guild as a viable entity in the industry.

In the fall of 1957, four of us who were toiling as directors in the Chicago area, invited George L. George to come to Chicago and tell us more about this new guild of directors, the Screen Directors International Guild, that had been recently formed in New York. George L. George was the guiding light of this new organization and the leader of its organizing efforts in the East. Most of us in Chicago had long ago given up any idea of scaling the lofty walls erected around, what we saw as, the sacred ground occupied by Hollywood's Screen Directors Guild.

 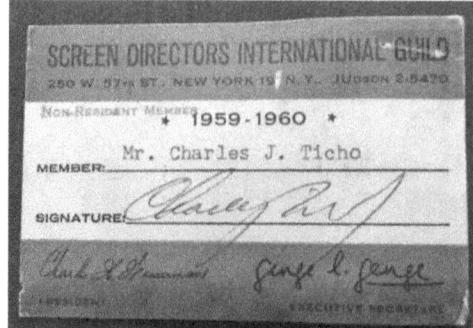

My very first guild identity card from the fledgling Midwest Chapter of the Screen Directors International Guild.

We were directors engaged in a wide variety of audio-visual products – TV commercials, industrial films, educational films, exhibits, slide films, multi-media programs, even 360-degree film presentations — but no theatrical or dramatic motion pictures. To us, therefore, in the cinema backwoods of the Middle West of the United States, it certainly seemed as if Hollywood's Screen Directors Guild presented us with a classic Catch 22: you could not get into the Hollywood Guild without feature film credits, but you could not be hired to direct a feature film without an SDG card. At least, that was how it seemed to those of us who had made attempts to claim our directorial star in the Hollywood sky. In addition there was the rather substantial $2,000 initiation fee that those of us, who were earning around $250 a week, could hardly afford.

After several years of fruitless correspondence with Joe Youngerman, the guiding light of the SDG in Hollywood, many of us arrived at the conclusion that it was time to seek other affiliations. Therefore, this new Screen Directors International Guild that had recently been founded in New York City looked like a welcomed alternative. Besides, the four of us, Bill Lippert and Ed Grabill from Wilding Pictures, Gordon Weisenborn and I, felt we had much more in common with the New York directors.

George L. George arrived in Chicago and the five of us met in a small inexpensive restaurant on the near North Side where, after a Dutch treat dinner, George spoke at length about the new guild and its activities in New York. His enthusiasm and optimism was infectious. He described the progress that SDIG had made, the modest contract they had been able to achieve and the plans they have for the future that included a health and welfare plan. It all sounded very exciting. He urged us to assemble a cadre of potential members and, once we had a substantial number, to formally become a guild. Later on, we would be able to join the New York organization and, perhaps, negotiate a contract with the local production companies. Then, George thanked us for the dinner and departed for the hotel and then New York.

Of course, four directors doth not a guild make. I was elected vice president and undertook (more precisely, was assigned) the task of recruiting more members. Now, in those days, the number of freelance directors in Chicago could be counted on the fingers of one hand. As a matter of fact, I think, that Gordon Weisenborn was the only one. Nearly everyone else, who wished to earn a living in this film trade, had to have a staff job with one of the local production assembly line companies such as Niles, Wilding Pictures, Sarra, Cal Dunn Studios, Coronet Instructional Films, Encyclopedia Britannica Films, Dallas Jones, Jam Handy, and a few other smaller operations. Lose one of those positions and you could look for work for quite a while. Recruiting members for the union, therefore, was a difficult and delicate procedure. Many directors and assistant directors did not even want to talk to me. They made me promise never to mention their names in connection with this union idea and hung up the phone. Most others simply would not join for fear of reprisals. It became obvious that a new strategy was needed.

The logjam began to break up slowly after I began to guarantee to all potential members that I will keep their involvement completely confidential and would not issue a membership list until we had at least one hundred members signed up. Within the confines of the Chicago film industry that number just about included everyone who could call himself (or herself, in one instance) a director. I suspected, that most individuals who agreed to this arrangement probably banked on the probability that I would never achieve our goal of 100 members and that the whole idea would go away.

Undaunted, and perhaps foolishly, I proceeded to man the phones and the typewriter. For the next twelve months or so, I was the only person who knew who our members were. Not even the other officers of our organization were privy to this information. All I ever reported to them at our meetings was what number I had reached. When I signed up a new member, I would fill out a card that I would, at the earliest opportunity, put into my family's bank safe deposit box. At each of these occasions I would count the cards and rejoice as the number slowly grew. Of course, we did not have a meeting of the membership during all this time. Caution reached such a level that most new members paid the $50 initiation fee in cash lest there be a check that might reveal their involvement.

I persevered. I even spread our wings to include directors and assistant directors in Detroit, Toronto and St. Louis. By the middle of 1959 we had

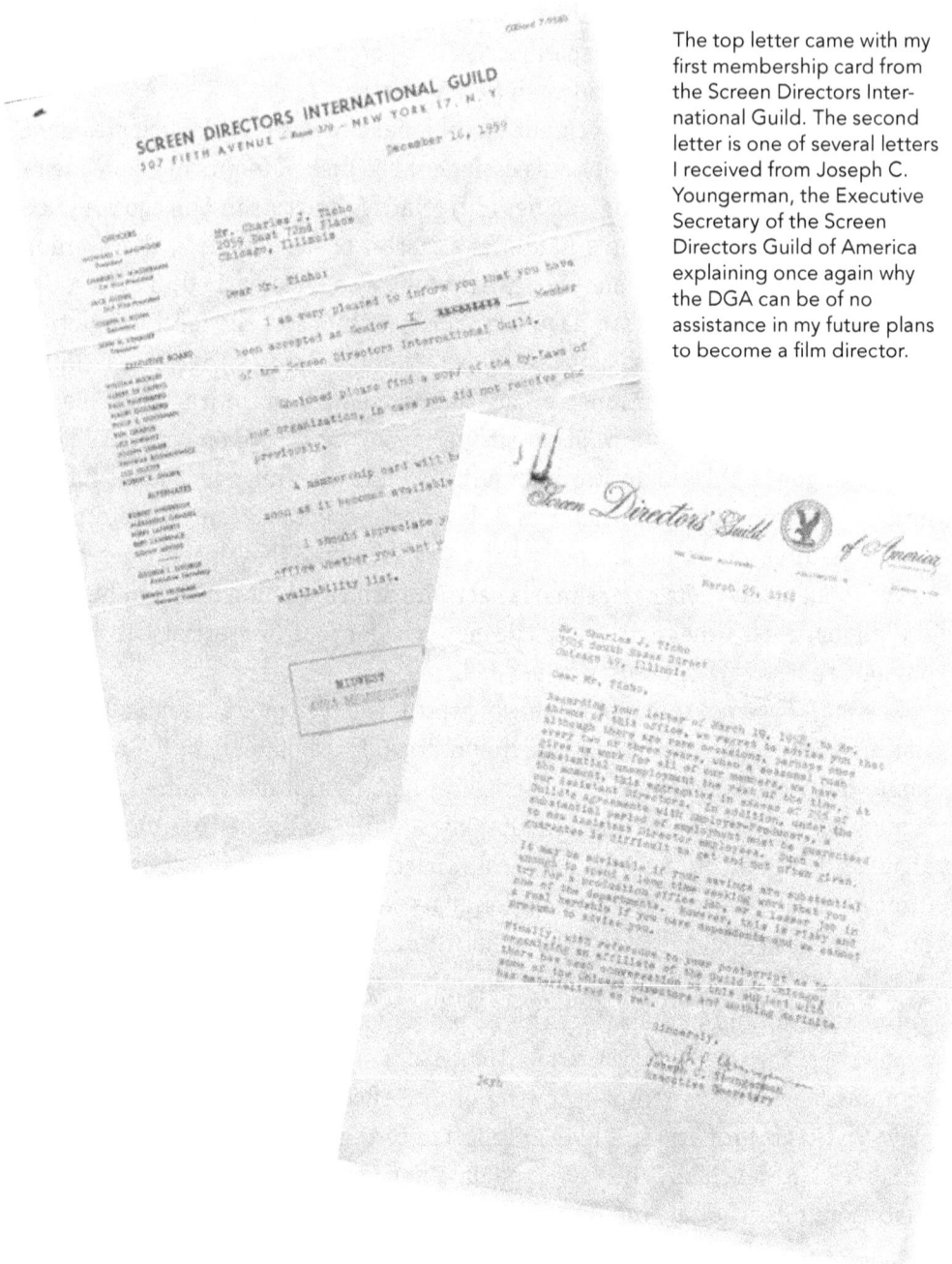

The top letter came with my first membership card from the Screen Directors International Guild. The second letter is one of several letters I received from Joseph C. Youngerman, the Executive Secretary of the Screen Directors Guild of America explaining once again why the DGA can be of no assistance in my future plans to become a film director.

exceeded the goal of one hundred members. With a great sense of pride and accomplishment I presented the list of 104 signed up and paid up members to our officers. This was shortly followed by a formal invitation to all the members to attend the first general membership meeting. Fifty-six hardy, fearless and somewhat surprised souls showed up — just four above the minimum required to make a quorum. The membership voted to formally incorporate and apply for affiliation with the New York SDIG organization.

Most of 1959 was taken up with negotiations to formally affiliate the Midwest Chapter with the New York SDIG organization. These discussions turned out to be almost as difficult as the recruiting of new members. New York was reluctant to surrender an appropriate share of control of the directorial market in the East while we, in Chicago, now with nearly 140 members, refused to be treated like poor country cousins. But good common sense prevailed. One of the highlights of my early directorial career was being able to rise at the first annual SDIG banquet in New York at the St. Moritz Hotel in late October 1959 to announce, with my wife at my side, the marriage of the two organizations. The Midwest Chapter of SDIG was now a full partner of the Screen Directors International Guild.

In early 1962, the Midwest Chapter felt confident enough to hold its first meeting with its employers to discuss future arrangements. The owners were, as yet, unimpressed and not very receptive to the guild's proposals. All this would change within a year after a two-day walkout of all the directors and assistant directors in the area. Shortly thereafter a contract, patterned after the New York one, was signed and sealed. But, by that time, I was no longer in Chicago.

Little did I know or anticipate that, shortly after we completed the affiliation agreement with the New York guild, I would become the first Chicago based director to take advantage of the new arrangement with the New York organization. Niles had opened a New York studio that was failing. In the spring of 1962, I moved with family, furniture, new daughter and my new SDIG card to New York to rescue that operation.

When SDIG merged with Hollywood's Screen Directors Guild, the existence of the Midwest Chapter enabled the newly formed organization to proudly state that it was a Guild of the whole country. Hence the name of today's Directors Guild of America.

I could not help gloating a little bit. Not only had I been instrumental in the launch of a successful guild operation in the Middle West, but also had just been inducted into the exclusive DGA fraternity, without the need to present three letters of recommendation, without any feature film credits — and at Chicago's original $50 initiation fee.

Tit For Tat

For 14 years, from 1962 to 1976, I was in charge of the New York studio of Fred A. Niles Communications Centers. My move from Chicago to New York was actually more a matter of desperation rather than an intelligent business decision. While I greatly admired Fred Niles during the seven years I worked for him in the Chicago headquarters, we really did not get along very well. I wanted to move ahead and Fred did not seem to want to give me the opportunity. I was organizing the film directors in Chicago into a guild and, I assume, that did not make me very popular with Fred. But, most importantly, I was making some very strenuous financial demands and Fred was reluctant to agree to them lest my salary mess up the pay schedule of the large staff in Chicago.

Moving me to the New York branch in 1962 served several purposes. It got me out of Fred's hair; I was now running my own operation and, if I earned more money in New York, it would not affect Chicago's pay scales. Also, Fred promised that if New York showed a profit, I would be able to share in the proceeds. Of course, this immediately made me very much aware of what we sold, what we produced, and what profit our projects made. Each and every year, while I was in charge of the New York operation, it showed a healthy profit, and every year, I waited for the promised profit-sharing plan to go into effect. I managed to get raises in my salary but was unable to share in the success of the branch. By 1971, after nine years of waiting, I was getting a little impatient.

During this time, we in New York sold a rather complex set of tourism promotional films to the Greek National Tourist Office. Our assignment was to produce four 15-minute films in English and then translate them also into French, German, and Spanish. This was a major project and promised to be quite profitable. Also, I was looking forward to spending some time touring Greece during the production. Over my bitter objections, Fred assigned the project to a staff director in Chicago. This meant that the New York branch would not get credit for the production, and I could not visit Greece.

Unfortunately, the director who did go to Greece lacked the finer points of handling a client and apparently offended a great number of people over there. I never learned exactly what happened, but I realized that matters were not going well. The client kept putting off making any payments on the contract. They insisted that we first must produce all four films, and then they demanded the translations and then they wanted to receive the prints. The Chicago office kept supplying the client while we in New York kept telling them that we were not receiving any payment. Then we learned that the contract may not be enforceable, and it looked like we might never get paid.

Now, the problem was passed back to me. "It's your project," I was told, "see what you can do." After a few months of searching I located an intermediary — basically a man who had the connections to bribe the right people to get some of the money paid out to us. He claimed that, for a percentage, he could assist us in collecting the money owed. We promised to consider his services and that I will visit Athens to meet with him and the client. But first, I flew to Israel to meet my brother Steven and spend a few days showing him the country. This was Steven's one and only tour of Israel during which he gave me some free lawyer's advice to use in Athens during my meeting with the intermediary.

The intermediary arranged a meeting with the head of the Greek National Tourist Office and I asked him to meet me at my Athens hotel the night before. I arrived in Athens in the afternoon and met with the intermediary. We discussed procedures, his involvement and his compensation. In the morning I welcomed him with an 11-page contract that I typed the night before. I wanted to be sure that, before I paid this man anything, we must see some money.

At first he refused to sign, but when I got up from the table and told him I was leaving for New York, he changed his mind and agreed to the terms of the contract. We met with the director of the Greek National Tourist Office at 10 o'clock and by noon I had an agreement to receive a substantial payment right after lunch. It was not everything that was owed to us, but enough to cover all of our production expenses and the intermediary's fee.

Using Steven's advice, I now started looking for a way I could immediately cash the check that I was about to receive. I was afraid of further tricks from the Tourist Office or the intermediary. To my great surprise and pleasure, as I was searching for a lunchtime restaurant, I stumbled on a branch of the Chicago First National Bank. That was the same bank with which Fred Niles did business in Chicago. I walked in and spoke with the manager. I learned that the bank closed at two in the afternoon. I could not possibly arrive with the check by then. However, when the man learned that I was about to deposit several million drachmas into an account, he showed me where the back door was located and told me to come there. Instead of eating lunch, I opened a savings account in my name, signed the signature card, and took extra signature cards to take to Chicago so that Fred Niles could also sign on the account. At about 3 o'clock, I arrived at the back door of the bank to deposit the millions of drachmas safely into the account, grabbed a taxi for the airport and the flew back to New York.

By 1973, I was tired of waiting for the promised profit-sharing plan and announced that I was leaving the Niles organization unless one could be agreed to. Finally, I won the battle and when the year ended I received a grand total of $1,800 as a bonus. The following year, I did a lot better and my bonus was over $30,000. When my bonus went up an additional $8,000 the following year, the company decided to revoke the agreement. By then I had had enough. After a 21-year career at Fred Niles Communications Center, on Thanksgiving Day 1976, I resigned from the company and my new production company, Performance Designs Incorporated, was born.

The last thing I did at Niles was to request the six weeks of vacation pay owed to me. My request was ignored. For the first time, I turned to my director's guild for support. "This is a matter that is not covered in our contract," was the guild's response. I resigned myself to the fact that I would never see that vacation money.

That is, until one day some two years later, when I got a very friendly phone call from the comptroller at the Niles organization in Chicago. It seems, he said, that there are several million drachmas that have been sitting for several years in an account in Greece. Fred Niles now wanted to use these funds and, it appears, Niles never sent in the signature card and I was the only one authorized to sign on the account. Could I please sign the withdrawal form they are mailing to me?

"Of course," was my most eager response, "however, if you remember, there is this one small outstanding matter regarding my vacation pay…"

Crime Does Pay

Yes, crime does pay — sometimes.

One of the most miserable things that producers of convention programs have to put up with is "The Proposal." What is that and why is it so objectionable?

A client extends an invitation to a producer to submit a proposal for the design of a program that a company or an association wishes to stage. When this is done with just one selected production company, the request presents no problem. The client wants to see what the producer has in mind and the proposal will be used as a base for discussions, suggestions, amendments and, ultimately, for the budget and the final design of the program.

Problems arise, however, when the client invites three, four, or even more production companies to submit their proposal. Now it becomes a competition, a major gamble and a substantial investment for the production companies. The production companies are, in effect, asked to develop the concept, create a program, design the staging, suggest the entertainment, plan out the graphics, suggest the costs and do it all on a completely speculative basis. The client may review these proposals and may even invite you in to discuss your ideas. But, more often than not, you get a nice letter thanking you for your effort, telling you that someone else has been selected, and promising that, perhaps, you'll be invited next year once again. Thanks a lot! Production companies waste hundreds of thousands of dollars in this fashion every year.

Here are two examples that will illustrate what I mean and why I decided many years ago that my company, Performance Designs Incorporated, would not play this game. If a client wants our ideas, they will have to pay for them. If you want a proposal, here is what it will cost you if we don't get the assignment. Some potential clients said: "no, thank you" and we did not do any business with them. But others appreciated what we had to offer and became loyal long-term customers of PDI.

One example was a client that we started to service in the early days of the computer age. They were first known as the Sperry Corporation and then, during the years, they changed names several times as they battled IBM for the world's large computer market. Throughout the many name changes and acquisitions, this corporation called on us to assist them in the staging of sales meetings and other events. Yes, we submitted proposals and, on some occasions, a proposals had to be revised, But we worked diligently, each time, to deliver the best end results. We produced their sales meetings when the company was known as Sperry Univac and worked with them right through several decades and several more name changes right up to Unisys.

The other example will show why we became so determined not to submit speculative proposal. Let's go back some years to 1979.

We were invited to submit a proposal to the Consumer Finance Association. After several meetings with the convention director, we prepared an elaborate and, we thought, exciting concept. The client reviewed our suggestions and, to our great delight, selected us for the project. We, in turn, selected a writer and assigned him to start the research and begin writing a script. At this point the client asked us to engage Alvin Toffler, who was a well-known author and speaker at that time. His recent book, *Future Shock*, was a best-seller. Toffler was represented exclusively by the Leigh Bureau Agency. We contacted them and a few days later received a confirming letter that Toffler had accepted the assignment to be the speaker at this convention and that his fee would be $12,000. We advised the client of this arrangement.

A few weeks later, we were shocked to receive a letter from the client accusing us of dishonesty and removing us from the project. I rushed to call the client to learn the details of this accusation. At first the client did not want to discuss it but he finally told me that he had learned from the Leigh Bureau that Toffler's fee was $10,000 not $12,000 and said that he could not work with a supplier who was dishonest. I protested that I was not being dishonest and mailed a copy of the confirmation letter from the Leigh Bureau to the client. No matter, the client did not wish us to continue on the project. I was hurt by this unfair treatment. After taking a few days to cool off, I called the client, and we agreed that the association would pay for our expenditures to date. We sent them a modest bill for about $1,200 and waited for payment. Six months passed, but the client ignored our statements and reminders. I finally gave up the idea of ever getting paid.

When the Fred Niles Company decided to withdraw my hard-won profit-sharing plan, they did give me a substantial raise. But I was also presented with a lawyer's letter demanding that, in the event I stopped working for Niles, I would have to remain out of the audio-visual business for two years. This was obviously designed to prevent me from "stealing" the Niles clients that I had served through the New York office. I could not agree to such an arrangement and for a month or so we were in intense negotiations. I finally decided that the only way to solve this impasse was to leave the organization.

> *... the only way to solve the impasse was to leave the organization ...*

During these lengthy negotiations I was asked to step aside as the head of the New York studios and take on the task limited to finding new business opportunities for the company. While I was in this strange position, I received a call from an old client at the RCA Service Company. He told me that he had a project for me to produce. In keeping with my unusual position at Niles, I directed him to the chief salesman in the office. A few days later, I resigned and was gone from Niles.

My good friend Paul Tyras offered to let me use a part of his office space at 666 Fifth Avenue, and Performance Designs Incorporated opened for business on Dec. 1, 1976. I was very pleased with this name. My wife, Jean, was busy at that time with her fashion designing. So, I was designing performances, and she was performing designs. My branch became PDI Productions and Jean's branch became Jean Ticho Designs. We were both busy and happy.

After settling down, I started calling people that I knew, including the client at RCA. I called him just to tell him that I was no longer at Niles. "I thought there was something wrong," said Jack, my contact at RCA "I did not like the way things were going at Niles, and I did not really care for their proposal. It did not look like your work." I offered to prepare a proposal of my own instead. Jack hesitated. "I am not sure what the legal ramifications might be if you'd been involved in the preparation of the Niles proposal and are now competing against them." I assured him that I had nothing to do with the Niles proposal that he received and told him that I would send him my proposal in a few days.

"Alright, but I can't promise anything. I've got to check with our lawyers," said Jack and hung up the phone.

I prepared a proposal in a couple of days and sent it to the RCA office in Cherry Hill, New Jersey. Months went by and I did not hear from Jack. Then, I suddenly got a call from Jack's assistant: "Okay, Charlie, let's go to work. We like your proposal and we can proceed." I was ecstatic. This was a $56,000 project — a great deal of money and PDI's first big project. The production went very smoothly and two months later I was in Cherry Hill to deliver the completed job. To celebrate, all of us went out to a fancy restaurant for lunch. During the lunch the client stated several times how lucky they feel that I could do the project for RCA.

I finally asked what he meant by this remarks that "they were lucky." "Don't you know what happened?" he asked. I shook my head. "Well, we liked your proposal very much and wanted to work with you, but our attorneys told us to forget your proposal as well as the Niles proposal. Whichever company you select, the lawyers told us, you'll have legal problems. Besides, they said, there must be other production companies around that can do this job. So, we were soliciting ideas from other companies when we got this nasty letter from Niles telling us that you had nothing to do with their proposal and that you had no right to use it. We showed this letter to our lawyers, and they said: Niles just gave RCA permission to award the job to PDI. That's why we think we were lucky."

RCA wasn't the only old client from Niles who stayed loyal to me. As a matter of fact, it was almost a year and a half before I succeeded in landing a completely new client. But, by that time, PDI was already well on its way. As mentioned earlier, one of the clients that remained with PDI was the Univac Corporation. One of the projects we were awarded was a big meeting in Honolulu, Hawaii, to launch the expansion of Univac's international operations.

I was sitting in the plane, along with my assistant Bill Gerstenmaier, on the way to Hawaii when I happened to open my date book. At that time, I was not using a computer to keep track of appointments, just a small notebook. I opened this book to note some appointments I had made in Hawaii. As I turned the pages I noticed that I had apparently erased an earlier notation for my arrival

Throughout the many name changes and acquisitions this corporation called on us to assist them in the staging of sales meetings and other events including a memorable one in Hawaii.

day in Hawaii. I took a closer look and, after some struggling, I managed to decipher what I had written and erased. To my total amazement and surprise I realized that this very afternoon, the very day when I will arrive in Hawaii to start the Univac project, happens to be the very same day when the opening session of the Consumer Finance Association convention was to take place at the Sheraton Hotel in Honolulu. What an incredible coincidence! I had completely forgotten about this ill-fated project!

I told Bill that as soon as we arrive at the Honolulu airport I was going to rush right over to the Sheraton Hotel to see what this former client had selected to do instead of our proposal. I asked Bill to go to the Hilton Hotel with my baggage and I would rejoin him there later. As soon as the plane touched down I was in a taxi heading to the Sheraton Hotel. I arrived just about 20 minutes before the start of the Consumer Finance Association meeting. Knowing hotels inside and out, I had no trouble sneaking into the Grand Ballroom through the kitchen door without a badge. I found a seat near the back and sat down to see what clever ideas my competitor had come up with.

Well, I was in for another surprise and shock that day because, as the program unfolded, I realized that they were doing our proposal! They were using our concept, our ideas! Even the sets were built based on our drawings! The actors and even their costumes matched what we had proposed and the script faithfully followed our outline. An hour later, during the intermission, I rushed to a pay phone to call Bill. "Bill, grab your camera and come over to the Grand Ballroom of the Sheraton Hotel," I told him in a great hurry, "and when the session ends, please get me some photographs of the stage settings."

I hung up and rushed back into the ballroom for the second half of the meeting that continued to follow our outline. I was pleased with my good luck that I had managed to sneak into the meeting and discovered this violation of common decency and business practices.

This was the first time, and the only time, that I have sued anybody. As soon as I returned to New York I went to see a lawyer. When all the depositions were taken and all the lawyers had met and discussed the case, we settled for $45,000 and the $1,200 they owed on the original bill. After the lawyers got their share, PDI got a little more than what we would have earned had we actually produced the event.

Yes, sometimes, crime does pay.

Gravestones In The Desert

In 1984, while Berlin was still divided into West and East with a fortified wall dividing the two sections, I visited Berlin on business and decided to try and locate and visit the graves of my maternal grandparents.

As an American citizen, I had no problem getting permission to cross the boundary into Communist-controlled East Berlin. A simple ride on the "S-Bahn" (the Berlin elevated railroad) brought me to East Berlin. I underwent a very strict and thorough examination by the East German border guards who reminded me several times that I have permission to remain only until midnight. I felt like Cinderella. I was also instructed that I must exchange at least 25 West German marks for 25 East German marks. They made the visit as unpleasant and scary as possible.

With map in hand, I finally departed and visited the offices of the East Berlin Jewish community hoping to learn the location of the graves. From there I was sent on a long-distance streetcar ride that carried me carried me to the Jewish Cemetery. At the very imposing offices of this cemetery, I was first told that the names of my grandparents did not appear on their register. I then remembered that they were buried in the Agudath Cemetery and asked the clerk to check that register.

"Well, yes," said the clerk, "the graves are in that cemetery, but there is no need for you to go there since the place is locked." I had visited several Jewish cemeteries in Poland, Russia, and Romania in the past, and I had learned that there were few Jewish cemeteries in Eastern Europe that were truly "locked." So, I asked for directions anyway and started to walk. I reached the cemetery after a 45-minute walk and, as expected, had no difficulty entering it through a large hole in the fence.

I was shocked, however, by what I found. I remembered a photograph of my Uncle Julius standing in front of my grandparent's gravestones right after World War II.

General Julius Klein parents' gravestones in Berlin right after WWII.

In that photograph everything appeared normal and in perfect order. Now, all I found was devastation.

All the gravestones had been knocked down, and the weeds and undergrowth reached over my head. It was like a jungle. I forced my way through the bushes and vines to the center aisle that was paved and, therefore, clear of weeds. In the front was a large gravestone marking the site of a recently buried Torah and sacred books. That gravestone was also knocked down. I spent a fruitless hour or so pushing my way through the thickets trying to find some trace of the graves.

I could not help thinking: "Nobody knows I am here. If I should fall and crack my head open, I'd be here forever before anyone would find me."

I finally gave up. There was no way that I could ever find my grandparent's graves. As I was exiting the cemetery, I learned that in a Communist country there is no such thing as "nobody knows I am here." A man had apparently been observing me for some time from the apartment house across the street.

I guess I was not quite as "alone" as I had thought. I should have known better. In a Communist country where everyone is watching everybody else and suspicion is the order of the day, someone was sure to be observing what I was doing.

"What are you looking for?" the man asked. I hesitated for a moment. Was he the infamous Stasi East German secret police? I assumed the safest thing to do was to tell the truth.

When I told him that I was searching for graves, he insisted that we re-enter the cemetery and renew the search. Once again, the effort was unsuccessful. During our search the man explained to me that the damage to the cemetery was recent and that students from the local high school had invaded the cemetery and vandalized it. The police were called but did nothing. The students did not leave until all stones were knocked down and on the ground.

When we were ready to part company, the man offered to take my picture in front of the cemetery. I, in turn, offered to take his picture. This he refused to allow. He apologized and explained that he had been a prisoner of war under the British during World War II and that he was under constant suspicion by the Communist regime even now some 40 years later.

"You can return to America," he explained, "but I have to remain and live here, and I don't need any more trouble."

I was puzzled but let it go at that.

I spent the rest of the day visiting museums and had a late dinner in an open air restaurant on the Mombijou Platz where my mother used to live decades ago. I arrived at the S-Bahn station ready to head back to West Berlin and civilization. At the checkpoint, I was asked to declare all the currency I was carrying with me. This I did with great care. There was no way I wanted to get into any trouble with the authorities because I had an undeclared penny somewhere on me. Nevertheless, when I turned in my declaration, the guard escorted me to a room, searched me and through my possessions, and questioned me at length. He was finally satisfied with my answers and told me that it was against the law for anyone to take East German currency out of the country. I was told that I must return the few coins I had left from the East German money I was forced to exchange when I first crossed the border. This I did and was allowed to leave East Berlin, all the time thinking about the man at the cemetery and how right he was not to have had his picture taken.

Had the guard been just a little more suspicious he might have asked for the film in my camera and the man who helped me may have been in deep trouble having associated with an American.

Acknowledgements

At my age, and I am pushing 95, I could not have completed this book without the guidance and support of a dedicated group of people. They have spent hours, days, and many weeks keeping me from making one foolish error after another.

Two of them go back to my first book *From Generation to Generation: A Family's Story of Surviva*l. Pam Lott, our talented daughter-in-law, brought her master's degree talents in journalism and visual communication and managed to keep both my first book and this new project on track and to conclusion. Gayle F. Hendricks, who has a master of fine arts degree, somehow managed, once again, to find sufficient time away from her teaching obligations to gather text, illustrations, and style it into something that made continuity possible.

Then there is our daughter and art director, Robin Ticho, who collaborated with Lisa Massey Buffer, photo journalist, and Pam to create the cover for this opus.

I must also acknowledge award-winning journalist Angel Ackerman, who scanned the script for errors and contradictions.

Thank you for all your help and support.

Last, but certainly not least, I salute my dear wife of 61+ glorious years, for putting up with my incredibly messy work area while I labored on this project.

All their combined talents and patience made this book possible.

Pam Lott, left, and Lisa Massey Buffer review test photos of the cover on an iPhone.

Pam Lott (l-R), Stevie Daniels, Gayle F. Hendricks and I at the book launch for my first book *From Generation to Generation: A Family's Story of Survival.*

www.ingramcontent.com/pod-product-compliance
Lightning Source LLC
Chambersburg PA
CBHW081344070526
44578CB00005B/716